Debating the Dasam Granth

AAR RELIGION IN TRANSLATION

SERIES EDITOR
Anne Monius, Harvard Divinity School
A Publication Series of
The American Academy of Religion
and
Oxford University Press

BETWEEN HEGEL AND KIERKEGAARD
Hans L. Martensen's Philosophy of Religion
Translations by Curtis L. Thompson and David J. Kangas
Introduction by Curtis L. Thompson

EXPLAINING RELIGION
Criticism and Theory from Bodin to Freud
J. Samuel Preus

DIALECTIC, OR, THE ART OF DOING PHILOSOPHY
A Study Edition of the 1811 Notes
Friedrich D. E. Schleiermacher
Translated with Introduction and Notes by Terence N. Tice

RELIGION OF REASON
Out of the Sources of Judaism
Hermann Cohen
Translated, with an Introduction by Simon Kaplan
Introductory Essays by Leo Strauss
Introductory Essays for the Second Edition by Steven S. Schwarzchild and Kenneth Seeskin

DURKHEIM ON RELIGION
Émile Durkheim
Edited by W. S. F. Pickering

ON THE GLAUBENSLEHRE
Two Letters to Dr. Lücke
Friedrich D. E. Schleiermacher
Translated by James Duke and Francis Fiorenza

HERMENEUTICS
The Handwritten Manuscripts
Friedrich D. E. Schleiermacher
Edited by Heina Kimmerle
Translated by James Duke and Jack Forstman

THE STUDY OF STOLEN LOVE
Translated by David C. Buck and K. Paramasivam

THE DAOIST MONASTIC MANUAL
A Translation of the Fengdao Kejie
Livia Kohn

SACRED AND PROFANE BEAUTY
The Holy in Art
Garardus van der Leeuw
Preface by Mircea Eliade
Translated by David E. Green
With a New Introduction and Bibliography by Diane Apostolos-Cappadona

THE HISTORY OF THE BUDDHA'S RELIC SHRINE
A Translation of the Sinhala Thūpavamsa
Stephen C. Berkwitz

DAMASCIUS' PROBLEMS AND SOLUTIONS CONCERNING FIRST PRINCIPLES
Translated by Sara Ahbel-Rappe
Introduction and Notes by Sara Ahbel-Rappe

THE SECRET GARLAND
Āṇṭāḷ's Tiruppāvai and Nācciyār Tirumoḻi
Translated with Introduction and Commentary by Archana Venkatesan

DEBATING THE DASAM GRANTH
Robin Rinehart

AAR
AMERICAN ACADEMY OF RELIGION

Debating the Dasam Granth

Robin Rinehart

OXFORD
UNIVERSITY PRESS

OXFORD
UNIVERSITY PRESS

Oxford University Press, Inc., publishes works that further
Oxford University's objective of excellence
in research, scholarship, and education.

Oxford New York
Auckland Cape Town Dar es Salaam Hong Kong Karachi
Kuala Lumpur Madrid Melbourne Mexico City Nairobi
New Delhi Shanghai Taipei Toronto

With offices in
Argentina Austria Brazil Chile Czech Republic France Greece
Guatemala Hungary Italy Japan Poland Portugal Singapore
South Korea Switzerland Thailand Turkey Ukraine Vietnam

Published by Oxford University Press, Inc.
198 Madison Avenue, New York, New York 10016

www.oup.com

Library of Congress Cataloging-in-Publication Data
Rinehart, Robin, 1964–
Debating the Dasam Granth / Robin Rinehart.
p. cm.
Includes bibliographical references and index.
ISBN 978–0–19–975506–6
1. Daswen Pādshāh kā Granth—Criticism, interpretation, etc.
I. Title.
BL2017.456.R56 2011
294.6'82—dc22 2010013869

1 3 5 7 9 8 6 4 2

Printed in the United States of America
on acid-free paper

ACKNOWLEDGEMENTS

MY TRAVEL TO INDIA FOR research on this project was completed with the assistance of grants from Lafayette's Advanced Research Committee, and the writing of this book was supported by an Enhanced Sabbatical at Lafayette College.

At Lafayette, I am fortunate to have many friends and colleagues who are a constant source of advice, encouragement, and stimulating discussions, including Robert Cohn, Stephen Lammers, Asma Sayeed, Herman Tull, Bianca Falbo, Patricia Donahue, George Panichas, and Suzanne Westfall.

The Interlibrary Loan staff of Skillman Library at Lafayette College managed to track down countless texts in Punjabi, Hindi, and Brajbhasha. Staff at the British Library in London helped me locate early printed works on the Dasam Granth. Kurt and Ellen Poriles Weiler shared the late Royal Weiler's library of works on Indian literature with Lafayette College, making a treasure trove of scholarship easily available to me.

Among the community of scholars of South Asia, I would like to thank Corinne Demspey, Whitney Sanford, Bill Harman, Anna Bigelow, Lou Fenech, Doris Jakobsh, Michael Hawley, Jack Hawley, Gurinder Singh Mann, and Nikky Singh. I am especially grateful to Pashaura Singh for his encouragement and support, and his generosity in sharing texts and bringing important references to my attention. The late Selva Raj and the late Aditya Behl were both dear friends, now deeply missed, with whom I discussed this project.

I am grateful for the comments and suggestions of audience members at lectures and presentations I have given on the Dasam Granth at the University of Pennsylvania, Columbia University, Princeton University, Sikh studies conferences at the University of Michigan and at University of California—Riverside, meetings of the American Academy of Religion, the Conference on the Study of Religions in India, and at Lafayette College.

As a participant in 1999 Summer Program in Punjab Studies, sponsored by Columbia University and the University of California—Santa Barbara and led by Dr. Gurinder Singh Mann, I was fortunate to hear a series of lectures by Dr. J. S. Grewal, Dr. Indu Banga, and other scholars on the history and culture of the Punjab.

This book would not have been possible without the availability of scholarly work on the history of Sikhism and Punjabi language and literature. I am especially indebted to Dr. R. S. Jaggi for his formidable body of published work on the Dasam Granth and other Sikh texts and to Dr. J. S. Grewal for his work on Sikh history, as well as the Publications Bureau of Punjabi University, Patiala, and the Bhasha Vibhag of Punjab for their efforts in making Punjabi texts available in print. Mr. Saran Singh, President and Editor of the Sikh Cultural Centre in Kolkata, kindly provided me with copies of Dr. Trilochan Singh's articles on the Dasam Granth.

In India, my dear friend Nina Anand, her late husband, Ashok Anand, and Rajeev Bhagat provided invaluable support and logistical assistance. Also in India, I would like to thank the countless people who spoke with me about the Dasam Granth and helped me to understand the differing viewpoints on the text. In addition to many whom I cannot name here, I would like to thank Mary Fisher and Bhai Kirpal Singh at Gobind Sadan, as well as Giani Gurditt Singh, Roopinder Singh, Dr. Darshan Singh, and Dr. Jodh Singh, who allowed me to sit in on one of his graduate classes on the Dasam Granth at Punjabi University, Patiala. Although I heard many different views on the Dasam Granth from Sikhs in India, the people who spoke with me were invariably kind and generous in sharing their time and knowledge. I cannot thank them enough for sharing their views on a topic that is at times contentious and divisive.

Thanks to Anne Monius, editor of the American Academy of Religion series Religion in Translation, for her wise counsel, to the two anonymous reviewers of the book, who made invaluable suggestions, and to Cynthia Read of Oxford University Press for her guidance.

I would also like to thank my parents, my brother Mike, and Ward, Sarah, Steve, and Janice for their encouragement. Molly and Lilith were a constant source of trenchant feline counsel. I give special thanks to Brad for everything.

I give sincere thanks to the scholars I have mentioned here for all that they have contributed to my knowledge; any mistakes or infelicities in this book are mine alone.

CONTENTS

ABBREVIATIONS

BN	*Bachitra Nāṭak*
CC 1	*Chaṇḍī Charitra Ukti Bilās*
CC 2	*Chaṇḍī Charitra 2*
CP	*Charitropākhiān*
DGK	*Dasam Granth dā Kartritav*
DGPP	*Dasam-Granth kī Paurāṇik Pṛṣṭhabhūmi*
DM	*Devī Māhātmya*
KA	*Krisnāvatār*
SNM	*Shastra-nām-mālā*
VDK	*Vār Durgā Kī*

TRANSLITERATION AND TRANSLATION

CHOOSING A SYSTEM OF transliteration for a work such as this poses challenges. Most of the Dasam Granth [Dasama Grantha] is in the Brajbhasha [Brajbhāṣā] language, but Punjabi speakers typically follow the conventions of Punjabi pronunciation when they read or recite the text. Secondary literature on the Dasam Granth in English uses a wide range of transliteration styles; transliteration styles for Punjabi and Hindi often differ significantly as well. Brajbhasha uses final short vowels [a, i, u] that are grammatically and metrically significant but generally not fully pronounced. Thus the title of the first composition in the Dasam Granth is written as *Jāpu*, but pronounced *Jāp*, usually with a slight pause at the end of the word.

Generally, terms, titles, and proper names are given with full diacritics in brackets the first time they are used. If a name occurs only once, it is given with diacritics. Phrases or lines quoted directly from the Dasam Granth in the original Brajbhasha use full diacritical markings in the format used for Sanskrit and modern Indo-Aryan languages, including final short vowels. If not part of a direct quotation from the Dasam Granth, Brajbhasha, Punjabi, and Hindi words are given without final short vowels (e.g. avatar rather than avatara [*avatāra*]). Titles of Sanskrit works preserve Sanskritstyle transliteration with the final inherent *a*, e.g. Mahabharata [Mahābhārata] rather than Mahabharat. I have preserved final consonant clusters from Brahbhasha such as the–*tra* in *Bachitra*. In the case of names and terms that are in common usage in works on Indian religions, I use the most common spelling, e.g. avatar, dharma, karma, Shiva, Vishnu, Durga. In some instances, the transliterated form of the word may differ from the typical pronunciation in modern Punjabi and Modern Standard Hindi. Thus "Shiva" is most commonly pronounced as "Shiv," and the elements of final consonant clusters may be separated, e.g. dharma is pronounced as "dharam"; *bachitra* is pronounced "*bachitar*."

The unvoiced unaspirated palatal consonant is transliterated as *ch* (e.g., Chandi [Chaṇḍī]), and the aspirated palatal consonant as *cch* (e.g., Chhibbar [Chhibbar]). Aspirated sibilants are usually not indicated in Brajbhasha orthography but are here transliterated as *sh*, for example, Shiva, *shastra*. When providing the transliteration with diacritics of words from Sanskrit or Hindi texts, I have preserved the distinction between *ś* and *ṣ*, for example, Vishnu [Viṣṇu]. Nasalization is generally indicated with *n*.

When a Brajbhasha word is significantly different from its form in Sanskrit, modern Punjabi, or Modern Standard Hindi, I have included the Sanskrit form in brackets (e.g., Kacch [Kaśyapa]).

Quotations from the secondary literature on the Dasam Granth in Punjabi, Hindi, and English preserve whatever form of transliteration is used in that text. Books and articles in Punjabi, Hindi, and Brajbhasha are listed in the references section at the end of the book with full diacritics.

Unless otherwise indicated, all English translations from the Dasam Granth are mine. Citations of the original include the composition title, chapter number if appropriate, and verse number.

Debating the Dasam Granth

Introduction

"Ma'am, is that a holy book?"

Airport staff searched every piece of carry-on baggage before they allowed passengers to board an international flight departing from New Delhi. They carefully opened purses, parcels, and packages and combed through everything inside. As the young lady searching one person's bag pulled out a book wrapped in fine cloth, she posed the question above and then quickly handed the book to the passenger, asking that she unwrap and open the book, then fan its pages to show that nothing was hidden inside. The inspector allowed the passenger to return it to her bag, even though airport staff were otherwise not allowing passengers to touch their things as they were inspected and repacked.

That a "holy book" should occasion special treatment at an airport in India, in an era when at airports worldwide nothing about one's person or possessions is the least bit sacred, is significant. The fact that airport personnel have been instructed not to handle holy books suggests that such books are special not only for the words they contain but also as objects in and of themselves, to be treated with deference lest offense be caused. At the airport, the simple fact of the fine cloth wrapping—not the actual content of the book—served to suggest the book's holiness. But in the world beyond airports, gaining such status is far more complex, and in many cases quite controversial.

This book is about a very controversial text in the Sikh faith called the Dasam Granth, attributed to the tenth and final human Guru [*gurū*] of Sikhism, Guru Gobind Singh. This text is so controversial, in fact, that some Sikhs assert it is not a "holy book" at all but part of a scheme to discredit Sikhism. The text itself is vast and complex, comprising more than 1,400 printed pages in a typical complete edition. The compositions within the book range from praise to a formless, indescribable god in the opening *Jap* [*Jāpu*], to detailed expositions of the avatars [*avatārs*] of Vishnu [Viṣṇu] and other deities and stories of the goddess Durga [Durgā], to a series of tales of women and the schemes they devise to pursue illicit liaisons with men. The reasons for the controversies surrounding the text are complicated as well. There is a long-standing and at times acrimonious debate among Sikhs as to whether or not the Dasam Granth is worthy of the wrapping that would indicate its status as a "holy book." In discussing the different sections of the text, Sikhs often make a distinction between "scripture" and "literature" (sometimes even using these English words in Punjabi), though how they apply such categorizations to the Dasam Granth varies.

Authorship has been one of the central issues in this debate. Did Guru Gobind Singh really compose everything within the Dasam Granth? Or, perhaps, did he compose only some of it, the remainder being the work of poets he sponsored in his court? Or is it the work of someone else entirely? What evidence is available to support these positions, and what kinds of arguments have Sikh authors made? The authorship question is central to how many people have sought to determine the "holy" status of the text; if Guru Gobind Singh was the author of the Dasam Granth in its entirety, then the fact of his authorship in and of itself makes the text "holy"; if he was the author of only some of it, the issue of "holy" status becomes more complex.

A second and related issue, indeed, one of the criteria some Sikh commentators have used to determine authorship, is the content of the different portions of the Dasam Granth. May they be seen as being in keeping with the spirit of the compositions of the earlier Sikh Gurus, those that are preserved in the Guru Granth Sahib [*Gurū Granth Sāhib*]? How, for example, can verses celebrating the deeds of deities and avatars associated with Hinduism be understood in the context of Sikh tradition? Perhaps even more challenging, how might stories of illicit love relations be understood in the context of a religious text? If the Dasam Granth is indeed the work of Guru Gobind Singh, why did he write such material? Or, even if he did not compose or tell these stories himself, why would he sponsor the composition of such material? What information about Guru Gobind Singh's life might shed light on the nature of his literary endeavors? How and why did the diverse body of compositions that make up the Dasam Granth come to be contained within a single text?

A third and equally complex issue concerns the role of the Dasam Granth in the development of Sikh practice and belief. How did Sikh tradition evolve during the initial stage of the ten Gurus, and to what extent might the Dasam Granth illustrate a phase in that evolution? May the Dasam Granth be taken as indicative of Sikh perspectives during Guru Gobind Singh's life, or might its compositions have been targeted at a wider audience? What role did the Dasam Granth play in the development of Sikhism after the period of the ten Gurus? What effects did the Singh Sabha reform movements of the late nineteenth and early twentieth centuries have on understandings of the Dasam Granth and its status in Sikh tradition? What role does the Dasam Granth play in current Sikh practice? To this day, a few portions of the Dasam Granth are used regularly in Sikh liturgy, though not all Sikhs are necessarily familiar with the broader context from which these portions are drawn.

Unraveling the controversies that swirl round this text is no easy task. There is a fairly substantial body of secondary literature on the Dasam Granth, in Punjabi, Hindi, and English, produced by both Sikh and non-Sikh scholars. Taken as a whole, however, this body of interpretive literature raises just as many questions as it answers, and it has reached what is thus far an insurmountable impasse over the issue of authorship. Much of the secondary literature on the Dasam Granth is framed in terms of the authorship debate, and the same sets of arguments have been made over and over. A particular scholar's conclusion regarding authorship in turn shapes conclusions about the text's authenticity as a "holy book." It is quite common for studies of the Dasam Granth to reach conclusions about the text's authorship and authenticity as a Sikh "holy book" on the basis of some combination of limited historical evidence, debatable claims about authorial intention and the meaning of particular passages, and theological assertions. Authorship analyses, particularly those which assume that Guru Gobind Singh authored only some of the text, are typically focused on individual compositions as judged against particular criteria, and therefore place less emphasis on the Dasam Granth in its entirety. Sorting through such claims about authorship and evaluating their merits against competing claims invariably leads into larger controversies about the nature of Sikhism as a distinct religious tradition and the narrative that best describes its historical development. At particular issue is the nature of Sikhism's relationship to Hinduism and the degree to which Sikhism has been understood as a distinct tradition at various points in its history.

Even if one leaves aside the controversies about interpreting the Dasam Granth, simply coming to grips with the text itself is daunting not only for its sheer length but for the great breadth of its subject matter. Because the text figures heavily in analyses of the life of Guru Gobind Singh and the subsequent history of the Sikh community, or *panth*, in many studies of Sikhism, it is often mentioned, but not fully analyzed in the press of addressing other topics. The text is linguistically challenging as well; most of its compositions are in Brajbhasha [Brajbhāṣā], but there are also Punjabi and Persian compositions. Some native Punjabi speakers find the Brajbhasha of the Dasam Granth challenging.

Although arguments regarding authorship have been a primary focus of many analyses of the Dasam Granth, the goal of this study is not to solve the questions of the authorship of the Dasam Granth as a whole or its differing parts, or even to offer an argument in that regard. In fact, our present knowledge about the text may not be sufficient to reach a fully satisfying answer to the authorship questions. What I will argue, however, is that the unending debate about issues of authorship and authenticity, framed within an analytical model that proposes Guru Gobind Singh as the author of all, some, or virtually none of the Dasam Granth, has obscured aspects of the text that raise a different set of questions and allow us to think about the text in its entirety.

In addition to the authorship debate, a second factor that has dominated the majority of scholarship on the Dasam Granth, by both Sikh and Western scholars, is the issue of the text within the context of Sikh history subsequent to its compilation. To put it another way, the Dasam Granth is almost always placed on a forward trajectory in which it is interpreted according to later developments in the religion. Of course, it makes perfectly good sense to treat the Dasam Granth in the context of subsequent Sikh history; it is a part of Sikh heritage, and its significance naturally lies in large part in its ongoing use and interpretation. However, the Dasam Granth, because of its controversial content, including Hindu mythology and tales of wayward women, has often been seen as an anomaly requiring explanation.

The questions about authorship and the use of the Dasam Granth in Sikh practice are extremely important, and I do not mean to downplay their significance in any way. But the range of answers we suggest to questions about the Dasam Granth may be expanded substantially if we place the work in a still wider context that looks not only forward but also to the past. The Dasam Granth was not woven out of entirely new threads. Like any text, it has its antecedents. It is this aspect of the text's history that has received the least attention, and which opens new avenues of analysis of the text and its relationship to wider Indic literary traditions. This approach allows us to develop new frameworks for understanding the Dasam Granth and to move beyond the interpretive impasse over authorship and authenticity.

In the specific context of Sikhism, the Dasam Granth stands in relation to the earlier compositions of the Sikh Gurus and other poets that were first compiled in a text known as the Adi Granth [*Ādi Granth*] and later came to be known as the Guru Granth Sahib, the primary sacred text or "scripture" of Sikhism. Many analyses of the compositions within the Dasam Granth focus on this relationship, often framing it as the question of whether particular portions of the Dasam Granth are in accord with the "spirit of bani [*bāṇī*]" or the sacred words of the Sikh Gurus, qualifying them for "holy" or "scriptural" status. But the Dasam Granth also stands in relation to long-standing Indic literary traditions. With substantial portions of the text focused on the goddess Durga and the avatars of Vishnu, there is undoubtedly some relationship with the Puranic mythology of Hindu tradition. And with tales of wayward women, similar to those found in Sanskrit and Indian vernacular languages, there is also a relationship to wider Indic literary and storytelling traditions. There is also the issue of the text as a whole. How and why might the diverse contents of the Dasam Granth, from lofty praises of God to lusty tales of licentious women, have been woven together into a single anthology? Can a dichotomy such as "scripture" and "literature" fully capture the nature of such a text? The unrelenting focus on authorship has pushed such questions aside.

In order to explore questions about the Dasam Granth's relationship to wider Indic traditions and thereby enrich our understanding of it, we must not simply consider it on a forward trajectory but also look to its past and its relation to earlier versions of the myths, stories, and themes it presents to listeners and readers. We must also acknowledge that not all those who have heard, read, recited, or otherwise used the Dasam Granth have necessarily done so with the authorship issue as their primary concern. In this study, to demonstrate how we might begin to ask different questions that could lead to a new understanding of the Dasam Granth and its significance within Indian literature, I will focus on three specific aspects of the text that have connections to earlier Indic traditions.

To set the stage, chapter 1 provides background information on the life of Guru Gobind Singh as it relates to the Dasam Granth, as well as Sikh sources that mention the Guru's literary activities and the poets he sponsored in his court. This chapter also includes synopses of each of the compositions within the Dasam Granth, along with a summary of the history of the text and the controversies surrounding it. To illustrate the parameters of the discourse surrounding the Dasam Granth, this summary addresses the key findings of some of the most important scholarly studies of the Dasam Granth, particularly with respect to the evidence concerning extant manuscripts of the text and its authorship and compilation. For Sikhs, the authorship controversy is in large part a theological matter because reaching a conclusion about whether or not Guru Gobind Singh composed the portions of the text that address goddesses and avatars is central to interpretations of how one may express conceptions of divinity, as well as an understanding of Guru Gobind Singh as a religious leader and the subsequent development of Sikh practice (Rinehart 2004). The goal in this study, however, is not to present a particular theological reading of the Dasam Granth but rather to understand the range of arguments that Sikhs have made. Once again, I must emphasize that I do not intend for this study to solve the authorship question but rather to examine the discourse to the present, taking note of the available evidence and competing arguments, and suggesting possible new avenues of interpretation.

Chapter 2 explores a fascinating composition in the Dasam Granth called *Bachitra Natak* [*Bachitra Nāṭaka*], "The Wondrous Drama," part of which is known as *Apni Katha* [*Apnī Kathā*], or "My Story." *Bachitra Natak* presents an autobiographical account of the life of Guru Gobind Singh, preceded by a lengthy genealogy describing the Guru as a descendant of Ram [Rām], a well-known figure in Hindu mythology, whose life story is related in the many versions of the Ramayana [*Rāmāyaṇa*]. Much of the autobiographical narrative focuses on Guru Gobind Singh's battles with neighboring hill chiefs and forces allied with the Mughals. The fact that this composition considers Guru Gobind Singh's life means that it is of course crucial to a reading of the text as a whole; indeed, it introduces themes that recur throughout the Dasam Granth. It is also the core portion of the set of compositions within the Dasam Granth known as the *Bachitra Natak Granth* (discussed in more detail in chapter 1). Chapter 2 concludes with a discussion of the "autobiographical" nature of this narrative and its relation to earlier Indian literary traditions presenting royal genealogy and praise of kings. I argue that *Bachitra Natak*'s presentation of Guru Gobind Singh as a spiritual and worldly leader is key to a reading of the Dasam Granth in its entirety.

The Dasam Granth contains three separate compositions that tell the story of Durga and her battles with demons; the goddess is also mentioned in many other parts of the text. The goddess compositions are a significant portion of the Dasam Granth and among the more controversial because of the theological issues they raise. In Sikh exegesis, there has been debate as to whether these compositions advocate belief in and worship of a goddess, as well as speculation regarding the implications of the usage of the term *bhagautī* [Sanskrit *bhagavatī*], which Sikhs have translated both as "goddess" and as "sword." Chapter 3 examines these goddess narratives and their interpretation and compares their treatment of the goddess to other Indian goddess traditions. It also explores the cosmic significance of the goddess's battles with demons, how these battles are related to Guru Gobind Singh's battles as described in *Bachitra Natak*, the role of weapons in these battles, and how these narratives relate to Indic notions of kingship. Although these compositions have clear connections to goddess mythology in Sanskrit, they are largely absent from studies of the goddess in Indian tradition. A close study of the Dasam Granth's goddess compositions may contribute to greater understanding of the nature of myth and belief not only in Sikhism but in Hinduism as well.

The longest and most controversial composition in the Dasam Granth, *Charitropakhian* [*Charitropākhiān*], begins and ends with lengthy accounts of battles between deities and demons, and in between includes several hundred stories embedded within a frame story about a king betrayed by his new wife. These *charitras* include many accounts of women who use duplicitous means to pursue illicit liaisons. Versions of some of its tales may be traced to Sanskrit texts such as the *Hitopadesha* [*Hitopadeśa*] that teach practical wisdom through storytelling, as well as regional oral and written romance tales and anecdotes about historical figures. The sometimes graphic nature of the *charitras* has led to the exclusion of *Charitropakhian* from many printed editions of the Dasam Granth, and many commentators have seen it as entirely separate from the seemingly more religiously oriented compositions of the rest of the text. I will argue, however, that when read in its entirety, *Charitropakhian* does indeed show clear thematic connections with other parts of the Dasam Granth. Chapter 4 includes an introduction to the stories found in *Charitropakhian* and an analysis of this composition as a whole, its relation to the rest of the Dasam Granth, and its relation to broader Indic storytelling tradition.

Finally, the conclusion explores how the seemingly disparate portions of the Dasam Granth may fit together. I argue that the themes enumerated in *Bachitra Natak*, especially the role of the Gurus in promoting and protecting dharma, may provide a key to understanding the Dasam Granth in its entirety as a exploration of the nature of both spiritual and worldly leadership, and therefore bearing a relationship to the types of anthologies produced at royal courts throughout India but also illustrating a new Sikh conception of the role of the leader with both spiritual and worldly responsibilities.

The concluding chapter also explores how the Dasam Granth relates to similar textual anthologies in Sanskrit and Indian vernacular literature. Nearly everyone who has written about the Dasam Granth has acknowledged the relationship the text has to Indian traditions, particularly traditions most commonly associated with Hinduism. Many Sikh authors have argued that its diverse contents reflect Guru Gobind Singh's desire to preserve and protect Indian heritage during a time of political instability and religious conflict, either by composing the text himself or by sponsoring poets who composed it. With noteworthy exceptions such as R. S. Jaggi's *Dasam-Granth kī Paurāṇik Pṛṣṭhabhūmi* (1965), the analysis of the nature of the text's relationship to wider Indian traditions has not moved beyond fairly broad characterizations, typically something like "most of the Dasam Granth comes from the Puranas [Purāṇas]," characterizations that are almost always situated solidly within arguments for or against Guru Gobind Singh as author. Analyzing specific aspects of the Dasam Granth's relationship to and place within the larger body of Indian literature affords new means of reading the text as a whole.

Analyzing the Dasam Granth in the broader framework of Indian literature also helps to move our understanding of the text beyond the limited analytic frameworks and categories in which it has been cast, such as authorship, and scripture or literature, that is, "holy book" or not. Placing the Dasam Granth in this wider context also highlights the importance of the text in our understanding of crucial issues within the history of Indian literature, such as the relationship between classical Sanskrit and the vernaculars, and the development of Brajbhasha literary traditions. It is also an important part of the development of literature not only in Sikhism but in the greater Punjab region of northwest India.

This focus on the Dasam Granth in the wider context of Indic literary traditions is *not* an argument for or against a "Hindu" influence in Sikhism. As with arguments regarding authorship, assertions about the degree of Hindu influence in the Dasam Granth and subsequent Sikh history are significant in a more theological context advocating particular forms of Sikh belief and practice, as well as understandings of the relationship between Hinduism and Sikhism. The goal here, however, is to build upon a basic point on which there is widespread agreement: a substantial portion of the Dasam Granth has clear connections to literary traditions associated with what is now termed "Hinduism" and, more broadly, Indic literature.

There are limitations to framing any analysis of the Dasam Granth in terms of the relationship between Sikhism and Hinduism. The meaning of the term "Hinduism" itself is by no means self-evident, as much recent scholarship has addressed; it encompasses a vast range of theological positions and practices. Current understandings are in part a result of developments in colonial and postcolonial India that are predated by the Dasam Granth itself, so we must be careful to avoid anachronistic applications of the term. Nonetheless, if we keep in mind that the term "Hindu" in Guru Gobind Singh's time did not yet carry all the associations it acquired in later history, it is clear that the Dasam Granth illustrates an important phase in the exploration, development, and demarcation of religious boundaries in precolonial Punjab. The use of Hindu mythological themes within a Sikh text should be a matter of interest to scholars of both Sikhism and Hinduism, for important issues are often negotiated on the boundaries between religious traditions, especially when those boundary lines are contested.

The Dasam Granth has until recently been largely overlooked as an illustration of the ongoing negotiation of religious boundaries between Sikhism, Hinduism, and Islam. The argument here focuses primarily on the connections between the Dasam Granth and Indian literary traditions. It is important in addition to note, however, the presence of various forms of Islam in the Punjab during the time the Dasam Granth was composed and compiled. The Dasam Granth reflects the presence of Islam in the Punjab in several ways. For example, the *Bachitra Natak* account of Guru Gobind Singh's birth notes the earlier efforts of both Hindu and Muslim spiritual leaders, and it highlights Guru Gobind Singh's battles against forces led by Muslim leaders or involving Muslim warriors. Poetic imagery drawn from the practice of Islam appears in a number of compositions; warriors, for example, are at times described as being like the towering minarets of a mosque. In addition, some of the anecdotes in *Charitropakhian* concern Muslim characters.

The Dasam Granth has also largely remained absent from wider discussions of vernacular literature and even studies of Brajbhasha literature, although Dharam Pal Ashta (1959, 309), one of the first scholars to publish an English-language study of the text, described it as the "biggest work in Braj, surpassing even the *Sur Sagar*." The Dasam Granth's relative neglect outside the realm of Sikh studies may be due in part to the fact that the text has been most frequently transmitted in the Gurmukhi [Gurmukhī] script, which is typically used for the Punjabi language, while Brajbhasha compositions are most often in the Devanagari [Devanāgarī] script. In turn, scholars conversant with Punjabi and Gurmukhi script have typically focused their attentions on matters related to the history of Sikhism rather than the development of Brajbhasha literature. The Dasam Granth has also not received much attention in studies of goddess mythology or avatars, both central themes of the text. Thus, a greater understanding of these issues as they are presented in the Dasam Granth is important and may allow us to reflect more deeply on the nature of belief in gods and goddesses and their mythologies, evolving understandings of the role of the avatar, and the ongoing exploration of religious boundaries.

Because substantial portions of the Dasam Granth address gods, goddesses, and avatars associated with Hinduism, many Sikh interpreters have sought to define what the text suggests about Sikhism's relationship with Hindu traditions. Unfortunately, most such analyses have tended to make Hindu tradition rather more monolithic than it is or has been in the past. Thus, we find terms such as "dharma," "avatar," "Purana," and "Tantra" presented as if they were self-evident, clearly defined concepts and categories of text and practice, which, in fact, they are not. Acknowledging that such concepts are contested and variously defined and redefined within Hindu traditions allows a more nuanced reading of such terms as they are used in the Dasam Granth. Arguably, it may also afford the opportunity for less sharply targeted polemic among Sikh interpreters of the Dasam Granth, for if it is acknowledged that there were diverse views within Hinduism, there is more room to acknowledge that even in using so-called Hindu concepts in the Dasam Granth, Sikh tradition may well have been articulating a new and distinctively Sikh interpretation of them.

A question that has run through many Sikh analyses of the Dasam Granth is whether the compositions within it that address Hindu mythological themes in some way indicate belief in or reverence for the gods, goddesses, and avatars of Hindu traditions. This is a very difficult question to answer. First, it is almost always entangled with the authorship question; those who read the text as advocating belief in gods, goddesses, and avatars typically argue that Guru Gobind Singh therefore was not the author of sections in the text that focus on these topics because he would not have endorsed such beliefs. In contrast, those who believe Guru Gobind Singh was the author most often argue that the god, goddess, and avatar passages do not promote belief in these figures. Second, even if the authorship question were to be fully resolved, it would still not provide a conclusive answer to this issue of belief, both because defining authorial intention is a highly problematic venture, and because whatever the author(s) of these compositions may have intended, he or they could not control how an audience, whether readers or listeners, might interpret the text.

Often we are too quick to make assumptions about what people "believe" about their texts, without acknowledging the very real possibility that a person may take something from a text without necessarily believing whatever it asserts, or may interpret it differently than the author intended. Put another way, some portions of the Dasam Granth can mean different things to different people. A devotee of the goddess could listen to or read the sections that detail the goddess and her defeat of demons and take these sections as an expression of his or her faith in the goddess. Someone else who does not believe in the existence of the goddess could listen to or read the very same text and nonetheless find some sort of meaning within it, perhaps through an allegorical interpretation. This is in fact the dominant view among Sikh interpreters—that the stories about gods, goddesses, and avatars triumphing over demons were meant to inspire warriors in battle and more generally to emphasize the triumph of good over evil. This issue of whether such stories imply belief in and worship of gods, goddesses, and avatars may be a useful question to consider in the realm of not only Sikhism but Hinduism as well. Under what circumstances might such mythical narratives be meaningful to people, but not necessarily "believed" as an assertion of the existence or ultimate authority of particular deities?

The question of whether people "believe" in myths is connected to the challenge of deciding whether or not the Dasam Granth is a "holy book." Some Sikh authors, such as Surindar Singh Kohli, who published a partial English translation of the Dasam Granth in 2005, have termed it the "second scripture of the Sikhs." Others, however, are less comfortable with designating the entire text as "holy" or "scripture." As I noted earlier, in conversations with Sikhs about the text, I have found that many people prefer to categorize some parts of it as "scripture" and other parts as "literature," using these terms not just in English but also in Punjabi, an issue to which I will return in the concluding chapter. While some Sikh critics of Western scholarship decry the use of "Western" analytical models in the study of Sikhism, it is significant that Sikhs themselves have adopted terminology such as "scripture" and "literature" in their analysis of their own tradition, suggesting that the characterization of any model of analysis as "Western" or "Sikh" may be an oversimplification.

Much recent scholarship on Sikhism of necessity addresses recent controversies about how Western scholars and Sikh scholars trained in the West have represented Sikh history and practice, and whether these scholars have imparted particular biases into their work. The Dasam Granth has often directly or indirectly factored into these controversies about the representation of Sikhism. Large portions of the Dasam Granth (e.g., those concerned with Hindu mythology) are related to forms of Sikh practice targeted by the Singh Sabha reformers of the late nineteenth and early twentieth centuries as being too closely intertwined with Hinduism; as a result, most people writing about the text since the reform movements have in some way either affirmed or responded to the critical lens of the Singh Sabha movement. The Dasam Granth's place in various narratives of the development of Sikhism is thus contested. As such, there are many tantalizing references to the Dasam Granth in studies of other aspects of Sikh tradition, many of which raise important questions about the text and its reception, or suggest continuity between ideas expressed in the Dasam Granth and later Sikh praxis, particularly during the period of the Sikh kingdoms in the eighteenth and early nineteenth centuries. But these references are often all too brief, lost in the press of exploring equally important matters or of asserting a particular argument about the authorship and authenticity of the Dasam Granth. While the field of Sikh Studies is growing both in India and in the West, and much has been written about the Dasam Granth, there is still much more to be learned from this significant and controversial text with respect not only to Sikh literature but to Indian literature as a whole.

Additionally, the sheer length and breadth of the Dasam Granth have meant that scholarly studies that have dealt with the whole text have, perhaps of necessity, sometimes devoted more focus to various forms of description such as long lists of meters and summaries of the compositions within the text at the expense of sustained analysis. Ashta's important work *The Poetry of the Dasam Granth* (1959) illustrates this phenomenon well. Much of the book is dedicated to lists and summaries. Nonetheless, his work can be tremendously helpful to someone seeking a basic understanding of the content of the Dasam Granth. Ashta's work was an important early step in scholarship on the text, and it was one of the first efforts to consider the Dasam Granth in the wider context of Brajbhasha literature. Rattan Singh Jaggi's groundbreaking early published works on the Dasam Granth, particularly his Hindi *Dasam-Granth kī Paurāṇik Pṛṣṭhabhūmi* (1965) and Punjabi *Dasam Granth dā Kartritav* (1966) are also tremendously valuable. Jaggi, an advocate (in his early work at least) of the view that Guru Gobind Singh authored only select portions of the Dasam Granth, has been critical of the work of Ashta, who believed that Guru Gobind Singh authored the entire text. At times, particular scholars' views on authorship appear to have influenced the extent to which they engage analyses of the Dasam Granth by scholars who support a different position.

While acknowledging the importance and significance of the authorship debate, in this study, I treat the Dasam Granth as a text strongly associated with Guru Gobind Singh and therefore an important part of the history of Sikhism. Chapter 1 includes a discussion of the differing arguments regarding authorship, but I do not present a particular argument in this regard in order that I may instead focus on a different set of questions. This approach of reading the Dasam Granth without focusing on determining the authorship of each composition allows key thematic continuities to emerge and come into focus. The sections of the Dasam Granth addressed in subsequent chapters in particular illustrate a clear concern to explore the nature of spiritual and temporal leadership in the context of a broad cosmic framework in which the maintenance of proper order or dharma is critical. This overarching concern for elucidating the responsibilities of a leader in turn provides a lens through which we may understand how the diverse compositions of the Dasam Granth—from lengthy praises of weapons to tales of wayward women—may fit together as a coherent whole.

1

The Life of Guru Gobind Singh (1666–1708) and the History of the Dasam Granth

THIS CHAPTER BEGINS WITH A brief account of significant events in Guru Gobind Singh's life, with special focus on those that are relevant to the Dasam Granth. This account of the Guru's life is followed by synopses of the different compositions in the Dasam Granth, and the chapter concludes with a brief history of the text and its interpretation, noting some of the most important Sikh sources that mention Guru Gobind Singh's compositions and the possible circumstances surrounding their compilation. This provides a basic framework for understanding the Dasam Granth and the many ways it has been interpreted.

The Life of Guru Gobind Singh

Whatever position one takes on the authorship of the Dasam Granth, the text is clearly associated with Guru Gobind Singh, and therefore some understanding of his life is critical to how people have read the Dasam Granth. While it is beyond the scope of this project to construct a full critical biography of Guru Gobind Singh, we must nonetheless note some of the limitations inherent to constructing even a short sketch of the Guru's life. The earliest sources for Guru Gobind Singh's life do not always present a consistent picture, and there are particular events in the Guru's life of which there are widely divergent portrayals, most notably the foundation of the Khalsa [Khālsā] in 1699.[1] There has been considerable scholarly debate regarding the reliability and particular biases of most of the earliest sources used for constructing a biography of Guru Gobind Singh. Among some of the earliest accounts of Guru Gobind Singh's life in Western sources, the dates vary for key events, such as his birth and some of the battles in which he took part. Because Guru Gobind Singh led military campaigns and at times urged his followers to take up arms, an understanding of his life and mission is central to various historiographical narratives about what Gokul Chand Narang (1946, 19) termed "the transformation of Sikhism" from a "religious sect into a political organization," and this too is a matter of some controversy in understandings of the development of Sikhism. Also problematic in some biographical accounts is the tendency to assert particular psychological motivations for Guru Gobind Singh's actions (e.g., in the period following the tragic deaths of his four sons) with no concrete evidence on which to base such assertions. An additional complicating factor is that many of the accounts of Guru Gobind Singh's life that are presented in various secondary sources addressing the Guru's life and works do not always fully identify the primary sources from which they are drawn.[2]

These challenges notwithstanding, accounts of Guru Gobind Singh's life are important in understanding different interpretations of the Dasam Granth because elements within his biography are used to support particular arguments about the text's composition. Yet another caution is in order, however, because some elements of his biography are derived from an autobiographical portion of the Dasam Granth in *Bachitra Natak* called "My Story," or *Apni Katha*. Even authors who are uncertain about whether Guru Gobind Singh actually composed *Bachitra Natak* tend to rely upon it as a primary source. It is also important to note that much of the biographical tradition surrounding Guru Gobind Singh dates from a period when some version of the Dasam Granth was already in circulation, and therefore some portions of the biographical tradition may perhaps in part seek to explain certain parts of the text. Still, there are certain generally accepted facts about the Guru's life that become the basis for particular arguments about the Dasam Granth; these are outlined briefly here, with areas of controversy noted. For the sake of consistency, this account will use the dates provided in the "Chronology of Guru Gobind Singh" in J. S. Grewal and S. S. Bal's (1967, 263–266) *Guru Gobind Singh (A Biographical Study)*, noting points at which other sources provide different dates.

The Punjab of the seventeenth century was a religiously diverse environment that included the followers of Guru Nanak [Gurū Nānak] and his successors, as well as Hindu groups such as Shaivas [Śaivas], Vaishnavas [Vaiṣṇavas], and Shaktas [Śāktas], who were particularly prominent in the Punjab hills. The presence of Shakta goddess worshipers in the hills is especially important for interpretations of the Dasam Granth because the text includes several compositions concerning the goddess.[3] Islam in various forms was also an important feature of the religious landscape, including popular practices such as the worship of holy men, or *pirs* [*pīrs*]. There was diversity and conflict within Sikhism itself in terms of interpretations of the teaching of the Gurus, as well as different views regarding the leadership of the community; for example, Guru Gobind Singh's father, Guru Tegh Bahadur [Gurū Tegh Bahādur], had been challenged in his position as Guru. While we thus can identify communities of Sikhs, Hindus, and Muslims in the Punjab in Guru Gobind Singh's lifetime, it is important to remember that the conceptions of community identity and boundaries in operation at the time—both within particular traditions and between them—were not necessarily the same as those that developed subsequently in colonial and postcolonial India.

During Guru Gobind Singh's lifetime, the Punjab was under the rule of the Mughal empire, with the emperor Aurangzeb in power for almost of all of Guru Gobind Singh's life. At the local level, however, Mughal authority tended to be indirect, through the submission of numerous small kingdoms that paid tribute to the Mughals.[4] These small kingdoms, particularly those in the Punjab hills, had a long tradition of shifting alliances and conflict, and they battled one another fairly regularly. Guru Gobind Singh and his followers became involved in some of those battles; some are described in the *Apni Katha* section of the Dasam Granth, and the theme of battle is significant in other Dasam Granth compositions as well.

Guru Gobind Singh was born in Patna in eastern India (modern-day Bihar) in 1666.[5] His mother's name was Gujari [Gujarī], and his father was the ninth Sikh Guru, Tegh Bahadur. The young Gobind remained in Patna for several years with his mother and other relatives, returning to the Punjab in 1672, where they settled at Makhowal (later renamed Anandpur; in present-day Rupnagar district of the Indian state of

Punjab). In 1675, when Gobind Singh was just nine years old, his father was executed by the Mughals in Delhi. Soon thereafter the young Gobind assumed the position of Guru, at first leading with the counsel of his mother and his uncle Kripal [Kripāl], and then assuming full leadership as he grew older. Most sources concur in reporting that as he grew up, Guru Gobind Singh continued an education that included instruction in the martial arts and the languages of Brajbhasha and Persian, and, according to some sources, Sanskrit and Arabic as well.[6]

Like his father, Guru Tegh Bahadur, Guru Gobind Singh maintained a court at Anandpur (see, e.g., Fenech 2008, 160–164). Features of the Guru's court mentioned in some sources suggest the court was recognized as a site of both spiritual and political authority (e.g., building and maintaining forts, training armed forces, and keeping an elephant that had been presented to the Guru, a traditional symbol of royalty in Indic culture). Guru Gobind Singh maintained armed forces, which at times included men who were not Sikhs. The character of Guru Gobind Singh's forces is significant to interpretations of the Dasam Granth because one of the most frequent arguments about the text is that much of it was tailored specifically to this audience of soldiers, not all of whom were familiar with the Sikh practices and beliefs of the times. Many sources, discussed in more detail later, also report that Guru Gobind Singh sponsored a number of poets in his court. This is another key element of many interpretations of the Dasam Granth, for a number of scholars have argued that the composition of many portions of the text may be attributed to these court poets rather than to Guru Gobind Singh.

The Guru's presence at Anandpur, which included armed forces and symbols suggestive of political power, was apparently seen as a potential threat to the leaders of some of the neighboring hill kingdoms and led to conflicts with some of them.[7] Guru Gobind Singh and his followers left Anandpur for some time, establishing a fort at a site that came to be known as Paonta, where they remained from about 1685 until 1688. Many sources consider this to have been a time of significant literary composition for both Guru Gobind Singh and his court poets, and many of the compositions in the Dasam Granth are often dated to this period.

From the 1680s until the early 1700s, Guru Gobind Singh and his forces were involved in a number of battles, some of which are detailed in the *Apni Katha* portion of *Bachitra Natak*, discussed in more detail in chapter 2. Guru Gobind Singh and his wives Mata Jito [Mātā Jīto] and Mata Sundari [Mātā Sundarī] had four sons, Ajit Singh [Ajīt Singh], Jujhar Singh [Jujhār Singh], Jorawar Singh [Jorāwar Singh], and Fateh Singh. Some sources also mention Mata Sahib Kaur [Mātā Sāhib Kaur] as a third wife.[8] The two elder sons joined Guru Gobind Singh's forces in battle as teens. In Sikh tradition, the four sons are typically referred to with the honorific title of "Sahibzada" [Sāhibzādā].

The 1699 establishment of the order of the Khalsa on the spring festival day of Baisakhi [Baisākhī] is a central event in Guru Gobind Singh's life. The Guru had called his followers to Anandpur to celebrate the festival, at which he instituted a new order of initiation and abolished the power of the *masands*, the leaders of local Sikh congregations who in some instances had become corrupt. Evidence for the exact events of the establishment of the Khalsa and what factors led to it is limited (Grewal and Bal 1967, 182–189).[9] While there are still unanswered questions about the exact nature of the events of Baisakhi 1699, their memory in Sikh tradition has become the foundation for rituals of initiation into the Khalsa. Khalsa initiation rituals typically include recitation of certain parts of the Dasam Granth. The foundation of the Khalsa, however, is not described in the Dasam Granth itself; the *Apni Katha* section of the Dasam Granth does not address events as late as 1699.

Some early Sikh sources, such as Kesar Singh Chhibbar's 1769 *Bansavalinama* [*Bansāvalīnāmā Dasān Patshāhiān Kā*], state that Guru Gobind Singh worshiped the goddess before establishing the Khalsa. Versions of this story appear in many early Western accounts of Sikhism as well.[10] The question of whether or not Guru Gobind Singh's establishment of the Khalsa involved ritual worship of the goddess has been especially controversial. More recently Sikh historians have contested the accuracy of such accounts or have argued that if Guru Gobind Singh was in any way involved with worship of the goddess, it was solely for the purpose of demonstrating its futility and the ways in which Brahman [Brāhmaṇ] ritual specialists exploited people through the performance of elaborate rituals. Because compositions about the goddess Durga and her manifestations are a significant part of the Dasam Granth, the issue about Guru Gobind Singh's purported goddess worship is important to various interpretations of the text.

After the establishment of the Khalsa, Guru Gobind Singh's conflicts with the neighboring hill chiefs continued, leading to a siege of Anandpur late in 1700. Guru Gobind Singh and his followers had to leave Anandpur sometime in 1701. They were able to return in 1702 but were still enmeshed in local conflicts. Some of the rival hill chiefs sought the assistance of Mughal forces. There was a second, protracted siege of Anandpur, and Guru Gobind Singh, his family, and followers finally left Anandpur at the end of 1704. Mughal officials had promised the Guru and his family safe passage, but as they left Anandpur, Guru Gobind Singh's mother, Mata Gujari, and his two younger sons were separated from the rest of the group and taken into captivity in Sirhind. According to some Sikh sources, a great deal of written material was lost as Guru Gobind Singh and his followers left Anandpur. The turmoil in this phase of the Guru's life often plays an important part in arguments about the authorship and subsequent compilation of the Dasam Granth. (Sadly, the theme of lost material continues throughout the history of the text, with manuscripts apparently having been lost or destroyed during battles in the nineteenth century, at partition in 1947, and in 1984 with the Indian army's Operation Bluestar at the Golden Temple in Amritsar.)[11]

Late in 1704, Guru Gobind Singh's two elder sons, Ajit Singh and Jujhar Singh, were killed in battles that took place after the evacuation of Anandpur. Guru Gobind Singh's younger sons, Zorawar Singh and Fateh Singh, were executed at Sirhind, and Mata Gujari died there as well.[12] These tragic events were the basis for what is one of the less controversial parts of the Dasam Granth, the Persian *Zafarnama* [*Zafarnāmā*], Guru Gobind Singh's letter to Aurangzeb, in which he criticized the Mughal emperor and his officials for their failure to keep their word that they would provide the Guru and his family safe passage. The letter also explained that the Guru's battles were not with Aurangzeb but with the hill chiefs.

For most of 1705, Guru Gobind Singh stayed on the move.[13] Some sources report that at one point he was assisted by some Pathans [Paṭhāns] with whom he had previously had dealings. The Pathans helped the Guru disguise himself as "Ucch kā pīr," or "the Muslim holy man from Ucch." Then he took shelter with Qāzī Pīr Muhammad, with whom he had previously studied Persian and the Qur'an (e.g., Narang 1946, 156).

In 1706, Guru Gobind Singh settled for nine months at a site now known as Damdama; it was here that he recited the Adi Granth to Bhai Mani Singh [Bhāī Maṇi Singh],[14] adding his father Guru Tegh Bahadur's compositions. J. D. Cunningham (1990, 77–78), a British army officer who wrote one of the early (1915) Western accounts of Sikhism, reported that Guru Gobind Singh also worked on his own "supplemental *Granth*" at this time. Accounts of this phase are significant to understandings of the Dasam Granth for two main reasons: first, because later tradition reports that it was Bhai Mani Singh who first compiled the Dasam Granth, and second, because there was subsequently some question as to why Guru Gobind Singh did not include any of his own compositions in the Damdama recension of the Adi Granth.

During this period of the Guru's life, the Mughal emperor Aurangzeb was engaged in conflicts in the Deccan region. Late in 1706, Guru Gobind Singh left Damdama to meet with him, but Aurangzeb died before a meeting could take place. In 1707, Guru Gobind Singh met in Agra with Bahadur Shah [Bahādur Shāh], Aurangzeb's eventual successor. He traveled with him to Rajasthan in early 1708.[15] Later that year, he traveled southward to Nander, where he met the Bairagi [Bairāgī], who later took the name Banda [Bandā] and led Sikh forces. In Nander, Guru Gobind Singh was stabbed by a Pathan. Although he initially appeared to be recovering from his injury, the wound reopened after several days, and Guru Gobind Singh died in October 1708. According to many traditional Sikh accounts, prior to his death, Guru Gobind Singh proclaimed that the lineage of human Gurus would come to an end, and that the *panth*, or community of Sikhs, and the Adi Granth would assume the role of Guru after his death.[16]

The Contents of the Dasam Granth

This section outlines the compositions found within printed editions of the full Dasam Granth, followed by a brief discussion of additional compositions found in some of the early manuscripts but not typically included in print.[17] The ordering and total number of compositions vary in the earliest manuscripts of the Dasam Granth. Here they are listed in the order in which they are found in current printed editions of the full text.[18] Although the text is now most commonly known by the title Dasam Granth (or *Srī Dasam Granth Sāhib*), it earlier was sometimes referred to as *Bachitra Natak* (a title that in some instances referred only to select portions of the text, discussed later) or as the *Dasven Pātshāh kā Granth* (*Book of the Tenth Ruler*).

Most of the Dasam Granth is generally understood to have been composed at Anandpur and Paonta and completed by the late 1690s, except for the *Zafarnama* and a few other verses noted later. Some studies of the Dasam Granth include dates for specific portions of the text and/or a listing of the order in which portions were composed, but these dates and order vary within early manuscripts. Those compositions about which there is some consensus regarding dates and/or ordering are noted in the following.

The compositions in the Dasam Granth are in verse using a wide range of meters.[19] Most, with a few exceptions noted later, are in Brajbhasha (some Sikh scholars have also used the terms "Hindwī" and "old Hindi" for Brajbhasha) in the Gurmukhi script.[20] By the time of Guru Gobind Singh, Brajbhasha had become a prestigious literary language, used at some royal courts in north India, and this may be one reason it was the dominant language of the Dasam Granth. Ashta (1959, 280) attributed the use of Brajbhasha rather than the Punjabi language of the late seventeenth century to Guru Gobind Singh's early years in the Patna area where a Bihari dialect was spoken. (For those who believe that Guru Gobind Singh did not compose the majority of the Dasam Granth, the language of the text may be taken as evidence that most of the text was composed by poets with Vaishnava or Shakta leanings who therefore used Brahbhasha rather than the Punjabi language.)

English translations of select portions of the Dasam Granth are available in a number of books on Guru Gobind Singh, the history of Sikhism, and Sikh literature (e.g., Duggal 1999; Macauliffe 1990; Mansukhani 1997; McLeod 1984; Shackle and Mandair 2005; Nikky-Guninder Kaur Singh 1995). There is as yet no published complete English translation. Jodh Singh and Dharam Singh's two-volume *Sri Dasam Granth Sahib: Text and Translation* (1999) is a translation of the text through the *Chaubis Avatar* [*Chaubīs Avatār*] section. Surindar Singh Kohli's *Dasam Granth: The Second Scripture of the Sikhs Written by Sri Guru Gobind Singh* (2005) is a translation of all but *Charitropakhian* and *Hikaitan* [*Hikāitān*]. Both Singh and Singh and Kohli chose to omit *Charitropakhian* and *Hikaitan* because of the controversial nature of these two compositions.

There are several editions of the original text with modern Punjabi commentaries and translations. Pandit Narain Singh Ji Giani published his eight-volume *Sri Dasam Granth Sāhib Jī Satik* from 1994 to 1997, and Bhai Randhir Singh's three-volume *Sabdārth Dasam Granth Sāhib* appeared in 1995. In 1999, Gobind Sadan, a New Delhi–based organization led by the late Baba Virsa Singh, published a five-volume edition of the entire *Srī Dasam Granth Sāhib* with a modern Punjabi translation by Rattan Singh Jaggi and Gursharan Kaur Jaggi. Gobind Sadan has commissioned an English translation of the entire text based on Jaggi and Jaggi's Punjabi translation but has not yet secured funding to publish it.[21]

In addition to editions of the full text of the Dasam Granth, many portions of the text are available individually or in editions with selected compositions. Collections of selected compositions may be known as *Das Granthī*; one such collection is a selection of compositions officially sanctioned by the Shiromani Gurdwara Prabandhak Committee (SGPC), including *Jap Sahib*, *Shabad Pātshahi Das*, *Akal Ustati*, *Bachitra Natak*, *Chandi Charitra* 1, *Chandi Charitra* 2, *Chandi di Var* (alternate title *Vār Durgā Kī*), and *Giān Prabodh*. Editions of individual compositions or collections of selected compositions are more widely available than editions of the text in its entirety.

Unless otherwise noted, all English translations of Dasam Granth passages are mine; they include the composition title, chapter number if appropriate, and verse number.

Jap Sahib [Jāpu Sāhib: *frequently spelled* "Jaap" *in English*] *("Revered Spoken Prayer")*

While the exact dating of this composition is uncertain, many Sikh authors consider it to be the Guru's first composition. It is one of the least controversial portions of the Dasam Granth. As its title suggests, it may be seen as parallel to Guru Nanak's *Japjī*, the opening composition of the Guru Granth Sahib (both titles come from a verb meaning "to pray" or "to recite"). The 199 verses of the *Jap Sahib* offer praise to a formless, all-pervading God. Many Sikhs know it by heart and recite it daily, and it may be recited at Khalsa initiations. Ashta (1959, 35) and others[22] have suggested that the *Jap* is modeled on the Sanskrit text *Viṣṇu Sahasra Nāma*, or "thousand names of Vishnu," part of a genre of Sanskrit texts listing various names and epithets of Hindu gods and goddesses.

Akal Ustat [Akāla Ustati] *("Praise of the Timeless Lord")*

Akal Ustat describes God as *Akal Purakh* [*Akāl Purakh; puruṣa*], or the timeless primal being or lord, and *Sarabloha*, "Lord of All Steel." God is also described as manifesting in various other gods and goddesses, as well as in people of different religious affiliations such as Hindu and Muslim. While there are occasional references to Muslim practices and the Qur'an, the preponderance of references are to Hindu mythology. As in many compositions of the earlier Sikh Gurus, ritualism is criticized as an ineffective means of gaining knowledge of God. Most Sikh commentators believe that this composition is incomplete, and some have speculated that parts of this text are later interpolations or may actually belong in other parts of the Dasam Granth. A number of Sikh commentators have argued that Guru Gobind Singh authored all of this text except verses 211–230, which praise the goddess Durga.[23] Portions of *Akal Ustat* may be used in Khalsa initiation rituals.

Bachitra Natak [Bachitra-Nāṭaka] *("The Wondrous Drama)*

The title *Bachitra Natak* is used in several ways. It refers to an individual composition of fourteen chapters within the Dasam Granth that includes a portion entitled *Apni Katha* ("My Story"). Some Sikh authors, however, have used the term *Bachitra Natak* to refer specifically to *Apni Katha* rather than the larger composition of which it is a part. To confuse matters further, other compositions within the Dasam Granth may be grouped under the umbrella heading of *Bachitra Natak Granth* (Jaggi 1966, 9–10). The following compositions contain verses that make reference to their being a part of the *Bachitra Natak Granth*: *Chandi Charitra Ukti Bilas*, *Chandi Charitra* 2, *Chaubis Avatar*, *Brahmā Avatār*, and *Rudra Avatār*, thus suggesting that these compositions were intended to be taken as a whole (whether by authorial intention or the reading of a later compiler).[24]

In *Bachitra Natak*, the author, who, depending on one's perspective, may or may not be Guru Gobind Singh, describes his lineage going back to the beginning of creation, detailing his previous lives as well as his actions in his lifetime as Guru, including some of the battles with hill chiefs and the Mughals. The author states that he was born in order to establish dharma and defeat its enemies, and he describes himself meditating on the deities Mahakal [Mahākāla] and Kalaka [Kālakā] in the Himalayas when he received word that he was to take birth.[25] This composition is usually considered to cover events up to 1696;[26] many Sikh commentators have lamented the fact that it does not address the foundation of the Khalsa. Many Sikh and Western interpreters, including those who believe that Guru Gobind Singh did not compose all of the Dasam Granth, accept this as an authentic composition of Guru Gobind Singh.[27] This composition is discussed in more detail in chapter 2.

Chandi Charitra Ukti Bilas [Chaṇḍī Charitra Ukti Bilāsa]
("Enjoyment of the Recitation of Chandi's Deeds")

In eight chapters, this composition recounts the exploits of the goddess (known by the names Durga, Chandi, Chandika, etc.) and her slaying of demons. It closes with explicit mention of the *Mārkaṇḍe Purānā* and has often been interpreted as a partial translation or retelling of the *Durgā Saptaśati* section of the Sanskrit Markandeya Purana [*Mārkaṇḍeya Purāṇa*], an issue to be considered in more detail in chapter 3.[28] *Chandi Charitra Ukti Bilas* is also sometimes known as *Chandi Charitra* 1 (CC 1).

Chandi Charitra 2 [Chaṇḍī Charitra 2]

In eight chapters, this composition once again describes the goddess Chandi and her defeat of demons. While *Chandi Charitra Ukti Bilas* makes specific reference to the Markandeya Purana, this composition does not. It is discussed in greater detail in chapter 3.

Var Durga Ki/Var Sri Bhagauti Ji Ki/Chandi Di Var [Vāra Durgā Kī/ Vāra Srī Bhagautī Jī Kī/Chaṇḍī Dī Vāra] *("The Ballad of Durga"/"The Ballad of Revered Bhagauti"/"The Ballad of Chandi")*

This is the only Punjabi composition in the Dasam Granth. Of the several titles by which it may be known, *Var Durga Ki* is the one found in the oldest manuscripts (Jaggi and Jaggi 1999, vol. 1, 314), though it is more popularly known as *Chandi di Var.*[29] It covers the same basic events as the two previous compositions about the goddess Chandi, although it is considerably shorter. The opening verses of this composition begin the Sikh prayer of ardas [*ardās*] (prayer or petition). This and the two preceding compositions concerning the goddess are discussed in chapter 3.

Gian Prabodh [Giana Prabodha] *("Awakening of Knowledge")*

This composition contains 336 stanzas of two to eight lines each. It opens with verses giving salutations to the Lord [*nāth, dev, ādi purakh*, etc.]. Beginning at stanza 126, there is a conversation between a soul [*ātmā*] and supreme soul [*paramātmā*], and subsequent verses detail stories from the Mahabharata [*Mahābhārata*] concerning the rule of the king Yudhishthira [Yudhiṣṭhira] and his performance of sacrifices such as the *rājasūya* (performed at a king's ordination) and the *aśvamedha* or horse sacrifice. *Gian Prabodh* also relates the complex story of King Janmejaya initiating a snake sacrifice but abandoning it on the advice of a Brahman, his battle with a king of Kashi, his marriages and love for a maidservant, his performance of an *aśvamedha* sacrifice, his killing of Brahmans in retribution for their laughing at his wife when a gust of wind blew away her clothing, and his suffering from leprosy in retribution for killing Brahmans. *Gian Prabodh* further describes how some Brahmans who survived Janmejaya's wrath advised him to listen to the Mahabharata to cure his leprosy. Vyāsa, the legendary compiler of the Vedas, epics, and other texts, was called to begin the recitation, and told the king the story of the Kauravas and the Pandavas [Pāṇḍavas] and their battle. After King Janmejaya's death, one of his sons became king, but Janmejaya's son by his maidservant, Ajai Singh, proved more clever and won the kingdom in a dice game. King Janmejaya's two sons then fled and took shelter with a great Brahman pandit. A delicate series of negotiations followed that led to some of Brahmans removing their sacred threads and becoming Vaishyas [Vaiśya], some Brahmans who had dined with the king becoming Rajputs, and some Kshatriyas [Kṣatriyas] being sacrificed. *Gian Prabodh* next relates the story of King Jaga, who sponsored a great animal sacrifice or *paśumedha*. The king succeeding him was Munī, who consulted Brahmans as to what sort of sacrifice he should offer. They told him of a sacrifice that the goddess Chandi performed after she had defeated the demon Mahishasur [Mahiṣāsura], and recommended that the king begin a sacrifice that involved offering pieces of flesh into a fire while reciting Vedic mantras. *Gian Prabodh* ends at this point, without a complete description of King Munī, his sacrifice, or his reign, as was given for the earlier kings.

Some Sikh commentators believe that this composition is incomplete, and/or that it combines portions of what may have been intended as two separate compositions, perhaps by more than one author (Jaggi 1966, 83). *Gian Prabodh*'s concern with kings' lineages, their sponsorship of Vedic sacrifices, and the roles of the various *varnas* is noteworthy.

Chaubis Avatar [Chaubīsa Avatāra] (*"The Twenty-four Avatars"*)

This is one of the longest sections of the Dasam Granth. The opening lines include the pen-name Siām, which some take to be a reference to the name of one of Guru Gobind Singh's court poets, and others a pen name of the Guru himself. *Chaubis Avatar* describes various incarnations of the god Vishnu, some of which (Ram, Krishna [Kṛṣṇa]) are found in other listings of Vishnu's avatars, and some of which (Brahma [Brahmā], Shiva [Śiva], and Mahidī)[30] are generally not. The lord in charge of this process of sending and destroying avatars is named Kal [Kāla] (verse 3).

The full list of avatars treated in *Chaubis Avatar* is Maccha [Matsya], Kaccha [Kaśyapa], Nara Nārāiṇa, Mahā Mohanī, Bairāha [Vārāha], Nara Singha, Bāvana [Vāmana], Parasarāma [Paraśurāma], Brahmā, Rudra, Jalandhar, Bisnu, Sheshmāī, Arihant Deva, Manu Rājā, Dhanantar [Dhanvantar], Sūraj, Chanda, Rām, Krisan [Kṛṣṇa], Nara [Arjan], Baūdha [Buddha], Nihakalankī [Kalkī], and Mahidī.[31] The accounts of most of these are relatively brief (though there are 588 verses describing Kalkī).

The descriptions of Ram and particularly Krishna constitute the longest portion of the *Chaubis Avatar*, and both include passages frequently cited by Sikh commentators in which the author states that he does not worship particular gods. As the story of Ram's incarnation comes to a close, the author notes that the story was completed on the banks of the Sutlej River at the base of Naina Devi (verse 861), and verse 863 of the section of *Chaubis Avatar* entitled "*Ram Avatar*" reads:

> Since I grabbed hold of your feet, I lower my eyes before no one else.
> The Puranas speak of Ram, and the Qur'an of Rahīm, but I don't believe in either of them.
> The Smṛtis, the Shastras [Śāstras], the Vedas, all proclaim various mysteries, but I do not recognize a single one of them.
> O Revered Sword-Bearing Lord [*asipāni*], it was through your grace that this story was told.

In a similar vein, verse 434 of the *Krishna Avatar* section reads:

> I will not first honor Ganesha [Ganesa], nor do I ever meditate upon Krishna or Vishnu [*kisan bisan*].
> I have heard of but do not recognize them. I am absorbed in contemplation at His feet. (434)
> Mahākāl is my protector. . . .

These verses are often cited as evidence that the Dasam Granth does not advocate worship of Vishnu and his avatars. Less commonly cited, however, is the preceding section of the text (*Krishna Avatar* verses 422–433), a series of verses in praise of the goddess [*devī*]. Indeed, there are several verses in praise of Chandi at the beginning of this section as well (verses 5–8), and verse 2306 describes how Krishna wakes in the morning, bathes, makes offerings, and then recites the *Satasaii* or *Durgā Saptaśati*. The opening verses of this composition state that a portion of it was composed at Anandpur, and it concludes with verses stating that it was completed in Paonta in the year 1745 of the Vikram era (1688 or

1689), that it was based on the *Dasam Skandha* of the Bhagavat Purana [*Bhāgavat Purāṇa*], and that it was composed for the sake of a war for righteousness [*dharam juddh*] (KA 2490–2491).

Brahma Avatar [Brahmā Avatāra] *("The Avatars of Brahma")*

This composition describes the following seven avatars of the god Brahma: Bālmīka [Vālmīki], Kasapa [Kaśyapa], Sukra [Śukra], Bachesa [Bṛhaspati], Biāsa [Vyāsa; this section includes the stories of some kings as well], Rikhi [Ṛṣi; an avatar who brought the six Shastras], and the renowned Sanskrit poet Kālidāsa.

Brahma Avatar and *Rudra Avatar* (described later) are sometimes grouped together as the *Upāvatār*, or "lesser avatars."

Rudra Avatar [Rudra Avatār] *("The Avatars of Rudra, i.e., Shiva")*

This composition, although longer than *Brahma Avatar*, addresses only two avatars of Rudra: Datta [Dattātreya; this section also describes twenty-three Gurus and ends with the poet using the name Syām] and Pārasnātha. The Pārasnātha section includes a lengthy passage (verses 45–89) in which Pārasnātha praises the goddess Durga, and she grants him a boon.[32]

Although a detailed analysis is beyond the scope of this project, the sections of the Dasam Granth addressing avatars are worthy of further study, both because of the issues they raise regarding ongoing Sikh understandings (and rejections) of the relevance and role of avatars, and also because they offer an example of perspective on avatars at the time that would provide a useful basis for comparison with avatar listings in other vernaculars and regions.[33]

Shabad Hazare [Shabada Hazāre]; a.k.a. Sabad Hazāre, Shabad Pātshāhī Das, Bisanpade] *("A Thousand Hymns")*

This composition includes ten hymns, or *shabads*, of varying length. One theory regarding the title is that perhaps originally 1,000 hymns were intended; Ashta (1959, 144) suggested that the word *hazārā* should be taken to mean "fountain." The hymns in this composition include reference to the *rāgas* in which they are to be sung, as do the verses in the Guru Granth Sahib. The title *Shabad Hazare* is also used for a collection of seven hymns from the Guru Granth Sahib. *Shabad Hazare* is not found in the earliest manuscripts of the Dasam Granth (Jaggi 1966, 206). Some of these hymns are thematically similar to poetry about the god Vishnu and his incarnations.

Shabad 6 is noteworthy in that it is in Punjabi rather than the Brajbhasha of the other hymns, and it is often said to have been composed by Guru Gobind Singh after the tragic deaths of his four sons:

> Tell the beloved friend about the state of his devotees.
> Without you, we feel sick wrapping ourselves in our quilts, it's like living in a snakepit.
> The flask is a thorn in the side, the cup a dagger, it's like enduring the butcher's blows.
> Better to sleep on the ground near the beloved; staying in the village is like being in a furnace.[34]

Savaye (Savaiye, Tetī Savaiye, Srī Mukhvāk Swaiyā)

The word *savayā* refers to the type of poem found in this composition. These poems praise a god who is beyond the imaginings of texts such as the Vedas, Puranas, and Qur'an. The verses challenge those who worship specific avatars or incarnations and who display their religiosity publicly without true knowledge of the mystery of God. Some commentators (e.g., Ashta 1959, 211) have taken *Savayā* 30, which describes greedy people who steal from the innocent, as a critique of the *masands*. These thirty-three verses may be used in the Khalsa rite of initiation.

Khalsa Mahima [Khālsā Mahimā; Khālse dī Mahimā; *or by Its Opening Words, "jo kichu lekhu likhio bidhnā"*] *("Praise of the Khalsa")*

This text is not found in the earliest manuscripts of the Dasam Granth. It is a short passage of four stanzas containing a statement to a Brahman, assuring him that while he will be given gifts, others are responsible for the speaker's success. The closing lines describe the Brahman's anger and frustration. This is typically taken to be Guru Gobind Singh's address to a Brahman priest explaining why alms were given to Sikhs rather than Brahmans after a sacrifice to the goddess at the Naina Devi temple near Anandpur.

Shastra-nam-mala [Shastra-nāma-mālā] *("Garland of the Names of Weapons")*

This is a composition of 1,318 verses naming and praising weapons, along with invocations to be used with specific weapons. The opening chapter praises *bhagauti*, and subsequent chapters praise and describe specific weapons and describe their many names, often in the form of riddles. Weapons praised include various types of swords, the discus [*chakra*], the arrow [*bāṇa*], the noose [*pāsi*], and the matchlock rifle, or *tupak* [*tupaka*].[35] This composition is also sometimes titled *Srī Nāma-māla Purāṇa.*

The first chapter of *Shastra-nam-mala* equates various weapons and their powers with *bhagautī*. *Bhagauti* (a term discussed in greater detail in chapter 3) is described as the essence of knowledge, as the creator who first made the world and then the different paths or *panths*, as various avatars, and as Vishnu's form (SNM 1–27).

The section on the *tupak* or matchlock rifle is more than 800 verses, and its opening verses are typical of this composition:

> First, say "*bāhini*." Then, add "*ripu*" at the end.
> These are the names of *tupak*. Poets take these names. (SNM 461)

Many commentators have read these verses as complex riddles. For example, another verse concerning the *tupak* begins with these two lines:

> *Haripati pati pati patiṇi ādi bhaṇījīai.* (First say "*Haripati pati pati patiṇi.*")
> *Ariṇī tā ke anta sabada ko dījīai.* (Then add the word "*ariṇī*" at the end.) (SNM 1247)

Ashta, who translated *tupak* as "small cannon," explained the lines as follows:

The poet wants the reader to construe first *Hari pati pati pati patini* and add to this the word *arini*. The poet further concludes that thus the wise would know the name of *tupak* i.e., a small cannon. The word "cannon" can be arrived at in the following manner:

Hari—Elephant
Hari pati—(lord of elephants) *Airawat*
Hari pati pati—(Possessor of Airawat) *Indra*
Hari pati pati pati—(Lord of Indra, i.e., Kashyap his) earth
Hari pati pati pati patini (*patini* of the earth) army
Hari pati pati pati patini arini (The enemy i.e., destroyer of the army) cannon.[36] (Ashta 1959, 148–149)

Even some of the most enthusiastic analysts of the *Dasam Granth* have found this composition "tedious." Grewal and Bal (1967, 74–75) interpreted *Shastra-nam-mala* as an exposition of the notion that weapons may serve as the medium of worship of God when they are used in defense of righteousness.

Charitropakhian [Charitropākhiāna; Pakhyān-Charitra, Triā Charitra] *("Stories about Character")*

This is perhaps the most intriguing and to many people the most troubling portion of the Dasam Granth, and it constitutes nearly 40 percent of the text as a whole. It includes 404 *charitras*,[37] or biographical sketches; in this context, *charitra* may perhaps be best understood as "character sketch." (*Charitra* is in other contexts sometimes translated as "adventure.") The charitras include traditional romances (e.g., Yusuf and Zulaikha, Hīr and Rānjhā) and many stories about women who concoct schemes that allow them to meet their lovers. Some of the stories are quite explicit in their descriptions of sexual behavior. A few of the stories explore and even advocate the use of intoxicants. The final verse mentions that the composition was completed in 1696. The stories are discussed in greater detail in chapter 4.

Some Sikh commentators have argued that these stories were used for the moral edification of Guru Gobind Singh's army; others have speculated that they were intended for entertainment. Still others have argued that they have no place in the Dasam Granth or Sikh literature at all. Due to *Charitropakhian*'s controversial nature, a number of printed editions of the Dasam Granth omit it entirely (e.g., the *Shabdārath Dasam Granth Sāhib* published by the Publications Bureau of Punjabi University). Pritpal Singh Bindra's two-volume *Chritro Pakhyaan: Tales of Male-Female Tricky Deceptions from Sri Dasam Granth* (2002) is the only published English translation of these stories.

Charitra 404 concludes with a set of verses known as the *Benti Chaupai* [*Bentī Chaupaī*], prayers that many Sikhs recite regularly. *Charitropakhian* was transmitted both as a part of the Dasam Granth and as a distinct volume.[38]

Zafarnama [Zafarnāmā] *("Letter of Victory")*

This is a Persian letter to the Mughal emperor Aurangzeb which Guru Gobind Singh is said to have composed in 1705 or 1706. In the letter, he chastises the emperor for reneging on a sworn oath to grant the Guru and his family safe passage from Anandpur. The soldiers who broke the oath are described as men without faith. Guru Gobind Singh opines that under such circumstances it is proper to take sword in hand. Most Sikh commentators consider this to be an authentic composition of Guru Gobind Singh.

Hikaitan [Hikāitān] *("Stories")*

This composition includes twelve stories in the Persian language. The tales are very similar in content to those found in *Charitropakhian*; indeed, many are Persian versions of the same tales.[39] Some authors (e.g., Cunningham 1990, 78) suggest that they follow *Zafarnama* in the Dasam Granth because the two were sent to Aurangzeb together because the stories would be instructive for the Mughal emperor. Another explanation is that they were grouped together in the Dasam Granth simply because both are in the Persian language.

Additional Compositions

In addition to the preceding compositions, some manuscripts contain additional sections that have not been included in printed editions of the Dasam Granth. Jaggi (1966, 100–101) noted compositions entitled *Samāhar Sukhmanā, Mālkāūs kī Vār, Bhagavant Gītā, Chhakkā Bhagautī, Sad, Sphoṭak Kabit* (a.k.a. *Asphoṭak Kabit*), and *Khayāl.* Mohan Singh (1971, 67) described the *Bhagavant Gītā* composition as "a literal, verse translation of the Bhagwad Gita interspersed with a rendering here and there of Madhusudhana's Commentary and with directly addressed words by the Guru to his Sikhs correlating his own teachings to them with those of Sri Krishna to Arjuna, and explaining their inner import and literary-*cum*-spiritual connection with previous thought."

There are other compositions attributed to Guru Gobind Singh that are not traditionally associated with the Dasam Granth. The *hukamnāmās* are letters that Guru Gobind Singh sent to different Sikh communities (for more on the *hukamnāmās,* see Ganda Singh 1996; Jaggi 1966, 133–135; Loehlin 1971, 61–67). Mohan Singh (1971, 69) noted the existence of a composition attributed to Guru Gobind Singh entitled *Premabodh,* biographical sketches of sixteen saints.

A text called the *Sarabloh Granth,* revered by Nihang Sikhs, which narrates some of the same events as *Chandi Charitra,* has been attributed to Guru Gobind Singh, though most Sikh scholars do not believe he was in fact the author (see Gurmukh Singh 1998a).

History of the Dasam Granth

How did the text now known as the Dasam Granth come into existence? The literature in Punjabi, Hindi, and English concerning the Dasam Granth is voluminous, ranging from arguments about its authorship to studies of particular portions of the text. This section includes a summary of some of the most important evidence about the compilation of the text that came to be known as the Dasam Granth and the development and main characteristics of the discourse surrounding it.[40] Much of the discourse is now taking place in cyberspace as well; an online search for "Dasam Granth" may yield upwards of 100,000 hits, with links to Web sites, blogs, discussion forums, and videotaped conferences.

There is much uncertainty and disagreement about the timing and circumstances of the Dasam Granth's compilation. Several sources dating to the eighteenth century mention events that have bearing on Guru Gobind Singh's literary activities, sponsorship of court poets, and compilations of poetic works. However, these sources do not provide definitive or consistent information, and Sikh scholars have questioned the reliability of some of them, with respect to both their historicity and their perspectives, in particular what some critics term "Hindu" or "Brahmanical" biases. In addition, some eighteenth-century sources that do cover the life of Guru Gobind Singh do not provide information about any texts that might have come to be known as the Dasam Granth. For example, one of the earliest sources addressing the life of Guru Gobind Singh, Sainapati's [Saināpati] *Sri Gur Sobha* [*Srī Gura Sobhā*], completed in 1711, does not address the compilation of compositions attributed to Guru Gobind Singh, or his court poets, although Sainapati himself is generally recognized as one of Guru Gobind Singh's court poets.[41] Similarly, Kuir Singh's 1751 *Gurbilas Patshahi Das* [*Gurbilāsa Pātshāhī Dasa*] does not focus on any book or *granth* compiled by the tenth Guru. The sources that do mention the compilation of texts connected to Guru Gobind Singh are from later in the eighteenth century, although several of them mention compilations of texts that were made during the Guru's lifetime.

The eighteenth-century text that provides the most detailed and disputed information regarding the Dasam Granth is Kesar Singh Chhibbar's *Bansavalinama* (1769), an account of the ten Gurus, as well as events in the decades after Guru Gobind Singh's death.[42] The work remains an important source for those who argue that Guru Gobind Singh composed the entire Dasam Granth. Like a number of texts from this era, it reflects a perspective that suggests the influence of a Puranic worldview. Chhibbar, a Sikh from a Brahman family of Jammu, was acquainted with Bhai Mani Singh and served Guru Gobind Singh's widow Mata Sundari in Delhi (Jaggi 1995, 280). Many Sikh scholars have criticized Chhibbar's Brahman perspective, as well as his haphazard approach to chronology.[43]

At several points in his account of Guru Gobind Singh's life, and in a later section of his text, Chhibbar refers to *granths* in some way associated with Guru Gobind Singh. According to *Bansavalinama* (*Bansāvalīnāmā* 14:267, Jaggi 1972, 215), Guru Gobind Singh completed his own *granth* in 1698.[44] Chhibbar further mentions a "large *granth*" called the *Samundra Sāgar* prepared by the Guru that was lost in a river in about 1701, with some pages later recovered by Sikhs. He also mentions a "small *granth*" in which the entire *Avatār līlā* was included. This *granth* was not bound, and many pages were lost in a battle. Later, Bhai Mani Singh was able to gather together some of this lost work containing the *Avatār līlā* as well as some pages that bore Guru Gobind Singh's signature. He then had prepared a *granth* that combined the Adi Granth and the tenth Guru's compositions (*Banavalinama* 10:377–384, Jaggi 1972, 135–136). Chhibbar twice mentions that Sikhs asked Guru Gobind Singh to combine his *granth* with the Adi Granth, but the Guru refused, explaining that while he was fond of his work, it was for entertainment or fun [*kheḍ*], while the Adi Granth was Guru and should therefore remain separate (*Bansavalinama* 10:389; 14:268, Jaggi 1972, 136, 215).

The challenge in interpreting these references in *Bansavalinama* is that it is not clear whether they refer specifically to the work that later became known as the Dasam Granth. The *Bachitra Natak* portion of the *Dasam Granth* does include several compositions about the avatars, but there they are not entitled *Avatār Līlā*. Nor is there evidence to determine what the *Samundra Sāgar* might have contained and what relation it bore to the Dasam Granth. Thus Chhibbar's work does not fully resolve the issue of the authorship of the Dasam Granth or what form it might have had during Guru Gobind Singh's lifetime.

Sarup Das Bhalla's [Sarūpa Dāsa Bhallā] 1776 *Mahima Prakash* [*Mahimā Prakāsha*] (cited in Jaggi 1966, 169–172) states that Guru Gobind Singh enlisted pandits and others to compile the knowledge of the Vedas, Puranas, and Shastras, and put them into the language of the time in Gurmukhi script. This text specifically mentions a poet named Siām, a name (also spelled Syām) that occurs in a number of Dasam Granth compositions. *Mahima Prakash* also mentions the "Twenty-four *Avatāras*" and "Four Hundred Four *Calitras* " (i.e., *charitras*) in the context of the efforts of these pandits and poets enlisted by the Guru. All or perhaps some of these works were then compiled in a text called *Bidiā Sāgar*, or "Ocean of Knowledge." Guru Gobind Singh then said that he had arranged to have these works put together. Jaggi (1966, 171) took this to mean that he was endorsing them as worthy of study, which in turn people came to understand to mean that the Guru himself had composed them.[45] Like *Bansavalinama*, therefore, *Mahima Prakash* does not in and of itself definitively prove or disprove anything in particular about the anthology that came to be known as the Dasam Granth, although there is a composition in it entitled "Twenty-four Avatars," *Charitropakhian* does indeed have 404 episodes, and the name Syām or Siām does occur in some Dasam Granth compositions. It is also not clear whether the work entitled *Bidiā Sāgar* to which Sarup Das Bhalla refers might be related to or the same as the *Samundra Sāgar* mentioned in *Bansavalinama*.

In part on the basis of Chhibbar's statements about Bhai Mani Singh, however, much Sikh tradition has ascribed the compilation of the Dasam Granth to him, noting that he was assisted by Bhai Shihan [Shīhān] Singh and Mata Sundari, Guru Gobind Singh's widow. Those who argue for Guru Gobind Singh as the composer of the Dasam Granth in its entirety have often cited a letter Bhai Mani Singh is said to have written to Mata Sundari in 1716. This letter includes mention of finding the *Krishna Avatar*, the 303 *Charitras*, and the *Shastra-nam-mala*. Thus it is cited as evidence that these texts are indeed Guru Gobind Singh's work, on the assumption that Bhai Mani Singh would have recognized the Guru's handwriting and would have been familiar with what he composed. The origins of this letter, however, are obscure. It apparently made its first public appearance in the late 1920s. Jaggi (1966, 39–45) analyzed a photocopy of the letter and argued convincingly that the handwriting and style of writing are not at all characteristic of Bhai Mani Singh's time.[46] Thus the Bhai Mani Singh letter does not in and of itself offer conclusive proof of the circumstances of the compilation of the Dasam Granth.

Bhai Santokh Singh's [Bhāī Santokh Singh] voluminous 1843 *Sri Gur Pratap Suraj Granth* [*Srī Gura Pratāpa Sūraja Grantha*] (published in an abridged form as *Sūraj Prakāsh*), mentions that Guru Gobind Singh spent several hours a day composing and translating poetry on Krishna and other avatars (Bhai Santokh Singh 1999, vol. 2, *Ritu* 2, *Amshu* 4, 4710–4711). This text also mentions the fifty-two poets at Guru Gobind Singh's court and a weighty book of their compositions entitled *Vidiā Sāgar* (Bhai Santokh Singh 1999, vol. 13, *Ritu* 5, *Amśu* 52, 5725). In his *Panth Prakāsh* (1880), Giani Gian Singh [Giānī Giān Singh] (1822–1921) also mentioned the fifty-two poets (Giani Gian Singh 1987, 677) and wrote that the text that is now known as the *granth* of the tenth Guru was not compiled in a single manuscript during the Guru's lifetime (cited in Jaggi 1966, 30 n. 1; 305).

Thus in the early Sikh sources that provide information that may be related to the compilation of the Dasam Granth, there is not fully conclusive evidence. There are some references to court poets and a collection of their work that was lost, as well as mention of Guru Gobind Singh's own poetic efforts and study of Sanskrit texts. There are also references to collections of Guru Gobind Singh's work, but it is not entirely clear what compositions they may have contained and what, if any, relation they bore to the Dasam Granth.

A slightly later source, Bhai Kahn Singh Nabha's [Bhāī Kāhn Singh Nābhā][1] 1930 *Gurshabad Ratnakar Mahan Kosh* [*Gurshabada Ratnākara Mahān Kosha*], provides an intriguing story in its entry on the Dasam Granth. First, Nabha explains (Nabha 1990, 616), Bhai Mani Singh carried out the wishes of Mata Sundari that he gather whatever he could of Guru Gobind Singh's writings, and then he put both those compositions that presented the Guru's teachings and those that were translations from Sanskrit into a single volume called *Dasven Pātshāh kā Granth*. Then, after Bhai Mani Singh's death in 1738, some Sikh leaders at Damdama questioned the contents of the compilation. Some argued that the text should remain as it was, but others thought it should be separated into different parts. Despite a lengthy debate, the Sikh scholars were unable to reach a consensus. Then, a Sikh named Mahtab Singh arrived at Damdama and was asked what he thought about the plan to either separate or keep together the text. He announced that he was on his way to Amritsar to kill a Muslim who was desecrating the Golden Temple, and that if he succeeded in killing the Muslim and returning alive, the text should be left as it was. He indeed killed the Muslim and returned alive, so according to tradition, the Dasam Granth was left as Bhai Mani Singh had compiled it, in spite of reservations on the part of some Sikh leaders. Although this story appears relatively late in the history of the Dasam Granth, it is striking that it reveals the view that learned Sikhs must have been concerned about the content of the text from early on, and that decisions about its status as "holy" or otherwise were very difficult to make. In this story, at least, an event entirely unrelated to the contents of the Dasam Granth became the basis for a decision about its fate.

In addition to Sikh texts that mention Guru Gobind Singh and his literary pursuits, another important source of answers about the authorship and origins of the Dasam Granth is the available and surviving manuscripts. In this regard Rattan Singh Jaggi's research is extremely important. Jaggi wrote his doctoral dissertation, *Dasam-Granth kī Paurāṇik Pṛṣṭhabhūmi* (The Puranic Background of the *Dasam Granth*) in Hindi for Punjab University, and it was published in 1965. Jaggi then published a revised and expanded version of that research in Punjabi in 1966 entitled *Dasam Granth dā Kartritav* (The Authorship/Creation of the Dasam Granth), which remains one of the most widely cited studies of the text. Jaggi's research included the first identification and systematic study of the earliest extant manuscripts[47] and a careful evaluation of the research on the text published up to that point, along with an assessment of the reliability of some traditional sources that include statements about the compositions of Guru Gobind Singh.[48]

When Jaggi conducted his research in the late 1950s and early 1960s, he identified and was able to view four early manuscripts of the Dasam Granth.[49] He concluded that other available Dasam Granth manuscripts were either copies of these four, or were no more than about 150 years old, that is, dating to the early 1800s (Jaggi 1966, 91). The four manuscripts are known as the Bhai Mani Singh Vālī Bīr, that is, the manuscript understood to be the original version compiled by Bhai Mani Singh, and the Motī Bāg, Sangrūr, and Paṭnā bīṛs (named for the locations at which they are held). Two of these manuscripts are said to include pages in Guru Gobind Singh's own handwriting, although Jaggi concluded that the pages were inauthentic.[50]

Jaggi examined the Bhai Mani Singh Vālī Bīṛ in 1959. The manuscript is dated 1770 Vikramī (1713 C.E.), but the date is in different handwriting from the rest of the manuscript, and thus does not establish the date conclusively (Jaggi 1966, 3). In a 1990 publication, Jaggi (1990, 3) argued that this manuscript seemed to be about 250 years old, that is, dating to roughly 1740. Bhai Mani Singh died in 1737 or 1738. Jaggi concluded that the *Bhai Mani Singh Vālī Bīṛ* is not the original version of the compilation of the Dasam Granth attributed to Bhai Mani Singh.[51]

In his examination of these early manuscripts, Jaggi (1966, 91, 98–101, 206–208) found that there was variation among the manuscripts with respect to the ordering of compositions, the division of compositions into sections, the number of verses within individual compositions, the opening lines of invocation in particular compositions, and lines in which the poet's name is mentioned. He suggested (1966, 112) that the variation and errors within the different manuscripts could support the conclusion that Guru Gobind Singh was not the author of this text, because if he had been, scribes would have taken more care in making consistent copies. Jaggi (1966, 148) also noted many points in the Dasam Granth at which the poet requests that others should correct any of his errors; Jaggi took this as further evidence that Guru Gobind Singh was not the author of compositions within which this request occurs, because Guru Gobind Singh, who was able to dictate the entire Adi Granth to Bhai Mani Singh, was not likely to compose works that contained mistakes.

Another factor in arguments for and against Guru Gobind Singh as author of the Dasam Granth is the phrase "Srī Mukhvāk Pātshāhī Dasa" [literally, "spoken by the Tenth Ruler"], which occurs at the beginning of some Dasam Granth compositions. Some Sikh commentators have argued that the presence of this phrase serves as proof that the composition is indeed the work of Guru Gobind Singh. However, Jaggi's research on the early manuscripts of the Dasam Granth (1966, 44–47, 108, 209–215, 216–218) indicated that the phrase does not occur uniformly.[52] He also noted that any editor or scribe could add this phrase to a manuscript and that therefore the presence of this phrase does not necessarily prove anything about the authorship of a particular composition.

The substantial variation within the earliest extant manuscripts led Jaggi (1996, 112) to conclude that the manuscript evidence in and of itself was likely not sufficient to resolve questions concerning authorship of the Dasam Granth. Jaggi's work remains the most substantial published assessment of Dasam Granth manuscripts. At present, therefore, the manuscript evidence does not provide definitive or conclusive evidence of who authored the compositions in the Dasam Granth. Intratextual evidence such as the use of pen names has been used as evidence both for and against Guru Gobind Singh as the author.

Just as the manuscript evidence has not yet yielded definitive evidence on which to make judgments about the origins and authorship of the Dasam Granth, so too, eighteenth-century and later references to the compositions of Guru Gobind Singh and his court poets and the work of Bhai Mani Singh do not provide consistent information about what texts may have been compiled under Guru Gobind Singh's leadership and who authored such texts, or how exactly the Guru's works might have been recovered after his death. As discussed earlier, while some of these sources mention no *granths* at all, others mention "big" and "small" *granths*, the names of specific compositions in the Dasam Granth, or names of compositions similar to Dasam Granth compositions (e.g., *Avatar Lila*), as well as a lost work entitled *Vidiā*, *Bidiā* or *Samundra Sāgar*. These sources also suggest that Guru Gobind Singh translated or had translated works from Sanskrit, and that written material associated with the Guru was lost in the evacuation of Anandpur, with some of it perhaps later being recovered.

Thus we have various eighteenth-century and later references to a compilation of Guru Gobind Singh's works, but the exact eighteenth-century form and status of the compilation that came to be known as Dasam Granth remain unclear. J. S. Grewal (1998, 265) has noted that Chhibbar's *Bansavalinama* indicates that a *granth* associated with Guru Gobind Singh was in existence when he wrote his text, but "who compiled it, why and for what purpose—these are important questions. And the question of its influence among the Sikhs during the late eighteenth century does remain to be answered." While Grewal does not believe that Guru Gobind Singh authored the entire Dasam Granth, he points out that even if historians demonstrate that Guru Gobind Singh did not author particular compositions within the Dasam Granth, they must take into account the fact that many of these compositions, such as *Bachitra Natak* and *Chandi di Var* (*Var Durga Ki*), enjoyed great popularity among Sikhs during the late eighteenth and early nineteenth centuries. Indeed, they still enjoy popularity among some Sikhs.

By the nineteenth century, there were many manuscripts of the Dasam Granth in circulation. Manuscripts that had both the Adi Granth and the Dasam Granth together were also common, and the two texts were sometimes kept together in gurdwaras [*gurdwārā*]. This is still the case in some locations, such as the gurdwara at Gobind Sadan in New Delhi. When mentioning the presence of the two texts in gurdwaras, however, most Sikh authors are careful to note that even under these circumstances the Adi Granth has higher status than the Dasam Granth.[53]

Early nineteenth-century Western accounts of Sikhism also mention the prestige in which the Dasam Granth was held at the time; Malcolm (1981, 40–41), for example, wrote in 1812 about the "Dasam Padshah Ka Grant'h" and described it as a "volume, which is not limited to religious subjects, but filled with accounts of [Guru Gobind Singh's] own battles, and written with the view of stirring up a spirit of valour and emulation among his followers," and reported that "is at least as much revered, among the Sikhs, as the Adi-Grant'h of Arjunmal."

It also appears that the Dasam Granth was important in the Sikh kingdoms of the late eighteenth and nineteenth centuries. According to Malcolm (1812, 95–97), at least as late as 1805, when Sikh chiefs convened councils or Guru-matas, those present bowed their heads before the "Adi-Grant'h and Dasam Padshah Ka Grant'h."

The Punjab came under British control in 1849. Changes in the educational system and the presence of Christian missionaries who sought to convince Punjabis to leave their native faiths helped create a heightened concern about religious identity. Among some Sikhs, there was particular concern that the Sikh faith, in the words of N. G. Barrier and Nazer Singh (1998, 211), was in "a state of utter ossification and inertia." Some Sikh leaders in particular feared that Sikhism had lost any sense of distinctive identity and was in danger of merging into Hinduism. To address these concerns, Sikh reformers established branches of the Singh Sabha in the 1870s. The efforts of the Singh Sabhas brought renewed interest to the history and development of Sikhism but also consequently highlighted differing views on the nature of Sikh identity. Singh Sabha leaders at times differed on their understanding of the nature of the relationship between Hinduism and Sikhism. The "Sanatanist" faction of the Singh Sabha did not see a need to draw strict boundaries between Hindus and Sikhs, while the Tat Khalsa Singh Sabha leaders were emphatic in their assertion that Sikhism was indeed a distinct faith.

The Dasam Granth, with its extensive consideration of the mythology of Hindu deities, was naturally a topic of interest in the context of the Singh Sabha movement. Indeed, the text was removed from some gurdwaras under the Singh Sabhas' influence. The concerns of the Singh

Sabha movement, along with the increasing availability of printing presses in the Punjab, led to inquiry into the available manuscripts of the Dasam Granth. Various organizations sought to study the history of the Dasam Granth in order to make determinations about its authenticity and proper format. Those who wished to bring out printed editions of the text found that there was substantial variation in the contents of different manuscripts of the Dasam Granth. Some of the earliest published works on the Dasam Granth were lists of variant readings, the goal being to find a proper way of reciting the text.

An organization called the Gurmat Granth Pracharak Sabha, established at Amritsar in 1885, sponsored research on Sikh literature. The Amritsar Singh Sabha (of the Sanatanist faction) enlisted the Gurmat Granth Pracharak Sabha to prepare an accurate recension of the Dasam Granth. To do so, they established the Sodhak [Soḍhak] Committee, which published a report authored by Giani Sardul Singh [Giānī Sardūl Singh] in 1897.[54] The committee had studied thirty-two manuscripts. As part of its deliberations, this panel concluded that all the material in the Dasam Granth was the work of Guru Gobind Singh.[55] The committee's work led to the creation of a relatively standard 1,428-page printed edition of the Dasam Granth in 1902 (in comparison, a standard printed edition of the Adi Granth has 1,430 pages) and also omitted some compositions found in some Dasam Granth manuscripts.

The production of printed editions of the Dasam Granth made the text more widely available for study and analysis, and the debate about the authorship of the text intensified. In his summary of research on the Dasam Granth up until the early 1960s, Jaggi identified two major factions among Sikh authors: those who believed Guru Gobind Singh authored the entire text, and those who believe that the so-called Puranic material was likely the work of court poets. This debate raged on in Sikh journals and books throughout the twentieth century. Since Jaggi first published his research in the 1960s, a third position has developed—that of those who believe that Guru Gobind Singh composed only a very small portion of the Dasam Granth and that most of the text may be understood as the later work of authors unfamiliar with Sikhism, perhaps even authors who sought to discredit Sikhism.[56]

Sikh authors have argued that Guru Gobind Singh composed only some of the Dasam Granth in different ways. In his book *Dasam Granth*

Nirṇay (1918), for example, Ran Singh [Raṇ Singh] argued that Guru Gobind Singh wrote *Jap*, *Akal Ustat*, the *Apni Katha* portion of the *Bachitra Natak*, *Gian Prabodh*, *Shabad Hazare*, *Savaiye*, *Khalsa Mahima*, and *Zafarnama*, but not the so-called Puranic compositions or *Charitropakhian*. As Jaggi (1966) showed in his detailed summary of various assessments of the Dasam Granth, Ran Singh and others making such assertions typically did so more on the basis of individual opinion regarding the content of particular compositions rather than critical analysis of the available textual and historical evidence.

Jaggi himself (1966, 168) concluded that the *Jap*, *Savaiye*, and *Zafarnama* are definitely Guru Gobind Singh's work, that *Akal Ustat* is the Guru's work except for the section toward the end praising the goddess, that the authorship of *Gian Prabodh, Shabad Hazare*, the *Hikaitan*, and *Shastra-nam-mala* is inconclusive based on available evidence, and that the remainder of the Dasam Granth is Puranic material composed by court poets, full of errors, inconsistencies, time-frame confusion, and other flaws. As noted earlier, Jaggi has conducted the most extensive research on the available manuscripts. In making his determination about those compositions Guru Gobind Singh did compose, he tended to use the extent to which particular compositions could be read as being in consonance with the spirit of *bani* in the Guru Granth Sahib as the criterion for authenticity. His conclusions were thus partly based on a theological presupposition.

Early Western scholars of Sikhism such as Ernest Trumpp (writing in 1877), Max Arthur Macauliffe (1909), and Joseph Davey Cunningham (writing in 1849; 1990, 325–329) typically argued that the Dasam Granth was only partly Guru Gobind Singh's composition. This has remained the majority view among scholars in the West, though there is some disagreement over which portions of the text may be considered the work of Guru Gobind Singh.

Among those who maintain that the Dasam Granth is all the work of Guru Gobind Singh, there are some standard arguments made with varying degrees of detail and supporting evidence. The assertion that the focus on Hindu mythology reflects Guru Gobind Singh's desire to inspire his followers to bravery in warfare is extremely common, as is the argument that the stories about wayward women in *Charitropakhian* (and the *Hikaitan*) were prepared for the specific purpose of the moral edification of Guru Gobind Singh's army. There are also arguments about how internal evidence such as the use of multiple poets' names (Rām, Siām, Kāl, etc.) throughout the Dasam Granth can be explained as different pen names of Guru Gobind Singh, not the names of court poets, thus making him the sole author of the text.[57] Trilochan Singh's four-part article "The History and Compilation of the Dasm Granth" (1955), published in *The Sikh Review*, is a classic and frequently cited argument for Guru Gobind Singh as the author of the entire Dasam Granth.

Those who consider Guru Gobind Singh the author of the entire text sometimes also cite the Sodhak Committee Report (1897) as official confirmation of their view. Another argument concerns an *akhand path* [*akhaṇḍ pāṭh*], or continuous reading of the entire Dasam Granth at the Akal Takhat in Amritsar in December 1944 to commemorate Guru Gobind Singh's birthday. The *akhand path* is taken as evidence for official acceptance of the text. Jaggi, however, has argued that the full story of this *akhand path* shows that it was not necessarily an official endorsement. According to Jaggi (1966, 38), there was indeed an *akhand path* of the Dasam Granth, but according to the rules of Akal Takhat *maryādā* or custom, the reading took place at the Diwān-sthān below the Akal Takhat, not at the Akal Takhat itself, where only *path* of the Adi Granth is performed. As with so many other details about the Dasam Granth and its history, therefore, the *akhand path* report has been used to support different positions, in this case, both the view that the *Dasam Granth* has received official sanction by virtue of its having been recited in the vicinity of the Akal Takhat, and that the fact that it was not read at the Akal Takhat itself is indicative of a lesser status for the text.

It is also significant that select portions of the text remain important in Sikh liturgy, such as the *Jap*, *Savaiye*, and *Benti Chaupai*, which may be part of daily prayer, as well as particular verses that are used in the rite of initiation into the Khalsa. The opening verses of *Var Durga Ki* [*Chandi Di Var*] form the beginning of the *ardas* prayer. In addition, some gurdwaras sponsor daily recitation from the Dasam Granth.[58] Overall, however, the portions used in liturgy are but a small fraction of the Dasam Granth in its entirety.

In the early twenty-first century, the debate over the authorship and status of the Dasam Granth shows no signs of diminishing, and the

Internet has provided a wider forum for discussion. The view that the Hindu mythological material, which in large measure focuses on the slaying of demons, was included as a means of inspiring people to fight injustice has moved beyond the realm of Sikh discourse. At the dawn of the twenty-first century, the Rashtriya Swayamsevak Sangh, a Hindu organization (often identified as "fundamentalist"), established a group called the Rashtriya Singh Sangat, which took the position that Sikhism is a part of Hinduism and recruited members in certain areas of the Punjab. Part of its plan was to publish translations of the Puranic portions of the Dasam Granth in various Indian vernacular languages in order to demonstrate that Sikhism and Hinduism have much in common. In January 2001, however, after tremendous public controversy, the group backed away from its stance and made a statement to India's National Minorities Commission affirming the separate nature of Sikhism and Hinduism. Some Sikh organizations have seen particular Sikh leaders as being complicit in such efforts to diminish or eliminate any sense of boundary between Hinduism and Sikhism.[59]

The debate about the status of the Dasam Granth takes place not only in India but also in Sikh communities around the world. In a number of publications, Gurbaksh Singh Kala Afghana, a Canadian Sikh, has argued that Guru Gobind Singh did not compose the entire Dasam Granth and called for a reform of many Sikh practices. Kala Afghana's publications, particularly his lengthy *Bipprān kī Rīt Ton Sacc dā Mārg* ("From the Customs of Brahmans to the True Path"), have been promoted and discussed by various Sikh Internet discussion groups.

In April 2000, the Institute of Sikh Studies in Chandigarh passed a resolution proclaiming that "except for the well-known *bani* of the Guru included in it, *sakat*, *vaishnav* and *brahmanical* scholars have composed the bulk of the *Dasam Granth*. It is clear that this is done with a sinister design to mislead the Sikhs and to derail Sikhism.... Enlightened Sikhs have been clear that the whole of it is neither scripture nor canon and that except for the Guru's writings included in it, [it] has no relevance to Sikh thought or doctrine."[60] Subsequent publications from this organization have further developed this argument.

The vocal and heated debate about the Dasam Granth has at times led to official action on the part of Sikh leaders. In May and August

2000, the *jathedār* of the Akal Takhat, Joginder Singh Vedanti, issued a directive to Sikh scholars that they should not comment publicly on the text. In October 2000, Joginder Singh Vedanti ordered Kala Afghana to stop the sale, publication, and dissemination of his works until he was given permission to do so.[61] He also announced plans to form a committee that would investigate the matter and issue a definitive statement on the authenticity of the text and its place within Sikhism.[62] It appears, however, that this committee has only recently been established, according to a statement by SGPC president Avtar Makkar in June 2008.[63]

In November 2006, the Akal Takhat asked that Sikh intellectuals provide a response to persons who were creating mischief by promoting misleading views about the Dasam Granth.[64] One critic of the Dasam Granth, for example, had offered a reward to anyone who could prove that Guru Gobind Singh was not the text's author.[65] In part to answer this call for a response, in February 2008, the Sri Dasam Granth Sahib International Seminar Series was held in Sacramento, California, with speakers supporting the view that the entire Dasam Granth is the work of Guru Gobind Singh. In June 2008, Akal Takht leaders requested that members of the Sikh community not fan the flames of controversy further.[66]

Thus debates about the Dasam Granth remain heated and unresolved, and to a great extent still revolve around the question of authorship. Advocates of each position regarding the authorship of the text—that Guru Gobind Singh wrote all, some, or virtually none of it—express their views with great passion. It is clear that for many Sikhs, their understanding of the status of the text ("holy book" or otherwise) is a key component of their personal understanding of what Sikhism is, the nature of its scriptures, and how they should practice their faith. It is also clear, given the ongoing official requests that Sikhs desist from stirring up the debate, that a resolution to these debates will be difficult to achieve.

While the Dasam Granth itself and the references to it in early Sikh sources may not resolve the difficult questions about authorship and authenticity that continue to plague the Sikh *panth*, there is much that we can learn from about how the text relates to other forms of Indian literature. It is to that topic that I now turn.

2

The "Wondrous Drama" of Guru Gobind Singh

BACHITRA NATAK, OR "THE WONDROUS DRAMA," is a work in sixteen chapters detailing Guru Gobind Singh's genealogy, birth, and life. The phrase *Apni Katha*, or "My Story," first appears in the second chapter, and then again at the beginning of the sixth chapter, which opens with the story of the Guru's birth. The *Natak*, or "drama," of the title does not mean that the composition is in the format of a play or drama, but rather implies a "drama" more in the sense of a *lila* [*līlā*] as applied to divine figures, suggesting sport or play. Much of *Bachitra Natak* is in the first person, and it is therefore typically described as an autobiography. In a text often attributed to Guru Gobind Singh, therefore, this composition is extremely important, and the themes it expresses are echoed throughout many other compositions in the Dasam Granth. This chapter will summarize the events of *Bachitra Natak* (referring to the author as the "poet" in order to focus on the themes of the text rather than debates regarding its authorship), and conclude with a discussion of the central themes of the composition and how they may be analyzed, as well as how these themes relate to the Dasam Granth in its entirety. As we shall see, this composition is especially important with respect to the concept of dharma and the role of leaders whose responsibility it is to nurture and maintain it. While many analyses of *Bachitra Natak* have highlighted the composition as an early and therefore noteworthy example of autobiography in Indian literature, *Bachitra Natak* in fact may be more profitably situated within the well-established Indian genre of texts extolling the exploits of rulers.

Bachitra Natak begins well before Guru Gobind Singh's lifetime with an account of his ancestry in the Sodhi [Soḍhi] lineage, and then details events in Guru Gobind Singh's life up until about 1697. As with much of the Dasam Granth, interpreters have typically read this section through the lens of subsequent Sikh history. Thus a reader familiar with other accounts of Guru Gobind Singh's life is likely to read a more extended biographical narrative into events described only briefly in *Apni Katha*. Translations into modern Punjabi and English typically fill in names and dates not explicitly mentioned, illustrating how events in *Apni Katha* relate to the turbulent political situation in the Punjab and surrounding regions during Guru Gobind Singh's lifetime as local rulers made and broke alliances and conspired with or against Mughal authorities. Many biographies of Guru Gobind Singh themselves use the *Apni Katha* portion of *Bachitra Natak* as a primary source. The focus here will be the key themes revealed in the narrative of the Guru's life. The author of this composition described himself as Tegh Bahadur's son and as the Guru but did not use the name Guru Gobind Singh (this being generally understood as the name the Guru adopted only after the establishment of the Khalsa in 1699). *Bachitra Natak* opens with a verse in praise of the sword:

> I salute the sword [*khaṛag*] with great affection in my heart.
> I shall complete this book if you help me. (BN 1:1–2)

More than a hundred verses lauding the lord as Kal [Kāla] complete the first chapter, titled "Praise of Revered Kal." Kal is here described in negating terms as without form, without flaws, and also with positive attributes such as "sword-holder" and as wearing a rosary, roaring so loudly the messengers of the god of death, Yam [Yama], tremble.

The second chapter, titled "Description of the Poet's Lineage" or "Description of the Origin of the Sodhi Lineage," describes the ancestry of the Sikh Gurus. The opening verse describes the Lord's greatness, and the poet then continues his praise of the Lord who bestows power and talent:

> The dumb recite the Six Shastras, the lame climb mountains.
> The blind see, the deaf hear, if Kal bestows his mercy. (2)

Lord, how can I relate your greatness with my meager intellect?
I haven't the power to praise you; may you yourself make this story better. (3) (BN 2:2–3)

The last line of the eighth verse in this second chapter reads, "Now I shall tell my own story, of how the Sodhi lineage came into being" (BN 2:8). In the verses that follow, we first learn about the origins of this world. The narrative thus links the Gurus' ancestry to greater cosmic forces responsible for creation itself:

When Kal [kāla] first set creation in motion, it was with *oṃkāra*.
[Kālasaina], great in strength, of incomparable beauty, was the first king. (10)
Kalket [Kālaketu] was the second, Krūrbaras [Krūrabarasa] was the third in this world.
Kaldhuj [Kaladhuja] was the fourth king, from whom the whole world came into being. (11)
His body was splendid with a thousand eyes, a thousand feet.
He slept on Sekh Nāg [Śeṣanāga], [thus] the world declares him the lord of Sekh. (12)
He dug out the wax from one of his ears, from which Madhu and Kīṭabh [Kaiṭabha] took form, and when he dug out the wax from his other ear, this entire creation came into existence. (13)
Kal killed them [Madhu and Kīṭabh], and their flesh [*med*] flowed into the ocean.
The greasy substance floated on the water, and that's why the earth is called *medhā*. (14)
The man who does good deeds is called a god on this earth.
But those who do bad deeds in this world, everyone calls them demons [*asura*]. (15) (BN 2:10–15)

This passage introduces several key themes. The emphasis on the central role of kings and their battles with demons from the very beginning of creation is noteworthy. The equation of good people with the gods and those who do bad deeds with demons is another theme that will be highlighted throughout *Bachitra Natak* and becomes especially significant in interpreting the events of other portions of the *Bachitra*

Natak Granth. The story of the king Kaldhuj sleeping on a serpent and slaying the demons Madhu and Kaitabh [Kaiṭabha] is also associated with the god Vishnu in Hindu mythology, and this story recurs in the first of the goddess compositions, *Chandi Charitra Ukti Bilas*. In particular, the story of the demons Madhu and Kaitabh, their creation out of Vishnu's earwax, and his slaying them is part of the mythology of Durga as related in the *Durgāsaptaśati*, which is discussed in more detail in the next chapter. Thus the opening chapters of *Bachitra Natak* mention topics that will recur elsewhere in the Dasam Granth.

The remainder of this second chapter lists more kings and their descendants in the Sodhi lineage into which Guru Gobind Singh would be born. More than once the poet expressed his fear that the story would become too long if he were to name everyone; the lineage stretched back through all the cosmic eras, or *yugas*, had its origins in the Sūraj [Sūrya], or sun dynasty, and included figures such as Ram and Sita [Sītā] and their twin sons Lav [Lava] and Kush [Kuśa], who here are described as founders of the Punjabi cities Lahore and Kasur and rulers of a great kingdom. The story of Ram and Sita and their sons is of course well known from sources such as Vālmīki's Sanskrit Ramayana and numerous vernacular versions, and in fact there is one such version in the *Chaubis Avatar* portion of the Dasam Granth itself.

The descendants of Lav and Kush in turn ruled for many generations. Among their descendants was a man named Sodhi Rai [Soḍhi Rāi], founder of the Sanaudh [Sanauḍh] dynasty. His descendants, known as Sodhis, continued to rule, conquering other kings and performing the traditional Vedic *rājasūya* and *aśvamedha* sacrifices many times, thereby fulfilling one of the central dharmic responsibilities of rulers as described in classical Hindu literature regarding dharma. The chapter closes with an explanation of how the Sodhis began to fight among themselves, driven by greed and self-interest.

A great battle among rival factions of the Sodhis is the subject of chapter 3. The verses describe their conflict in great detail—the weapons, the fallen wounded and their bloody injuries, the sound of battle. As warriors shouted, ghosts and evil spirits danced on the battlefield, and the goddess roared in the sky. The battle between the different factions of the Gurus' ancestors is waged on earth by humans, but significantly also closely observed by the gods. Finally, Lav's descendants were victorious, and in their defeat, the survivors among Kush's descendants fled to Kashi (i.e., Benares or Varanasi) to study the Vedas, thereby becoming known as the Bedis [Bedīs]. The ancestors of the Sikh Gurus are thus here portrayed as kings who performed the traditional Vedic sacrificial rites.

Chapter 4 of *Bachitra Natak* explains that after the Bedis had gone to Kashi, a Sodhi king of the Madra or Punjab kingdom sent a letter to the Bedis asking that they forget their differences. The Bedis agreed and returned to Punjab, where they recited the four Vedas for the Sodhi king. After this recitation, the king decided to retire to the forest, taking *bana bāsa* [Sanskrit *vanavāsa*], the third of the traditional four life stages, or ashrams [*āśramas*], for males of the twice-born *varnas* [*varṇas*], bestowing his kingdom on the Bedis. The newly enthroned Bedi king then proclaimed that in the fourth and final era, or Kaliyuga, to come he would be called "Nanak" and worshiped by all. The chapter ends with the declaration that the retiring Sodhi king would eventually be reborn as a Guru.

Thus in *Bachitra Natak*, the Sikh Gurus are placed within the framework of the classical Indian theory of the four *yugas*, or eras, in which dharma steadily declines. The ancestors of the Gurus were both kings and spiritual experts, their expertise at this stage being in Vedic recitation. By retiring to the forest, the Sodhi king was following the classical *āśramadharma* model according to which men of the twice-born *varnas* (Brahmans, Kshatriyas, and Vaishyas) ideally move from the student stage to the householder stage, to a stage of semiretirement in the forest, followed by the sannyas [*sannyāsa*] or renunciation stage. Up to this point, the narrative portrays the Gurus' ancestors as dedicated to fulfilling the classical responsibilities of the Kshatriya *varna* such as sponsoring Vedic sacrifices.

Despite the reconciliation between the Sodhis and the Bedis, however, strife came about once more. In the fifth chapter, we learn that after some time the Bedis lost nearly all their kingdom during a chaotic period when Brahmans did the work of Shudras [Śūdras], Kshatriyas did the work of Vaishyas, Vaishyas did the work of Kshatriyas, and Shudras followed the dharma of the upper three *varnas*. To anyone familiar with Indian literature on the *varna* system, a state of affairs in which people are not following their proper *varnadharma* indicates that dharma as a whole, the proper cosmic order, is in a state of decline, and that some remedy is necessary. In much classical Hindu mythology, the remedy is an avatar, a figure sent by a god who "crosses down" to right dharmic wrongs.

Finally, when the Bedis kingdom had been reduced to but twenty villages, Nanak was born.[1] He is described as one born (or "manifest"—*pragaṭe*) into the Bedi clan, with terms that echo those used to characterize avatars:

> He propagated dharma in this Kali age and explained the proper path.
> Those who followed the path he set forth were never troubled by evil [*pāpa*]. (BN 5:5)

Guru Nanak is here presented as a leader setting out a new path to follow, indicating a break with the leaders of earlier generations. Subsequent verses explain that Nanak took the form of the next eight Gurus of Sikhism: Angad, Amar Dās, Rām Dās, Arjun, Hargobind, Hari Rāi, Hari Krishan, and Tegh Bahadur, and that the wise could see that they were really all one (BN 5:7–12). The ninth Guru, Tegh Bahadur, Guru Gobind Singh's father, "protected the forehead mark [*tilak*] and sacred thread" and sacrificed his life for dharma (BN 5:13–14) in the Kaliyuga, or fourth era in traditional Indian reckoning, in which dharma is in its most highly weakened state. The *tilak* and sacred thread in particular are emblematic of the twice-born or upper three *varnas* in the Indian *varnadharma* system, especially Brahmans, and the protection of Brahmans is one of the central dharmic responsibilities of kings. Though the birth of Guru Nanak marks a new path, the Gurus are here still placed in a context in which the traditional obligations of the Kshatriya *varna* are valued.

The narration of Guru Tegh Badadur's death is followed by the story of Guru Gobind Singh's appearance on this earth:

> Now I shall tell my own story [*apnī kathā*], how I was brought here while performing ascetic practices.
> From Hemkunt mountain, with its splendid seven summits, (1)
> The place known as Seven Peaks [*saptasṛṅga*] where the Pāṇḍava kings performed yoga,

There I performed great austerities, and worshiped Mahākāla and Kālakā.[2] (2)
I performed austerities to the point that I attained a state of union,
My parents worshipped the Imperceptible One [*alakha*], and performed many types of yogic practice. (3)
They served the Imperceptible One, and Gurdevā was pleased with them.
When the Lord [*prabhu*] gave me the command, I took birth in Kaliyuga. (4)
I had no wish to come, for my mind and body lay at the feet of the Lord.
But the Lord made himself clear, and sent me to this world. (5) (BN 6:1–5)

The verses that follow relate how the Timeless Lord [Akāl Purakh] convinced a lowly "insect" why he should be sent to this world. When he first began the process of creation, the Lord explains, he created fearsome demons [*daīt*; *daitya*] who were soon so intoxicated with their own power that they ceased to worship him. So the Lord got rid of them and put the gods Shiva, Vishnu, and Brahma in their place, but they too were caught up in devotion to their own power and designated themselves as the supreme lords [*paramesura*; *parameśvara*] (BN 6:7–8). The Timeless Lord created other beings as well—the sun, moon, fire, air—and they became objects of worship, as did gods of stone, water, and even Dharmarājā (BN 6:10–11). Finally, when none recognized the Lord, he decided to create humans, but they too came under the spell of self-interest and believed that the Supreme Lord could be contained in an image made of stone (BN 6:13). The Lord then created perfected beings [*siddhas*] and wise ones [*sādhas*], but it turned out that whoever in the world gained a bit of wisdom simply started his own path; none realized the Supreme Lord, and enmity, disputes, and all-out egotism were on the rise (BN 6:14–15).

The Lord tried creating *rikhis* [*ṛṣis*], or sages, and whichever of them became a leader set out his own traditions [*simmrit*; *smṛti*], and those who followed these traditions abandoned the Lord. The god Brahma set forth the four Vedas, and those who followed the dictates of the Vedas also fell away from the Lord. Those who kept their minds on the Lord's feet, however, did not adopt these traditions (BN 6:18–19). The Lord further explains that he created various other religious leaders, including Gorakhnath [Gorakhnātha] (the traditional founder of the Kāṇphāṭ yogī sect), Ramanand [Rāmānanda] (one of whose poems is included in the Guru Granth Sahib), and Muhammad, the prophet of Islam. They and their followers were entangled in self-interest, never recognizing the Supreme Lord (BN 6:20–28). In *Bachitra Natak*, a range of religious organizations that could be grouped under the larger headings of both "Hinduism" and "Islam" are thus portrayed as having failed in their missions, leading to the necessity of establishing a more effective path for the protection of dharma through the lineage of the Sikh Gurus. One may read this significant passage as once again distinguishing between the efforts of the Sikh Gurus and those of other religious leaders.

> Having explained the failures of earlier leaders, the Supreme Lord then proclaimed:
> I have favored you as my son, and created you to promulgate the path.
> Therefore go to the world and set dharma in motion, and stop people from depraved actions. (BN 6:29)

The poet replied by accepting the Lord's command to be born in this world and to propagate his path. Thus on the one hand the Guru is portrayed in terms much like those of the avatars of gods such as Vishnu, who sends avatars when dharma is in a state of decline, but *Bachitra Natak* has already asserted that those avatars were unsuccessful. Thus even if the poet here is claiming avatar status, the suggestion is that he is a new kind of avatar. The poet's birth in a lineage of kings also suggests the path of dharma to be set forth will have both a political and a spiritual component. In setting the stage for the events in Guru Gobind Singh's life, the narrative here echoes themes found in the epic literature of India such as disputes among members of ruling lineages, kings who spend time in exile, would-be kings who perform austerities, as well as an ongoing exploration of the obligations of rulers.

The poet was quick to caution those who would call him the Supreme Lord, or *paramesura*, insisting that he was but the slave and servant of the Lord (BN 6:31–33), only carrying out the Lord's command, absorbed in reciting his many names (BN 6:34–40).

> All the earlier avatars just had people recite their own names.
> None of them vanquished the Lord's enemies, nor did they set people on the path of dharma.
> Whatever prophets [*ambīā*; i.e., plural of *nabī*] there have been came and left this world thinking only of themselves.
> None recognized the great Lord, and they knew nothing of karma and dharma. (BN 6:44–45)

The poet here explicitly grouped together avatars (most commonly associated with Hinduism) and *nabīs* (Arabic for prophet or messenger, most commonly used for the prophets of Islam). Subsequent verses highlight a range of futile religious endeavors, from recitation of the Qur'an to study of the Puranas, from the yogic practices of keeping matted hair to wearing heavy earrings. Those who perform such practices find no help from the Lord when they die; they go to hell [*naraki*] rather than heaven [*suragi*; *svarga*] (BN 6:47–58). Again, while the poet has in one sense described his mission in terms very much akin to those typical of an avatar, it is clear that his birth and role were meant to be different, explicitly contrasted with the birth of figures traditionally associated with Hinduism and Islam. The chapter closes with the poet's announcement that he shall now briefly narrate his own story.

In chapter 7, which is just three verses long, the poet tells us that his father journeyed eastward, bathing at various pilgrimage sites. At Triveni (the "triple braid" or confluence of the Ganges, Yamuna, and mythical Saraswati rivers; modern Allahabad) his father spent his days giving auspicious charitable gifts. There the poet was conceived, and he was born farther to the east in the city of Patna. He was then taken to the Punjab, lovingly raised by many nurses, and given various forms of education. When he began to perform acts of dharma, his father departed this world for heaven [*devaloki*] (BN 7:1–3).

In chapter 8, the poet again emphasized his role as a protector of dharma (using the term *rāj*, most frequently associated with kingship) before turning to a description of the battle of Bhangani.[3]

> When the responsibility of rule [*rāja-sāja*] came upon me, I promoted dharma to the best of my abilities.

I hunted different animals in the forest, killing bears, deer, and stags. (1)
Then I had to leave my home [*desa*], and we headed toward Paonta.
I enjoyed myself on the banks of the Kalindrī [Yamuna] river, and viewed various forms of entertainment. (2) (BN 8:1–2)

The description of the Guru's activities during this time is rather brief; we learn that the hunting continued along the Yamuna's banks, and that for no apparent reason this angered a king named Fateh Shah. So a battle began, depicted in far greater detail than previous events. Warriors on both sides wielded swords, daggers, and bows and arrows. Some fell in battle, others fled in fear. Ghosts and evil spirits were drawn by the bloody struggle, and huge vultures circled overhead (BN 8:4–28). A man named Hari Chand shot an arrow that struck the poet's horse, a second that grazed his ear, and a third that hit his waist but left no wound (BN 8:29–30). Angered, the poet fatally wounded his attacker with his own arrow. The poet's forces were victorious, returned to Paonta briefly, but then went to Kahlur, where the poet established the village of Anandpur. Good people were exalted, the wicked killed (BN 8:31–38). As in verse 15 of chapter 2, there is a distinction between the good and the evil, who are likened to the gods and the demons. Battle on behalf of good people is portrayed as part of the promotion of dharma, once again drawing attention to this central concern of the text.

Chapter 9 is the tale of the battle of Nadaun [Nādauṇ]. The opening verses depict a rivalry between the two local rulers Alif Khan [Khān] and Bhim Chand [Bhīm Chand]. Bhim Chand sought the poet's assistance and prepared for battle; other nearby rulers chose sides, and the battle began. As in the verse detailing his birth, the poet once again described himself as an "insect," who in this battle took up a gun [*tu-phanga*] and aimed for the heart of one of the local leaders, who then fell to the ground (BN 9:17). Then, the poet switched, took up his bow, and began shooting arrows. The enemy forces eventually retreated.

Pierced by arrows and spears, the brave fighters fell to the ground.
Their flowing blood dyed their clothes red as if they'd been playing Holi. (BN 9:20)

As in many other Dasam Granth tales of battle, the scenes of battle are vividly evoked. The bloodstained clothes of the fallen remind the poet of the dye-stained clothes of those throwing colored water at one another during the spring festival of Holi. Such comparisons of the death of enemies in battle to auspicious scenes such as celebrating the festival of Holi is a theme that occurs in many other Dasam Granth compositions.

Chapter 9 ends with the poet visiting the palaces of local kings before returning home to enjoy himself in Anandpur, where he passed many years (BN 9:22–24). Thieves in Anandpur were punished; others fled but returned when they could find no food. But the calm was disturbed when Dilawar Khan [Dilāwar Khān] sent his son to attack Anandpur as its residents slept. A man named Alam [Ālama] awakened the poet, and in turn the poet's men awakened and took up their weapons as they heard the shouts of the advancing attackers. Loud drumbeats sounded, the goddess Kali [Kālī] shrieked, and the scene on the river evoked for the poet the night of destruction [*Kālarātra*; the night when the world is destroyed, often associated with the goddess Durga]. The poet's warriors roared, and the frightened would-be attackers fled without taking up their weapons, plundering a village as they retreated (BN 10:1–9). The comparison between the battle scene on earth and the night of cosmic destruction is yet another example of an explicit equation of human and divine battles.

This theme is reiterated in the account of the intricacies of regional politics among the various chieftains of the Punjab and the gruesome sights and sounds of battle that form the basis for the dramatic eleventh chapter. After fleeing the battlefield, Dilawar Khan's son rushed to his father's side but was too ashamed to speak. Angered, Husaini [Husainī] (presumably an official under Dilawar's command) prepared for battle. He and his forces looted villages in the region, taking the villagers' food for themselves. Then he became embroiled in complex disputes with local chieftains and prepared to launch an attack. Attempts to reach a peaceful agreement among the rival factions were unsuccessful, and a battle began. By the end of the chapter, warriors named Husaini, Kripal Chand, Himmat, and Sangatia were among those who lay dead (BN 11:1–69).

The poet vividly described the sounds of this battle in short, staccato-like verses, from the beating of drums and blowing of horns to the sounds of weapons clanging against one another and the shouts of enraged warriors. As arrows flew, the wounded fell to the ground, the streaming blood from each fallen warrior merging into a raging red river. The conflict was so fierce, indeed, that it attracted attention far beyond the battlefield, awakening Rudra and Brahma from their meditation and causing hosts of celestial beings (including *kinnaras*, *jachas*, [*yakṣas*], and *vidiādhāras*) to laugh and dance (BN 11:49). The poet's imagery suggests yet again that the world of the gods and the world of humans are closely linked, and that celestial beings continually monitor the status of dharma in the world of humans, seeing their battles as parallel to those between the gods and demons.

The next chapter portrays a battle that took place after Dilawar Khan learned that his forces had yet to attain victory. Still more local chieftains took sides and fought, Jujhar Singh leading the forces against Dilawar Khan's, and the twelfth and final verse of the chapter depicts Jujhar Singh fighting valiantly with multiple weapons, and then himself departing for heaven [*devapuri*] (BN 12:1–12). The aftermath of this battle is the subject of chapter 13.

Chapter 13's opening verses explain that the Mughal emperor Aurangzeb, angered by the turn of events, sent his son to Madra Desa (Punjab). Frightened by the arrival of the emperor's son, residents fled to the hills. Aurangzeb's son in turn became angry and sent an official whose forces destroyed the homes of those who had fled in fear (BN 13:3–4). Those who fled in cowardice rather than staying to fight were the target of the poet's sharp derision:

> The homes of those who turned their faces away from their Guru will be demolished in this life and the next. They will be mocked, and they will not go to heaven. They will be disappointed in all matters. (5)
>
> Those who abandon service to the good [*sant*] shall remain hungry and sorrowful. None of their desires will be fulfilled in this world, and they will fall into hell in the end. (6)
>
> The world shall always mock them. They will live in the pits of hell in the end. The faces of those who turn away from the Guru's feet shall be blackened in this world and the next. (7)

> Their sons and grandsons will not prosper, they will bring grief to their parents and die. Those who bear malice toward the Guru die a dog's death; they shall repent when they are thrown into the pits of hell. (8)
> The Lord [*paramesura*] created both Baba's [Guru Nanak's] and Babar's successors. Recognize [Nanak and his successors] as the kings of spiritual matters [*dīnshāha*] and consider [Babar and his successors] the lord of the world [*dunīpatī*]. (9)
> Those who do not make offerings to Baba's [successors] will have [their wealth] taken from them by Babar's [successors]. They shall receive severe punishment, and their homes will be looted. (10)
> When those turncoats run out of money, then they'll beg from the Sikhs. The *malechas*[4] will loot the homes of the Sikhs who give money. (11) (BN 13:5–11)

The poet further describes the woes that would befall those who betrayed the Guru and how those whose devotion was steadfast would find success and be protected from the rapacious *malecha*s. The narrative suggests that in a situation in which there were multiple rulers demanding allegiance, some struggled to choose where to direct their loyalties. This is yet another point in the narrative at which the poet drew a sharp contrast between those who supported the Guru's unique mission and those whose evil deeds would consign them to hell. The distinction between spiritual and worldly kingship, between the power of the Gurus and the Mughals, is here defined as part of the cosmic drama, and it is the responsibility of good people to serve and be loyal to the Gurus.

After this fierce denunciation of those who were disloyal, the poet then returned to the story of the Mughal official named Mirza Beg, who had looted the homes of the people who fled to the hills. Aurangzeb's son sent another four officials. Those who had fled and effectively considered the four officials to be their Guru suffered great humiliation—their heads were doused with urine and shaved, and the urine was like "nectar" [*pāhuri*] that they took home. The officials inquired into who had fled without permission and paraded them around the city as if they were collecting offerings. They were beaten with shoes, leaving marks on their foreheads that the poet compares to a *tilak* placed there by their "gurus," the officials (BN 13:12–21).

> Those who never fought in battle, who acquired fame through bribes rather than earning it—no one knows which village they live in, or who told the Lord of Death [Jama] about them. (22)
> All the good people [*santān*] saw this spectacle of these people being mocked this way. The Lord [*nāthi*] could not stand to see the good people in distress, and lent his hand to save them. (23) (BN 13:22–23)

The chapter ends with the observation that those who keep the company of good people are protected, just as the tongue is protected by the teeth (BN 13:25). This implies that recognizing, supporting, and even fighting on the behalf of those who are good is a key component of following dharma and receiving the protection of the Gurus.

The final chapter of *Bachitra Natak* opens with verses in praise of the Lord [*Sarabkāla*] who protects the good and destroys the wicked, and who protected his servant the poet with his own hands (BN 14:1–2).

> Now I present to you all the wondrous events I have witnessed. Lord, if you look upon me with favor, your servant shall continue to recite. (3)
> I wish to bring to light all the spectacles I have seen. With the Lord's power, I will describe the previous births I have witnessed. (4)
> The infinite lord Sarabkāla is my father, the goddess Kālikā is my mother.
> The pure mind is my guru, and intellect is the guru's wife; they have taught me to do good deeds. (5)
> When that pure mind looked upon the intellect with favor, then the mind as guru refined my statements. Now I wish to describe the former deeds [*charita*][5] I have seen. (6)
> Sarabkāla, full of kindness, then showered his compassion on the one he knew to be his servant. He made me remember all my previous births. (7)
> What intellectual understanding did I have? Such wisdom as I have was given to me through the Lord's grace. Sarabkāla bestowed his compassion, and gave me the protection of steel at all times. (8)
> Sarabkāla is the protector at all times, the protection of steel [*loha*] is always vast. With your mercy upon me, I became fearless. I conduct myself with pride, I have become the king [*rāī*] of all. (9)

> I have narrated as books the previous births as I came to know of them. The Satijuga [*satyayuga*], which I saw first, I have narrated in the first *Debī-charitra*. (10)
>
> *Chandi Charitra* was composed first; I narrated it in order, from beginning to end. I told the full story before; now I wish to praise [the Lord] again. (11) (BN 14:3–11)

Here ends *Apni Katha*. The closing verses of this final chapter of *Bachitra Natak* suggest a close connection between this composition and other compositions found in the Dasam Granth, particularly those that are part of the *Bachitra Natak Granth*, including the stories of the avatars and the tales of the goddess, here referred to as *Debi-Charitra*. The composition that opened with a salute to the sword ends with praise of the protective power of steel. There is an explicit mention of the books or *granths* concerning the various births. This therefore suggests that one way to read the events related here in *Bachitra Natak* is as a reference point for the stories of the goddess and the incarnations.

Interpreting "The Wondrous Drama"

Bachitra Natak relates the story of at least part of Guru Gobind Singh's life but does so by placing his life in a substantially larger cosmic framework. It is not the story of just a single lifetime but of the eras, or *yugas*, of traditional Hindu mythology, moving from the first era or *satyayuga* to the fourth and present, the *kaliyuga*. Like most other models of the *yugas*, *Bachitra Natak* describes a supreme god who creates the cosmos in the hope that it will develop according to the principles of dharma, the cosmic order. In this narrative, the supreme god dispatches a host of religious teachers who bring texts such as the Vedas, Puranas, and Qur'an to humans but who fail in their mission to fulfill god's work, becoming caught up in ego and strife instead. The supreme god also entrusts particular lineages with the responsibility of rule in the hope that they will protect and preserve dharma, but they too succumb to ego and discord. Dharma continues to weaken as the *yugas* progress, despite the efforts of both kings and various avatars and prophets. A further sign of the decline is the mixing up of *varna* responsibilities. Even within the poet's own lineage, within which experts in Vedic recitation were born, there was discord in the time before the advent of Nanak and the Gurus. But *Bachitra Natak* reports that the advent of the Gurus marks a new effort on the part of the Supreme Lord.

The poet, despite his birth within a lineage that included ancestors such as the avatar Ram, is set apart from the failures of those earlier avatars and prophets, chosen specifically by the Lord to take birth and set forth a path. It is possible to read the poet's sense of mission here both in the general context of the passing of the *yugas* and in the specific context of the history of the Sikh Gurus. J. S. Grewal (1996, 53), for example, noted that we may read *Bachitra Natak* as confirming that Guru Gobind Singh "was convinced of his legitimate position as the true successor of Guru Nanak and of God's support for him in his arduous mission." That legitimacy is also attained through the sacrifice of the poet's father, Guru Tegh Bahadur, on behalf of the religious expression of those who wear the *tilak* and sacred thread. Such protection of Brahmans is one of the traditional dharmic responsibilities of male members of the Kshatriya varna of rulers and warriors. Still, this account of Guru Tegh Bahadur's death occurs within a narrative that sharply contrasts the nature of the Sikh Gurus' mission with that of religious leaders traditionally associated with both Hinduism and Islam.

Indeed, the poet's propagation of a path is in part focused on highlighting the futility of most forms of religious practice, whether it be the recitation of a Hindu or Muslim text such as a Veda, Purana, or Qur'an or wearing the garb of a particular sect, and also on battling the forces of evil through martial conflict. The later Sikh Gurus are portrayed as assuming both spiritual and military leadership positions. The poet's mission to propagate a true religious path involves fighting those who are obstacles on this path, an effort his ancestors such as Ram had made with only limited success. In J. S. Grewal's words,

> In Guru Gobind Singh's view of the cosmic drama, the creator of the universe intervened from time to time to reinforce good in its struggle against evil; and, depending upon the gravity of the situation the divinely appointed instruments of good were entitled to a legitimate use of physical force against the wicked; but those who had been appointed to that task in the past had failed to accomplish God's

> purpose which was not other than the establishments of His unqualified worship by mankind; therefore all previous dispensations had been superseded by the dharma instituted by Guru Nanak; it was left for Guru Gobind Singh to defend the claims of that dharma, even if it involved use of physical force against the enemies of this divine dispensation; and his Sikhs should be prepared for a struggle. (Grewal 1996, 54)

Here again we may note that *Bachitra Natak* suggests a clear continuity between traditional concepts such as dharma and the progression of the cosmos through the *yugas*, but also the ongoing development of a distinctive Sikh conceptualization of dharma and the role of the Gurus as its propagators and protectors. In *Bachitra Natak* the protector role is explicitly attributed to both Guru Tegh Bahadur and Guru Gobind Singh. Arguably, we can read this notion of protection not only in light of the traditional Hindu concept of the avatar but also in light of the notions of religious and temporal leadership that had developed from the time of the sixth Guru, Guru Hargobind. Guru Hargobind is traditionally credited with developing the concept of *miri-piri* [*mīrī-pīrī*], spiritual and temporal, worldly leadership, symbolized by two swords. Similarly, in *Bachitra Natak* Guru Gobind Singh assumes characteristics both of the spiritual leader and of a king or ruler, who has specific responsibilities with respect to dharma. The opening verse of the composition is in praise of the sword, the closing verse praises steel, and other verses in the first chapter offer praise to other weapons such as the spear, dagger, and bow and arrow (e.g., BN 1:87, 120). Indeed weapons and battle are a central theme in many Dasam Granth compositions, and in *Bachitra Natak*, battles are part of the dharmic responsibility of the Guru. The role therefore combines aspects of both spiritual and worldly power.

Bachitra Natak as Autobiography

Bachitra Natak is frequently described as an autobiography in the general sense that it is an account of part of a person's life presented in the first person. In an article on biography in Punjabi literature, for example, Ganda Singh (1979, 117) wrote, "This auto-biographical memoir is, perhaps, the first of its kind in Indian literature produced by non-Muslims." While the notion of *Bachitra Natak* as being the first of its kind is one way of highlighting its importance,[6] this designation of the text as autobiography is not particularly useful in understanding how *Bachitra Natak* fits into the wider context of Indian literature at the time, what some of its literary antecedents may be, or its role in the Dasam Granth as a whole. In declaring *Bachitra Natak* an autobiography, most Sikh commentators are implicitly comparing it to a later notion of autobiography as a genre, a move that is somewhat anachronistic. It does not provide a framework for reading the lengthy genealogy preceding the account of the Guru's life. *Bachitra Natak* has far more in common with traditional Indian genres of panegyrics of royal figures and spiritual leaders than it does with more recent forms of autobiography.

Bachitra Natak opens with a chapter in praise of God and then turns to the creation of the cosmos and the poet's lineage, a move that directly links him to significant events in the history of the cosmos. In this regard, the composition may be more profitably compared with poetic works that detail and praise the lineages of kings and religious leaders. Such accounts of lineages or *vamshas* [*vaṃśas*] are found throughout the Puranas, the epics, and in both poetic compositions (e.g., *mahākāvyas* composed at royal courts) and inscriptions in praise of kings and religious leaders [*praśasti*].[7] In such accounts, great leaders are frequently described as members of either the solar (*sūrya*) or lunar (*chandra*) dynasties, as is the case in *Bachitra Natak*, in which the Sodhis were part of the solar dynasty. The narration of lineages that directly link rulers to great kings of the past have traditionally served a legitimating function for rulers.

Verses in praise of great rulers also typically narrate the ruler's victories in battle, a central theme of *Bachitra Natak*. The chapters that precede the story of Guru Gobind Singh's life include narration of the battle between Kaldhuj and the demons Madhu and Kaitabh, battles among the descendants of Lav and Kush, and quarrels and disputes in the Bedi lineage before Guru Nanak's birth. Of the eight chapters that treat Guru Gobind Singh's life from the time of his birth, six are specifically devoted to descriptions of battles. *Bachitra Natak* reports that Guru Gobind Singh established the village of Anandpur after his victory in the battle of Bhangani, where, as befits a good ruler, he exalted good people and destroyed the wicked (BN 8:37–38, 162). Thus one central theme of

Bachitra Natak is the leader's responsibility to create a territory in which good people thrive, and the wicked are destroyed, with the leader fighting battles to ensure such a territory. This theme is illustrated both in the descriptions of battles, echoing the earlier struggles of leaders such as Ram and his descendants, and also more personally in the criticism of the people who abandoned the Guru as related in chapter 13.

Along with this theme of proper leadership as exemplified by creating a territory in which good people may thrive, there is an equally important theme of religious leadership that is expressed through the concept of the avatar, the figure sent by god to reestablish the proper dharmic order. Although the poet does not specifically describe himself as an avatar here, the context certainly implies that Guru Gobind Singh was born for a similar purpose. This is true of the specific context of *Bachitra Natak*, in which the poet takes birth at God's command, and of the larger context of the *Bachitra Natak Granth*, in which Vishnu, Shiva, and Brahma send avatars, and the goddess fights demons, all for the cause of the good, of proper dharma.[8]

The placement of Guru Gobind Singh in the avatar mode is one of the reasons that some Sikh commentators have been uncomfortable with the Dasam Granth, because it seems to be an example of a Sikh leader being cast into a Hindu framework. One possible reading, however, is that because *Bachitra Natak* so clearly portrays all previous avatars and prophets as having been failures in their missions, the role that is here described for Guru Gobind Singh represents a new conceptualization of the role of the figure sent by god in defense of righteousness. *Bachitra Natak* is a striking combination of long-standing Indic themes—the lineage, or *vamsha*, the decline of dharma through the ages and the avatars sent to restore it, the king who legitimizes his rule through his protection of dharma—and specific concerns of the late seventeenth century Punjab, with its warring hill chiefs, intrigues with Mughal officials, and the rising power of the Sikh *panth*, told in the first person. It explores the theme of a righteous ruler struggling to create a territory in which good people may thrive, and links the struggles of human rulers to those of the gods. *Bachitra Natak* ends with the poet mentioning his narration of the deeds of the goddess, a tale that makes even more explicit the parallels between the battles of righteous rulers and those of the gods.

3

Tales of the Goddess

THE CLOSING VERSES OF *BACHITRA NATAK* referred to both *Debī Charitra* and *Chandi Charitra*, and in standard printed editions of the Dasam Granth, *Bachitra Natak* is followed by three goddess-focused compositions. The first two are in Brajbhasha: *Chandi Charitra Ukti Bilas* [CC 1] and *Chandi Charitra* [CC 2], each with more than 200 verses divided into eight chapters, and both part of the *Bachitra Natak Granth*. The third, known both as *Var Durga Ki* and as *Chandi di Var* [VDK], is in Punjabi, and is 55 verses long.[1] In addition to these three compositions that are specifically about the goddess, there are other long sections within the Dasam Granth focused on her, including verses 211–230 of *Akal Ustat*, verses 5–8 and 422–433 of *Krishna Avatar*, the first chapter of *Shastra-nam-mala*, and the first *charitra* of *Charitropakhian*.

The extensive attention paid to the goddess in the Dasam Granth has raised for some Sikh commentators the question of whether these tales promote goddess worship and are therefore seemingly at odds with normative Sikh theology. If we consider the goddess tales in the wider context of the Dasam Granth as a whole, however, it becomes clear that while the question of whether or not goddess worship is advocated is significant, it is also important to note that these accounts of the goddess's exploits further develop themes raised in *Bachitra Natak* and elsewhere regarding the proper maintenance of cosmic order and the nature of leadership. Another significant feature of the goddess tales is their emphasis on the craft of poetry itself. The poet often requests that his readers or listeners take special note of his language and imagery, indicating an awareness of his audience. This concern with poetic imagery and aesthetic enjoyment is itself another indicator of the Dasam Granth's concern with the nature of proper leadership, the composition of poetry, or sponsorship of its composition, being a well-established obligation of the king in Indic culture.

The goddess is referred to by many names in these compositions, including Durga, Bhavani [Bhavānī], Chandi, Chandika, Chamunda [Chāmuṇḍā], Kali [Kālī], and Kalaka or Kalika [Kālakā or Kālikā]. As in various Hindu versions of goddess mythology, she takes different forms, and sometimes these forms merge into one another.[2] The first goddess composition, *Chandi Charitra Ukti Bilas*, ends with a reference to the *Markandeya Purana*, of which the *Devi Mahatmya* [*Devī Māhātmya* (DM); a.k.a. *Durgā Saptaśati*], is a part.[3] Many interpreters of the Dasam Granth have described the first two goddess compositions as "translations" of the *Devi Mahatmya*,[4] but while the subject matter is the same, the goddess narratives in the Dasam Granth are considerably shorter than the *Devi Mahatmya*, and their emphases and context are different.[5]

This chapter begins with an exploration of each of the goddess narratives. The discussion of the first, *Chandi Charitra Ukti Bilas*, includes a comparison with the sequence of events related in the Sanskrit *Devi Mahatmya* with references to Coburn's 1991 English translation. The chapter concludes with a discussion of how these narratives relate to one another, how they may be seen within the context of the *Bachitra Natak Granth* and the Dasam Granth as a whole, the controversy within Sikhism over whether these compositions indicate reverence for the goddess, and some observations on how goddess mythology in Indic culture has been related to political power and authority, particularly at the regional level. The close connection between goddess mythology and political legitimation in Indian culture suggests that the inclusion of these goddess narratives in the Dasam Granth in part indicates continuity with the themes of leadership expressed in *Bachitra Natak*. It also raises broader questions about how divine battles mirror earthly conflicts.

Chandi Charitra Ukti Bilas

The title of this composition may be translated as "the recitation of the sport of the deeds of Chandi" or "the enjoyment or sport of the recitation of deeds of Chandi." The word *ukti* (speech, recitation, statement, proclamation) suggests that this composition was meant to be read aloud and listened to, not simply read, but performed. The performative nature of the composition is highlighted in many verses in which the poet draws explicit attention to his imagery. The word *bilas* has connotations similar to those of the word *lila* in the context of the acts of gods and goddesses, suggesting sport or playfulness.

Jaggi and Jaggi (1999, vol. 1, 192) note that while the opening invocation of this text varies in different manuscripts, the majority include the phrase "srī bhagautī jī kī sahāi," "with the assistance of revered *bhagauti*." Kohli (2005, 64), Singh and Singh (1999, vol. 1, 206), and Bhai Randhir Singh (1995, vol. 1, 92), however, include only the invocation "ik oṃkāra vāhigurū jī kī fatahi." Interpretation of the phrase, "with the assistance of the revered *bhagauti*," varies in Sikh tradition. Some take the Brajbhasha word *bhagauti* to have the same meaning as the Sanskrit *bhagavatī*, the "holy one" or "goddess"; others take *bhagauti* to mean "sword," a contentious point addressed later in this chapter.

Like *Bachitra Natak*, CC 1 opens with a creation story, though not the same one. The opening lines of CC 1 praise the infinite, indestructible god who created Siva and Sakata [Shiva and Shakti], the four Vedas [*shruti cāra*], and the three qualities or *guṇas* of *rajo*, *tama*, and *sat* [*rajas*, *tamas*, and *sattva*; passion, inertia, goodness], who populated the three worlds, who brought forth day and night, the light of the moon and the sun, and the five elements, and who created enmity between the gods and demons and then sat back to watch the show (CC 1 1:1). The poet continues his supplication:

> Ocean of Mercy, if you bestow your grace upon me, I shall render the story of Chandika; may all my words be auspicious. (2)
> Whose light shines throughout the world, destroyer of Chaṇḍa and Chamuṇḍa, whose powerful arms slay the demons, who creates the nine realms. (3)
> You are Chandi, who carries people [across existence], the earth's liberator, the demon destroyer. Wherever one looks, there you are—the cause of Shiva's artistry [*īsa kalā*], Vishnu's Lakshmi [*kamlā hari*], the mountain's daughter [*adrasutā*; *Pārvatī*].[6]

> You are the qualities of darkness, passion, and goodness; you are the poetry woven in the poet's mind.[7] You are the philosopher's stone that turns the iron it touches in this world into gold. (4)
>
> She whose name is Chandika delights everyone and dispels fear. Enlighten my mind that I may compose the story of your wondrous deeds. (5)
>
> Now, if I have your permission, I will compose my book [*grantha*]. I will select and set pleasing words as if they were jewels. I will compose this work all in beautiful language, knowing in my heart your wondrous, infinite story. (6)

In these first verses of CC 1, the poet has alerted his listeners and readers to his intention to tell this story in beautiful language, and he will draw attention to the beauty of his imagery throughout the composition, emphasizing that it is not just the events of the story that are important, but the way they are told.

After these opening verses the story of the goddess begins. In outline, it is similar to the narrative of the *Devi Mahatmya*, though with considerably less detail than the Sanskrit text. For example, the frame story from *Devi Mahatmya* is abbreviated. In CC 1, the poet explains that a king named Surath [Suratha] renounced family and kingdom to meditate in the forest,[8] where he met up with a man named Samadhi [Samādhi]. Surath and Samādhi pondered the story of Chandi, asking a great sage to explain it to them (CC 1 1:7). CC 1 does not here mention the name of the narrator Markandeya.

In contrast, the *Devi Mahatmya* describes in greater detail the troubles that led to Surath and Samadhi leaving for the forest—Surath lost a battle, his kingdom was greatly reduced in size, and some of his ministers seized his treasury and army. Samadhi, of the Vaishya or merchant caste, was banished by greedy family members. The two met near the hermitage of the Brahman sage Medhas, and it was Medhas who explained the mysteries of the goddess after the two wondered why they were miserable and tormented by ego, the king longing for his kingdom, the merchant for the family that had betrayed him (Coburn 1991, 32–34).

In the first chapter of *Chandi Charitra Ukti Bilas*, the poet plunges directly into the tale of the demons Madhu and Kaitabh [Kaiṭabh], as narrated by the chief or lord of sages [*munīsura*, i.e., Medhas], thereby setting the stage for the battle he will describe. Hari [Vishnu] lay sleeping on a vast expanse of water; the world-creator [*bisu kartā*; *viśvakartā*] Brahma emerged from the lotus in his navel, and two demons named Madhu and Kaitabha came forth from Vishnu's earwax. Brahma was frightened, so he contemplated the World-Mother [*jagamātā*; an epithet of Durga]; Vishnu awakened from his deep slumber[9] and prepared to fight the demons. The battle raged on for 5,000 years, until the demons told Vishnu to request a boon from them. Vishnu asked for their heads, the demons agreed, and Vishnu put them on his lap, beheaded them, and then absorbed their radiance [*jota*] into his own body. Vishnu then established the rule of the gods and went to his heaven, Baikuṇṭha [*Vaikuṇṭha*] (CC 1 1:9–12).

In contrast to the relatively brief account in CC 1, the story of the slaying of Madhu and Kaitabh is more elaborate in the first chapter of *Devi Mahatmya*. Vishnu tricked the demons into allowing themselves to be killed because they asked that they be slain in a place where there was no water, thinking the whole earth to be submerged. Then Vishnu put them on his lap and beheaded them with his discus (Coburn 1991, 38–39).[10]

The tale of the buffalo demon Mahish [a.k.a. Mahishāsura; Sanskrit Mahiṣāsura] that follows in the second chapter of *Chandi Charitra Ukti Bilas* is similarly lacking in some of the detail of the Sanskrit text. The second chapter of *Devi Mahatmya* first narrates Mahish's victory over the gods. After the defeat, Prajāpati led a delegation of deities to Shiva and Vishnu. Angered, Shiva, Vishnu, and the other gods in turn produced the goddess from their own bodies and then gave her their weapons. The goddess then waged battle against Mahish and his army. While the demon army and their weapons are fully enumerated in the *Devi Mahatmya*, the description of the battle itself is rather succinct. The goddess slew different demons with different weapons; some lost limbs, other lost their heads and continued to clutch at their weapons. Finally, the battlefield was strewn with the fallen demons and their elephants, horses, and chariots, and torrents of blood formed a river. The goddess (here named as Ambikā) destroyed the demon army just as a fire devours a pile of grass and wood (*Devi Mahatmya* 2:66; Coburn 1991, 44).[11]

The second chapter of *Chandi Charitra Ukti Bilas*, however, is very much focused on depicting the carnage of this battle. The poet devotes eighteen verses to the initial battle between the gods and Mahish's forces (as compared with two verses in *Devi Mahatmya*) with a series of striking similes evincing the flesh and blood strewn on the battlefield.

> Fierce black elephants have fallen on the battlefield, their white flesh and marrow drenched with red blood, as if a tailor had cut different pieces of cloth and thrown them into piles during a deathly winter. (15)
>
> Indra, defender of the gods, angrily took all the gods with him toward the enemy army. Their faces covered by shields, swords in hand, they shouted and struck with their weapons. The demons were drenched in blood, and in the poet's mind it was as if Ram, victorious in battle, bestowed robes of honor on the bears. (16)

The poet has here drawn attention to the mental process of creating this imagery and has let listeners and readers know that the image of the bloodied demons is auspicious, comparable to Ram's gift to the bears who had assisted him in locating Sita after she had been kidnapped. The comparison is similar to that in BN 9:20 in which enemy warriors' bloodstained clothes are likened to the dye-stained clothes of people happily celebrating the festival of Holi.

As the struggle continued, the wounded lay writhing on the ground, blood streaming around them as jackals and vultures grew excited at the easy pickings of flesh (CC 1 2:17). The battle was so loud and fierce that it distracted other gods from their normal tasks, yet also reminded the poet of everyday scenes:

> As he watched the demon Mahakhāsura [Mahiṣāsura] wage battle, the sun stood still. Seeing the flowing stream of blood, the four-eyed Brahma forgot all his texts. Vultures saw flesh and cried out like students reading their lessons in school. The jackals tore at the flesh of the warriors' corpses like *siddhas* mending their patchwork quilts. (CC 1 2:18)

The demons emerged victorious from this battle, and in defeat the gods, evicted from their own abodes, went to live in Shiva's city. After a few days, the goddess came there to bathe. The gods paid their respects to her, told her of their troubles, and asked that she retake their residences for them. The goddess Chandika heard their pleas and, enraged at their plight, announced that she would destroy the demons (CC 1 2:18–23).

While at this point in the story in the *Devi Mahatmya* there is a lengthy series of verses describing how the gods created the goddess and then bestowed their weapons on her, in *Chandi Charitra Ukti Bilas* the episode is brief. The goddess Chandi pledged to kill the demons, and Vishnu's conch and all the other weapons came to her. Her mount the lion [*singha*] is described in great detail (CC 1 2:23–26). Preparing to fight, Chandi gathered up all her weapons, approached the demon's city, and sounded her gong to bring the demons to battle. Huge numbers of demons assembled and began aiming arrows at the goddess's lion. One demon unsheathed his sword and struck directly at the goddess and her lion, but Chandi grabbed him by the neck and threw him to the ground, the poet noting that she did so just like a washerman beats clothes on a wooden plank by the side of the river (CC 1 2:27–34). She skillfully wielded her sword to kill more demons, and seeing them wounded and bleeding in his imagination, it seemed to the poet that the king of birds (Vishnu's mount Garuḍa, enemy of serpents) had cut up the assembly of serpents and strewn them here and there (CC 1 2:35–36).

The poet continued to draw attention to the thought process that produced the images he presented to listeners and readers, using similes to evoke the battle scene. After suffering heavy losses, the demon army retreated to let their leader, Mahish, know what was happening, and he ordered that they surround the goddess. They rushed back into battle crying, "Kill, kill," and surrounded her on all four sides, like the halo that appears around the blackened moon during a solar eclipse.[12] Undaunted, Chandi fought on fiercely, letting loose arrows from bows in her right hand and her left, leaving so many demons bloodied on the ground that it seemed as if the creator had spit out an eighth ocean on this battlefield (CC 1 2:3 7–41). Chandi continued to slice and dice the demon warriors, and the conflict raged so fiercely that Shiva's meditation on Mt. Kailash was disturbed. When Mahish learned that his army was still losing, he entered the fray himself (CC 1 2:42–45).

As the mighty demon flung his mace at the goddess, he looked like Hanuman [Hanumān] uprooting a mountain and smashing it on the demon Ravan's [Rāvaṇa] chest. But Chandi wielded her sword, reddening the battlefield with blood so deep so that it appeared as if there were flames rising from a forest's floor.[13] Once again the scene gives rise to a simile in the poet's mind [*upamā upajī man mai*]; it appeared to him as if the World-Mother goddess's body were moving faster than her mind, like lightning in dark clouds. Still, the demons fought, but the goddess beheaded them with her discus, and the streams of blood flowed toward the sky as if Ram were making an offering of water to the sun (CC 1 2:46–49). This is yet another instance of comparing the bloody bodies of enemies to an auspicious scene; here, it is like a sacrificial offering. Finally, the goddess killed Mahish, and the surviving members of his army fled in all directions, like clouds blown by the wind. Kings from far and wide witnessed Indra's coronation as king once again, and the goddess disappeared from the scene, manifesting herself where Shiva was seated on his lion's skin (CC 1 2:50–52).

While in CC 1 Chandi's actions are the primary focus of the description of this battle, in the *Devi Mahatmya*, Mahish's actions in the battle are recounted more fully. In the course of the fight, the great buffalo demon changes from a buffalo to a lion to a man to an elephant, then a buffalo again. Chandi, meanwhile, drank an intoxicating beverage and beat Mahish until he was so contorted that he came forth from his own mouth (DM 3:27–3:38; Coburn 1991, 46–47). Indra then led the gods in a series of praises to the triumphant goddess, and the gods asked for her protection. As they bowed down before her in supplication, she asked them to request a boon from her. The gods asked that she come to their aid when they need it. The fourth chapter of the *Devi Mahatmya* then concludes with an introduction to the tale of the demons Shumbh and Nishumbh [Śumbha and Niśumbha], and how the goddess was born from Parvati [Pārvatī] or Gauri's [Gaurī] body (DM 4:1–36; Coburn 1991, 48–52).

The opening verses of chapter 3 in *Chandi Charitra Ukti Bilas* depict the comfortable life that resumed after the goddess slew Mahish, allowing the gods to restore the proper state of affairs in which they lived in their heavenly abodes. Sages could once again meditate on the gods in peace, and people recited the Vedas and performed sacrifices. The gods once more paid homage to Indra, and happiness prevailed until the powerful demons Shumbh and Nishumbh brought their army to conquer Indra's kingdom (CC 1 3:54–58). Thus at this point, *Chandi Charitra Ukti Bilas* has condensed into just more than two chapters the events of the first four chapters of the *Devi Mahatmya*. The goddess's battles against demon forces allow the proper order to be reestablished. The poet has highlighted the images of the bloody battles against the demons, and not the verses in praise of the goddess found in the *Devi Mahatmya*.

In the fifth chapter of the *Devi Mahatmya*, the sage Medhas explains that Shumbh and Nishumbh defeated the gods and took control of the three worlds, denying Indra his shares of the sacrifices humans offered to the gods. In contrast, the *Chandi Charitra Ukti Bilas* version again centers primarily on battle, describing in far more gruesome detail than the *Devi Mahatmya* how the two demons wrested control from Indra and the other gods, rather than addressing how the human/divine relationship is maintained through sacrificial ritual. As in earlier battle scenes, the poet described a battlefield strewn with flesh and blood, with a series of haunting images: demons circle the gods like dark clouds surrounding the sun, and every creature that delights in blood, from jackals and vultures to ghosts, bathes in the river of blood as if they were removing their sins with a bath in the Saraswati River. White matter oozed from the heads of the wounded like the Ganges river flowing from Shiva's head (CC 1 3:63–68). Amid such carnage, Shumbh and Nishumbh triumphantly took over the gods' kingdoms.

At this point in the story in the *Devi Mahatmya*, the vanquished gods remembered the boon the goddess had granted them and went to see her at her Himalayan abode. They lavished praise upon her, and as they were so doing, Shiva's wife Parvati arrived to bathe in the Ganges River. She asked the gods who they were praising, whereupon an auspicious form came forth from the sheath of her body, announcing that the hymn was made to her. Thus created from Parvati's sheath, the newly emerged goddess was known as Kauśikī, "She of the Sheath." Parvati, known previously as Gauri [Gaurī] or "pale," now turned black and was named Kālikā, the "Dark One."

The *Chandi Charitra Ukti Bilas* account of this episode differs from the *Devi Mahatmya*. Indra and the other gods, looking unkempt and miserable, vowed to seek the goddess's [here "Shivā"] help in regaining their kingdoms. They went to Shiva's city, hid in caves, and cried out for help. The goddess heard their cries and vowed to slay all the demons. Then Chandi manifested herself, and the goddess Kali burst out of her forehead. The poet explains that to his mind, it seemed that the lord of death [*jama rāja*] had taken birth as Death itself to destroy all the demons. Then Chandika commanded Kali to merge with her, just as the Yamuna River flows into the current of the Ganges (CC 1 3:73–77). The goddess, daughter of the mountain [*Girijā*], and the gods all realized that they could not regain their authority without a fight, and so the goddess began moving toward the battlefield like a black serpent. The description then shifts to the beauty of the goddess, her golden body appearing as if the creator had filled each limb with sweet nectar. Even the moon was not a suitable comparison for her face; Chandi looked as if she were Shacī, Indra's queen, sitting on her throne (CC 1 3:78–79).

But the goddess was fierce, too, and holding her sword, she looked like Yam holding his staff. Then, a demon came by on an errand, and stricken by Chandi's beauty, he fell to the ground unconscious. When he came to his senses, he pulled himself together, folded his hands, announced himself as the brother of King Shumbh, and suggested that Chandi marry his brother. But the goddess replied that she could not do so without waging war. So the demon rushed back to Shumbh and told him that since he had every other precious jewel save for a wife, he should marry this beautiful gem. Shumbh then asked his brother to describe her body. The brother was quick to oblige; her face was like the moon, her eyes like lotus blossoms, her hair more beautiful than the snakes curled round Shiva's neck, her gait like that of an elephant—the list goes on—and she was Shiva's wife. Hearing more about her beauty, Shumbh smiled and announced that a clever messenger must be sent to devise a ruse to capture her. Then Dhumralochan [Dhūmralochana; "Smoke-Eyes"] stood up in the demons' assembly and announced that he would go to get the goddess, either by talking her into coming back with him or, were that stratagem to fail, by dragging her back by her hair (CC 1 3:80–92). Dhumralochan announced:

> "If she makes me angry, then I'll wage war against her and make streams of blood flow on the battlefield. I'm so strong I can blow that mountain down with my breath." (CC 1 3:92)

And so Dhumralochan set out to fetch the goddess, accompanied by a four-part army. He and his soldiers surrounded the mountain like dark clouds, and Dhumralochan roared like the king of elephants. He stood at the base of the mountain and shouted loudly to the goddess that she could either marry Shumbh or fight a war. Chandi's response was to mount her lion and descend from the mountain carrying all her weapons. She engaged in fierce combat with the smoke-eyed demon and cut his lips. His teeth were white like the Ganges, his body dark like the Yamuna, and the red blood flowed over them to complete the triple braid, yet another reference to the confluence of the Ganges, Yamuna, and Saraswati rivers at Prayag or Allahabad, a further example of the poet likening demons' wounds to auspicious scenes. Dhumralochan soldiered on despite his wound; the goddess walloped him on the head; he revived, shrieked loudly, and pierced the goddess's lion with his sword. But Chandi took her sword in hand as well and lopped off his head, leaving the demon army to lament his demise (CC 1 3:96–100).

Although the basic outline of the story of Shumbh's wish to take the goddess as his wife and Dhumralochan's expedition to bring her to his king is roughly the same in the *Devi Mahatmya*, *Chandi Charitra Ukti Bilas* gives greater prominence to the character of Dhumralochan. In the sixth chapter of the *Devi Mahatmya*, when Shumbh learned about the beautiful goddess who would not marry without waging war, he angrily commanded his general Dhumralochan to drag the recalcitrant goddess by her hair. Dhumralochan set out to fetch the goddess, but she turned him to ashes by uttering a fierce sound, and she and her lion laid waste to his army. The lion tore apart warriors' bodies and drank their blood (DM 6:1–20; Coburn 1991, 59–60). In contrast, the Dhumralochan character in *Chandi Charitra Ukti Bilas* is a rather arrogant, almost comical figure who swaggers with pride and issues orders loudly. His death, too, is depicted more graphically; he is not just reduced to ashes but first dealt a sharp blow on his head, then beheaded, his severed head falling to the ground.

In the opening of the fourth chapter of *Chandi Charitra Ukti Bilas*, the description turns to the racket the demons made after Dhumralochan was killed. They were so noisy and disruptive that Shiva's meditative concentration was broken, and Garuda's (Vishnu's vehicle) feathers were ruffled. Chandi cast a fiery glance that burned the demons to cinders. This, the poet tells us, brought a simile to his mind—it was like bees being killed by poisonous smoke (CC 1 4:101). Chandi intentionally spared one demon from her deadly gaze so that he might tell Shumbh what had happened and continue the battle. Hearing the news that Dhumralochan and his army had been killed, Shumbh next sent another two demons named Chand and Mund [Chaṇḍa and Muṇḍa] to either arrest Chandi and bring her back or kill her (CC 1 4:102–107).

Chapter 7 of the *Devi Mahatmya* tells the story of the demons Chand and Mund and their battle with the goddess. When they prepared to attack, Kali emerged from the goddess Ambika's forehead and began slaying demons left and right, crunching them between her teeth. Chand and Mund rushed into the fray, letting loose arrows and discuses, but Kali grabbed Chand by the hair and beheaded him and then slew Mund too. The surviving demons fled, and Kali presented Chand's and Mund's heads to Chandika (Ambika), whereupon Chandika christened Kali "Chamunda" [Chāmuṇḍā] (DM 7:1–25; Coburn 1991, 61–62).

In *Chandi Charitra Ukti Bilas*, Chand and Mund's battle with the goddess is the subject of the fourth chapter, and the battle scene is described in terms very similar to those used for the narration of Dhumralochan's failed attack. The two demons assembled an army and besieged Mt. Sumeru, and Chandi heard their noisy approach and angrily gathered up all her weapons. She let loose one arrow, ten, a hundred, a thousand, hundreds of thousands, so many that the poet was at a loss for words and could only compare the falling demons to leaves falling from a tree in the wind (CC 1 4:108–111).

Mund launched an assault on the goddess and her lion, wounding both. His bloodied sword inspired the poet to make a comparison to Yam's tongue after he had eaten *pān* (which reddens the mouth). Undeterred by her wounds, the goddess let fly a torrent of arrows and prodded her lion to move forward. She sent demon warriors rolling in the dust and then struck Mund so ferociously that his head was severed, like a pumpkin cut from a vine (CC 1 4:112–114). Ghosts [*bhūta*] and flesh-eating demons [*pisāca*] shrieked as they feasted on the flesh of the fallen warriors, while Chandi quickly annihilated the demon forces as she made her way to confront Chand. He too lost his head to Chandi's spear, and to the poet it seemed as if Shiva had cut Ganesha's [Gaṇeśa] trunk from his head (CC I 4:115–116).

At this point in the story, there is a significant divergence between the *Devi Mahatmya* and the *Chandi Charitra Ukti Bilas*. While in the *Devi Mahatmya*, Kali emerges from Ambika's forehead just before the battle with Chand and Mund, at this point in *Chandi Charitra Ukti Bilas*, Kali has not made her appearance in battle. In the *Devi Mahatmya*, after Kali slew Chand and Mund and cackled as she presented their heads to Ambika/Chandika, Shumbh decided he had to regroup and assembled a vast army of demon forces from different demon families. The eighth chapter of the *Devi Mahatmya* explains that as Shumbh was preparing yet another surge against the goddess, the gods too were expanding their arsenal. Shaktis [*shaktis*], or female powers, sprang forth from the gods, creating the Mothers, or *mātṛikās*.[14] Chandika also emitted a fearsome shakti from her body. Chandika then enlisted Shiva as her messenger to Shumbh, directing him to issue to the demon king the ultimatum that he must either return the triple world to Indra and restore to the gods their share of the sacrifice, or else face yet another battle. Shumbh not surprisingly chose the battle option, and yet another bloody conflict began. When it appeared that the Mothers were winning the fight, the demon Raktabij [Raktabīja; "Blood-Seed"] joined the fray, complicating the situation with his unique talent for creating new forms of himself with each drop of blood that spilled from his body. The more the Mothers wounded him, the more of him there were, until they pervaded the entire world and terrified the gods. But Chandika just laughed, and told Kali to open her mouth. Chandika struck out at Raktabij, and with each blow Kali swallowed the blood that flowed from the wounds, as well as the other new forms of Raktabij that had been unleashed in the battle. She chewed up the many demon spawns until Raktabij himself fell to ground, his body bloodless and no longer a threat. The Mothers began to dance, intoxicated by the blood (DM 8:1–62; Coburn 1991, 63–67).

The prelude to this battle is described differently in the fifth chapter of *Chandi Charitra Ukti Bilas*. Significantly, the opening verses depict the etiquette of a demon king's court. When Shumbh learned that his forces had once again failed to vanquish the goddess, he conferred with

Nishumbh as well as his ministers, who advised that he assemble yet another great army, and summon the demon Raktabij. A messenger went to Raktabij to tell him that he had been called to the royal assembly [*sabhā*]. Raktabij quickly went to the assembly and bowed before King Shumbh, who told him he had a job for him to do. Shumbh and Nishumbh presented Raktabij with a crown as well as elephants and horses, and offered him betel leaf to chew. Raktabij happily accepted their gifts and proclaimed that he would detach Chandi's head from her torso. Shumbh and Nishumbh then presented Raktabij with more gifts,[15] and the demon set out for the fight (CC 1 5:117–127). Some accounts of Guru Gobind Singh's life describe similar negotiations taking place among rival chieftains in the hills of the Punjab, with disagreements similarly leading to conflict.

Once he agreed to battle Chandi, Raktabij adopted the same strategy of the earlier demon attackers. He took his army to the base of Mt. Sumeru and made a huge racket that alerted the goddess to the army's presence. Both sides prepared for war. Arrows flew in all directions, and blood streamed from Chandi's wounds as if snakes were cracking through the surface of a mountain. Still, she fought on with all her weapons, throwing down the demon warriors' howdahs from their elephants like Hanuman setting fire to Lanka and smashing down the upper stories of its palaces. She crushed demons' bones and drank their blood, until the dead and wounded lay strewn on the ground like mountains fallen in an earthquake (CC 1 5:128–135).

Raktabij's surviving forces began to flee in fear, but he brought them back with his vow to destroy Chandi. But his forces were no match for Chandi's wrath, and soon they and their elephants lay dead on the ground, torrents of blood gushing forth like the Vaitaraṇī stream that flows between earth and Yam's realm of dead spirits (CC 1 5:136–144). The poet has until this point composed similes comparing the carnage of battle to mythological scenes; here, he draws comparisons between Chandi's fight and religious practice:

> Chandi made the ferocious demon force flee, just as reciting God's name [*hari jāpa*] erases sin and affliction. (CC 1 5:145)
> Chandi's battle banished the demons just as dharma banishes anger and wisdom banishes delusion. (CC 1 5:146, line 4)

Thus fighting the forces of evil in a bloody battle is here presented as something that good people do, an auspicious act akin to religious devotion. It is yet another instance of valorizing fierce battle in the cause of maintaining proper order.

Still, the gory imagery of death and destruction continues; the warriors' white turbans bobbed in the stream of blood like the praise of warriors bubbling up in the Saraswati river (CC 1 5:148, lines 3–4). Raktabij renewed his efforts and swam across the ocean of blood, as if he were Mt. Sumeru and the gods and demons were using him to churn the milk-ocean. Chandi shot him with an arrow, and he fell to the ground. But he quickly came to his senses and injured Chandi's lion, its blood flowing on the ground. The poet pauses in the narrative to ask his listeners or readers to take special note of his imagery here:

> The poet has captured this scene with a breathtaking simile—it was like rain falling on an ochre-colored mountain, the mountain's color streaming onto the earth. (CC 1 5:156, lines 3–4)

The poet was indeed quite captivated with all the ways one could depict the flow of blood; he went on to compare the blood streaming out of demons to the flow of oil pressed from sesame seeds, to dye pouring from a broken pot, the demons' wounds glistening like flickering lights. The battle then took a serious turn, for a new Raktabij bubbled up from each drop of blood that spilled from him, new demons rising just as one's hair stands on end in the cold. Finally, Chandi sought assistance, and it is at this point that Kali makes her battle debut in CC 1:

> Chandi angrily fought a long battle, just as indestructible [Vishnu] fought Madhu. To vanquish the demons, she emitted a fiery flame from her forehead. Kali emerged from the flame; she shone like a light spreading fear among the cowards on the battlefield. It was as if the Yamunā River was bursting through the peak of Mt. Sumeru to gush down on the earth. (CC 1 5:165)

Her battle cry breaking Shiva's meditative concentration, Kali took her sword in hand. Chandi slashed out at the demons, and Kali drank their blood. The fifth chapter comes to a close with Raktabij's death (CC 1 5:167–172).

In the *Devi Mahatmya*, Raktabij's death brings about a final confrontation between Shumbh and Nishumbh and the goddess. The ninth chapter of the Sanskrit text opens with a reminder of the frame story as the king Suratha asked the sage Medhas to narrate what happened next. The sage explained that as Shumbh and Nishumbh took to the battlefield, the goddesses Ambika and Kali let out horrific sounds. Nishumbh attacked the goddess's lion, and she responded by breaking all his weapons and then killing him. Then Ambika and Shumbh confronted one another. The goddess wounded him with her lance, but he fought back, manifesting 10,000 arms with which he launched 10,000 discuses. At the beginning of the tenth chapter of the *Devi Mahatmya*, Shumbh taunted the goddess, telling her she was only fighting with the strength of others. Responding to this challenge, all the mothers and Kali then merged back into her, and she fought on. Shumbh's horse lay dead, his bow was broken, and he had no charioteer. He fought the goddess, but she slammed him to the earth and killed him. At first, the earth trembled, but then all became calm. The Gandharvas sang, the Apsarases danced, and sacred fires blazed once more (DM 9:1–39, 10:1–28; Coburn 1991, 68–73).

In *Chandi Charitra Ukti Bilas*, the slaying of the two demon brothers is detailed over two chapters. Nishumbh meets his end in chapter 6, and Shumbh is slain in chapter 7. As Nishumbh and his forces attacked Chandika with a volley of arrows, the goddess fought back, killing dark-as-mountain demons just as the sun's rays slay the darkness. The dark demons fled in terror, and the poet wondered how he might capture the scene; to him it was like an episode from the Mahabharata when the Pandavas fight the Kauravas, and it was as if the Kauravas had fled from the battlefield when they saw Bhīma's mouth full of blood (CC 1 6:173–180). It is at this point that the shaktis appear in CC 1.

> Seeing the ferocity of the battle, Vishnu decided to send shaktis to provide assistance.
> So ordered by Vishnu, all the shaktis came to fierce Chandi's aid.
> The goddess welcomed them respectfully, and said it was as if she had called them.

> And then it occurred to the poet how best to imagine the scene.
> It was like rivers flowing into the ocean in the rainy season month of Sāvana. (CC 1 6:184)

The shaktis then joined the fray, killing even more demons, and Kali chewed the wounded and dead while she dealt more fatal blows with her sword. Marrow oozed from the demons' heads, and the poet felt it was like snow sliding down from a mountaintop (CC 1 6:185).

Shumbh then commanded Nishumbh to regroup and wage the battle anew, but the demon brothers' forces were no match for Chandi's arrows and her sword. The battlefield was covered with so much flowing blood that the poet again imagined the splendor of the scene to be like Brahma creating an eighth ocean of blood after he had created the first seven (CC 1 6:189, lines 3–4). The poet continues with a stream of bloody images; he suggests that the earth wore a red sari of blood, that the eclipse-causing demon Rāhu swallowed the sun and the sun vomited blood, and that when Chandi stabbed a demon in the forehead, the blood flowed out like light coming from Shiva's third eye, flowing down the goddess's face and neck as if one could see the reddened saliva moving down the throat of a beautiful woman chewing betel leaf. Demons' severed heads flew like mangoes in a windstorm, and their bodies thudded to the ground like fruit shaken from a tree. Chandi then cut Nishumbh in half, like a soapmaker cutting a bar of soap with a metal wire (CC 1 6:190–202).

Shumbh was saddened and enraged when he learned of his brother Nishumbh's death, and he mustered up yet another army to take on the goddesses. Seeing themselves surrounded, Chandi laughed and signaled Kali with a glance. Kali tore at the demons, frightening some of them so much that they died in the stampede to escape her wrath. Shumbh shouted out, "Kill! Kill!" and entered the field of battle, as his demon soldiers swarmed like locusts. Shumbh came face-to-face with Chandi and told her he realized she had destroyed his entire army. She then commanded Kali and the shaktis to merge into her, and still the battle raged on (CC 1 7:205–214). Thus the sequence of events here is different from that in the *Devi Mahatmya*, the emphasis unmistakably on the flow of blood.

As the struggle between Chandi and Shumbh reaches its climax at the end of the eighth chapter of CC 1, the poet wields more comparisons to evince the continuing carnage:

> Chandika angrily fought several battles with Shumbh's forces.
> The jackals, witches, and vultures are the laborers, and Shiva dances in the mortar of blood.
> The corpses are piled up, forming a wall plastered with white fat and marrow,
> Creating a colorful house, as if Vishvakarma, architect of the gods, had designed this wondrous picture. (CC 1 7:216)

As the bodies stacked up, it came down to a battle between Chandi and Shumbh; their swords made sparks as they struck together, but Shumbh weakened as he lost blood, his face losing its luster, and Chandi picked him up. As in earlier scenes when the goddess wounded demons, the poet is inspired to compare the goddess's deed to that of another auspicious figure from myth; in this instance, the poet declared that it was just like Krishna picking up Mt. Govardhan to protect a herd of cows (CC 1 7:219). Then Shumbh's body fell from Chandi's hand to the earth before flying into the sky. All the gods watch as the two fought on until Chandi cut Shumbh in two with her sword, and he finally fell to the earth as if he had been sawed in half (CC 1 7:220–221). Chandi sounded the conch to mark her victory and then happily sounded a gong. The surviving demons ran away, afraid to fight without their king.

The eighth and closing chapter of *Chandi Charitra Ukti Bilas* diverges somewhat from the focus of the three final chapters of *Devi Mahatmya*. Both texts describe how the gods sang the goddess's praises for defeating the demons, but the praises are considerably longer and more detailed in *Devi Mahatmya*, where the gods ask for her continued protection. In the eleventh chapter of *Devi Mahatmya*, the goddess grants to the gods the boon that she will end their miseries and destroy their enemies, and then proclaims that in the future another pair of demons named Shumbh and Nishumbh will arise, and that she will be born from Yashoda's [Yaśodā] womb in the cowherd Nanda's house (DM 11:1–38; Coburn 1991, 73–77). She goes on to detail further occasions on which she will be born to destroy demons (DM 11:39–51; Coburn 1991, 77–78).

In the twelfth chapter of *Devi Mahatmya*, the goddess directs people to recite these tales of her glory, assuring them that she will protect them from all misfortune, particularly if they recite or hear the text on certain days in the lunar calendar. She promises to be present in any sanctuary dedicated to her. Those who hear or recite her deeds will become fearless, and their enemies will vanish. This *Mahatmya*, she announces, is the remedy for nightmares and bad astrological situations, and for children possessed by evil spirits, and recalling the goddess's triumphs can save someone from virtually any peril—forest fires, villains, kidnappers, lions and tigers, ocean storms. With this proclamation, the goddess disappeared, the gods reassumed their rightful positions, and the remaining demons went back to the netherworld (DM 12:1–32; Coburn 1991, 79–82). The *Devi Mahatmya* ends as the sage Medhas directs the king Suratha to seek refuge with the goddess. Markandeya then explains that King Suratha and the Vaishya Samadhi both began performing austerities on a riverbank, worshiping and making offerings (including their own blood) to an image of the goddess. At last she appeared before the two men and offered each a boon. The king asked for and received a kingdom that would persist even after his lifetime, and the Vaishya received the knowledge that would destroy ego and attachment. The goddess further proclaimed that in a future birth, the king would be the Manu Sāvarṇi, before disappearing yet again (DM 13:1–17; Coburn 1991, 82–84).

In *Chandi Charitra Ukti Bilas*, as the gods sang Chandi's praise, they mentioned reciting the *Brahama-kaucha* (CC 1 8:227, line 6), or "Brahma's armor."[16] The gods' wives performed *āratī* of the goddess and made offerings to her. Then, the goddess turned over all the royal paraphernalia to Indra and disappeared, indicating that he could officially resume his rightful position as ruler. The poet went on to proclaim victory to the goddess who had destroyed Madhu and Kaitabh, Mahish, Dhumralochan, Chand, Mund, Raktabij, Nishumbh, Shumbh, and demons in general (CC 1 8:228–230). Unlike the *Devi Mahatmya*, there is here no mention of the goddess's power over the universe; the focus is more specific to her demon slaying and the restoration of Indra as the rightful ruler. Nor is there the lengthy list of benefits that accrue to those who recite the tale of the goddess's deeds. These are the last three verses:

O Goddess Sivā! grant me the boon that I not shy away from performing good deeds.
May I achieve decisive victories when I fight my enemies in battle,
And may I ever instruct my mind to have the incentive to recite your praise.
When my time is at its end, may I die fighting on the battlefield. (231)

I have composed this poem of Chandi's deeds; it is full of angry sentiment [*rasa rudramaī*].
Each part is more full of sentiment than the last, and the similes are new from head to toe.
The poet composed this for enjoyment [*kautaka*]; here the story of seven hundred verses is complete.
For whatever reason a man reads or hears it, the goddess will surely grant his wish. (232)
I have made this book of seven hundred verses[17] which has no equal.
May Chandika grant to the poet the purpose for which he narrated it. (233)

These closing lines emphasize the centrality of victory in battle in this narrative of the deeds of the goddess. The poet's request that he perform good deeds and win in battle is reminiscent of the concern expressed in *Bachitra Natak* for protecting those who do good by fighting on their behalf. The poet has drawn attention once more to the similes he constructed in his verses and highlighted the sentiment of anger or *rudra* that has animated this tale.

Comparing this narrative with the *Devi Mahatmya* shows that CC I is not at all an exact translation of this text. While the basic sequence of the goddess's slaying of demons is the same, the details of the frame story and descriptions of battles differ significantly; the poet of CC I has particularly highlighted the enjoyment to be had in savoring the qualities of his poetry, a theme not found in the *Devi Mahatmya*. Many Sikh commentators have been especially careful to point out that CC I places much less emphasis on praise of the goddess than the *Devi Mahatmya*, emphasizing instead the goddess's victories in battles with demons.

Chandi Charitra 2

In the Dasam Granth, the *Chandi Charitra Ukti Bilas* version of the goddess's exploits is followed immediately by another known simply by the title *Chandi Charitra* 2. Although it is sometimes called a "summary" of *Chandi Charitra Ukti Bilas*, it is not much shorter in length. It may give some readers the impression of being a summary because it has no reference to the frame story of the king, merchant, and sage as found in the *Devi Mahatmya*, and it omits some components of the protracted battle between the demon king Shumbh and the goddess. Still, like both the *Devi Mahatmya* and *Chandi Charitra Ukti Bilas*, it does relate the goddess's slaying of Mahish, Dhumralochan, Chand and Mund, Raktabij, Nishumbh, and Shumbh. Its style, however, is rather different from that of *Chandi Charitra Ukti Bilas*—it is not as focused on the craft of similes, for one thing—and its opening and closing stanzas are of a different nature as well.

Chandi Charitra 2 does not open with benedictory verses to the timeless lord or to the goddess, nor does it describe the emergence and slaying of Madhu and Kaitabh. It simply starts right in with the demon problem that the gods faced when Mahish had conquered Indra and had taken over rule of the three worlds. The gods were frightened, and together they had all gone to live on Shiva's Mt. Kailash, throwing away their weapons and disguising themselves as yogis [yogīs]. Enduring physical hardship for many years, they meditated on the Mother of the Universe [*jagatra māti*]. When the goddess at last appeared to them, they fell at her feet and recited her praises (CC 2 1–5). The rhymed verses in the description of this scene are made up of short phrases devoid of the ornamentation found throughout much of *Chandi Charitra Ukti Bilas*, as this literal translation illustrates:

They worshipped the goddess. Brahma recited the Vedas. When they fell at her feet, their sorrows vanished (7).
They praised her. The goddess [*bhavānī*] was pleased. She took up all her weapons. She mounted her lion (8).
The gongs rang loudly. They sounded continuously. The demon king heard it. He prepared for war (9).

The sound of the words in these verses seems designed to create a mounting sense of tension. It is worth reading them aloud in the original:

> Karī debi arcā. Brahama beda carcā. Jabai pāi lāgai. Tabai soga bhāge (7).
> Binnati sunāī. Bhavānī rijhāī. Sabai sastra dhārī. Karī singha suārī (8). Kare ghaṇṭa nādam. Dhunam nirbikhādam. Suno daīta rājam. Sajiyo judha sājam. (9)

The description of the battle that follows continues in this rapid-fire, rhyming style as the demons begin letting loose arrows too numerous to count. The poet compared the arrows round the Mother's neck to a garland of flowers, and a few lines later, the demons' bloodstained clothing to the play of Holi (CC 2 12–13). But unlike the tendency of the poet in *Chandi Charitra Ukti Bilas* to draw attention to such images by noting their beauty and how they arose in his mind, these comparisons appear in the same terse style as the other verses with no explicit mention of the *kavi* or poet.

The goddess here is named differently as well—she is called the Mother, Bhavani, and Durga. In another divergence from the earlier narrative, in this version Kalika emerges out of a flame from the goddess's forehead during this initial battle with Mahish (CC 2 27). And in addition to bows and arrows, swords, spears, pikes, nooses, discuses, and the like, rifles [*tupak*] are part of the arsenal of weapons wielded in this war (CC 2 30). But the images of the battlefield strewn with the dead and wounded are quite similar:

> Giant vultures soar there, dogs and jackals howl.
> The rutting elephants are like winged mountains, the crows swoop down to et.
> The daggers are like little fish, the shields like turtles.
> The armor shines like a slithering crocodile, the blood-river is unfathomable. (CC 2 34)

The first chapter of CC 2 comes to a close with Kalika taking her sword in hand and killing Mahish in an instant, his "light" [*joti*] leaving his body (CC 2 37).

At the beginning of the second chapter, the poet details how the gods happily praised the goddess for her victory. She then disappeared after returning their kingdoms to them. Soon enough, however, the demons Shumbh and Nishumbh came to power, Indra lost his kingdom yet again, and the gods once more trembled with fear. Ashamed, they fled to live in the goddess's city. Angrily, she gathered up all her weapons, then merrily drank spirits [*pāni*][18] and roared as she took her sword in hand (CC 2 39–48). The goddess mounted her lion and rode into battle; the demons shouted out, "Kill" (CC 2 49–52). But there is no mention here of the demon king Shumbh hearing of the goddess's beauty and vowing to win her in marriage, no conversation in which she explains that she would only take as husband someone who could defeat her in battle, no scheming in the demon king's court. The battle is the primary focus, and the chapter continues as the demon Dhumralochan (here called by the alternate name of Dhūmranaina, *naina* being another word for "eye") took the lead in storming the goddess's mountain. The din he and his forces created was powerful enough to cause a pregnant woman to miscarry (CC 2 56). The conflict was over quickly; the Mother Kali blazed forth and sent virtually all the demon warriors to heaven, including Dhumralochan. Once he had died, the few survivors fled to tell their king what had transpired (CC 2 62–64).

Chapter 3 of CC 2 takes up the tale of yet more ill-fated demons, led by Chand and Mund, and for the first time the poet mentions the benefits of hearing this story:

> Having thus slain the demons, the goddess [Dhavalā, "the white one"] returned home.
> Whoever hears or recites this story will attain wealth and prosperity [*ridhi-sidhi*] in his home. (CC 2 65)

Meanwhile, the demon king mustered yet another army, bestowing gifts on Chand and Mund as leaders. This encounter, like the previous one, was over in virtually an instant. The demons struck out with their weapons and let arrows fly, but they were no match for the goddess. Kali killed Chand, Mund, and their army.

This leads to the fourth chapter, in which the two demon brothers Shumbh and Nishumbh, hearing that their forces had once again failed to vanquish the goddess, conferred and decided to send for Raktabij. They gave him gifts and outfitted him and yet another army with weapons. This army, too, marched to the base of Mt. Kailas and made a racket, which impelled the goddess to grab her many and various weapons and start slicing demons in halves and quarters. Her sword flashed like lightning, and Raktabij's blood gushed out, creating more and more raging Raktabijs, who all shouted out, "Kill! Kill!" (CC 2 78–90). The short, rhythmic verses here describe the conflict as blood streams, and the goddess roars in the sky (CC 291–100).

First, the poet set the scene of the battlefield: here there were the dead warriors, there, the wounded elephants and soldiers. Ghosts and evil spirits excitedly anticipated the feast of flesh and blood to come, and the air was thick with arrows (CC 2 101–108). The goddess yet again wore a flower garland of arrows, and blood-smeared horses and elephants lay on the ground, like mountains hiding in the sea, afraid of Indra (CC 2 109). The goddess's lion tore at the demons with his sharp nails, and their wounded limbs looked like flames of fire rising from the ocean (CC 2 110). The poet then sought to capture in words the sounds of the battle: the twang of bowstrings; the clang of swords and daggers striking one another, and sometimes hitting flesh; the shouts and roars of warriors; the sharp report [*taṛākaṃ*] of gunshots; the beat of drums; the sounds of conches and other instruments—all these sights and sounds filled the battlefield as Raktabij's drops of blood materialized new forms of the fierce demon. But Durga slew them all, and Kalika lapped up every last drop of blood:

> He lost blood, his limbs became weak.
> Finally, he staggered and fell, like a cloud to the earth. (121)
> All the gods were joyful, and showered a stream of flowers.
> The Drops-of-Blood demon died, and all good people were saved (122).

The slaying of demons has once more been explicitly linked to the salvation and prosperity of good people. But anyone familiar with the story of course would know that while the goddess won this battle, the war was far from over. Nishumbh and Shumbh, the demon brothers, had yet to enter the fray. When the brothers heard that Raktabij had been killed, they prepared for another invasion of the goddess's territory, and the sights and sounds of these preparations frightened the king of the gods Indra and made the sun and moon flee from the sky in terror (CC 2 124). The demon brothers' battles are the subjects of chapters 5 and 6.

Again arrows flew, blood splashed on the ground, and warriors shouted out "Kill!" Shumbh angrily stamped his foot on the ground and issued an order to Nishumbh: "Go quickly. Tie Durga up and bring her here" (CC 2 140). This command faintly echoes more detailed versions of the story in which Shumbh commands various demon warriors to either kill the goddess or bind and drag her to him so that she might become his wife. Here, though, there is no explanation of why Shumbh wanted the goddess brought to him.

Meanwhile, the gods grew concerned as the battles wore on. Trembling, Indra conferred with Shiva, who asked him how many warriors were available to fight and how they might ensure the goddess's victory. They decided that they should emit their shaktis, or powers, and send them into battle (CC 2 143–146).

> The *saktis* [*shaktis*] took swords in hand and quickly set off.
> [So too did] mighty vultures, and Kali's belching, flesh-eating
> assistants, male and female.
> Giant crows cackled, and headless bodies rose up blindly.
> A slew of gods and heroes began to shower arrows. (CC 2 147)

The shaktis bowed their heads in reverence to the gods, then entered the battle. Here the goddess killed demons, there her lion tore apart their flesh. Shiva's attendants [*gaṇas*] roared fiercely, and the demons trembled. The goddess slew Nishumbh, and the demon army fell in defeat (CC 2 148–156). Shumbh then sought to defeat the goddess and avenge his brother's death. The gods trembled in fear as he marched forward with all his weapons. Just as when Dhumralochan noisily entered the battlefield, in an image the poet apparently found compelling enough to repeat, the din was horrific enough to make pregnant women miscarry (CC 2 157–159). As the battle progressed, it remained so loud that even serpents in the netherworld could hear it (CC 2 162).

Flesh-eating spirits, witches, vampires, headless trunks danced.
The gods all laughed, and the demon king seethed as if he were blazing with fire. (163)
Shumbh grew angrier, [but] the goddess destroyed every demon he sent into battle, as if they were drops of water falling on a hot griddle. (CC 2: 164)

As shouts of "Kill! Kill" filled the air, the battle raged on. It was all leading to a direct confrontation between Shumbh and Durga:

Durga called for Shiva's messenger, and whispered into her ear,
"Send Shiva to the demon king."
When Shiva's messenger heard this, she made Shiva a messenger and sent him off. (195)[19]
From then on [the goddess's] name was "She Who Has Shiva as Messenger." All men and women know this. (196)
Shiva said to the demon king, "Listen. The Mother of the Universe has said, 'Either you return power to the gods or we'll start a battle right now.' " (197)
The demon king did not accept this proposition, and proudly set off to wage battle.
He arrived where Kali roared like death itself. (198)

The following verses craft now-familiar images of the sights and sounds of conflict, and the closing lines of chapter 7 describe Kali's fatal blow to Shumbh's head (CC 2 199–218). The chapter ends with a benediction:

Kali! In your frightful form, may you chew up the enemies of good people, just as you angrily killed the demon Shumbh. (CC 2 219)

Once again, the poet has reiterated the theme of how demon slaying is part of the effort to maintain a safe environment for good people.

The opening lines of chapter 7 in CC 2 depict how the gods celebrated the goddess's victory, showering her with flowers, praising her to no end, and reciting the "braham kavacha" *mantra*. At last there were no more demons (CC 2 220–222). Although this account of the deeds of the goddess began without benedictory verses, the final chapter includes thirty-four verses in praise [*ustati*] of the goddess with salutations to her many names and forms, and the weapons she used in battle. Among the goddess's names are Yoga-Fire [*joga juālāṃ*; CC 2 223), Supreme Goddess [*parama paramesvarī*; CC 2 236), Creator of the Fourteen Worlds of Illusion [*moha kai caudrahūṃ loga bandhiā*; CC 2 237], Knower of the Shastras and Wielder of Weapons (CC 2 242), and Hanuman's shakti (CC 2 243).

Many of the verses pay homage both to the goddess's beneficence and specific names and characteristics and to sites of her worship.[20]

> Salutations to Hanuman's shakti, salutations to the goddess of
> Kangra [Nāgra Koṭī].
> Salutations to the goddess of Kāmarūpā, of Kāmākshī, Karotī.[21]
> Salutations to Durga, the night of all-destroying time [*Kāla Rātrī*],
> with matted hair, the beneficent.
> Bestower of great wealth and power, the Sword-Bearer. (CC 2 244)
>
> You are holy, pure, ancient,[22] incomprehensible.
> Sovereign, the fulfiller, the power of Brahma, invincible.
> Formless, incomparable, nameless, placeless.
> Fearless, unconquerable, the great supporter of all dharma. (CC 2 252)

The series of verses praising the goddess ends with the poet's wish that the goddess forever be his protectress (CC 2 256); the remaining six verses of the eighth chapter describe once more the scene after the goddess was victorious over the demons. The poem closes with praise to the poem itself and a description of the benefits that accrue to those who read and recite it:

> A fool who recites this will attain wealth in his home.
> If a miser or an abstainer[23] hears it, he will fight fiercely.
> The yogi who recites it continuously through the night,
> Will attain the highest yoga and miraculous powers. (260)
>
> The student who recites this to attain knowledge,
> Will attain the essence of all the Shastras.

If a yogi, sannyasin, or Bairāgī recites it,
He will be blessed with all virtues. (261)

All good people who keep vigil continuously meditating on you,
Will attain the fruit of liberation at death, and union with god [*bhagavant*] (262)

As in CC 1, this goddess narrative places the greatest emphasis on the sights and most particularly sounds of her battles with demons, though it does have slightly more praise of the goddess. Each and every detail of flowing blood and oozing marrow is carefully drawn as the demons pursue their relentless desire to kill the goddess and her forces. But the goddess fights on behalf of good people, and the fatal blows she deals to demons have been likened to the good deeds that people may perform in her service.

Var Durga Ki/Chandi Di Var

The third account of the goddess in the Dasam Granth is the best known and most studied, and arguably of greatest importance for many Sikhs because its opening lines form the beginning of the oft-recited Ardas prayer.[24] The language of *Var Durga Ki* is closer to modern Punjabi than the previous two goddess narratives.[25] Interestingly, it also has more contemporaneous references (e.g., to Pathans and guns) and occasionally incorporates Perso-Arabic-derived vocabulary (e.g., *munāra, majlasa*). Like the preceding goddess narratives, *Var Durga Ki* details the deaths of Mahishasur, Dhumralochan, Chand and Mund, Raktabij, and finally Nishumbh and Shumbh, but it is far shorter. There is no mention of the demons Madhu and Kaitabh. The composition opens with praise of the first nine Sikh Gurus, and the following verses set the stage for the gods' demon troubles.

As in the *Bachitra Natak* account of the lineage of the Sikh Gurus, the gods' battles with the demons are placed in the framework of the *yugas*, or eras, of traditional Hindu mythology, in which there is an initial era of relative purity and goodness, followed by subsequent eras in which dharma falls into steady decline.

First I remember *bhagautī*, then I turn my attention to Guru Nanak.
I seek the aid of Guru Angad, Guru Amardas, and Guru Ramdas.
I recall Guru Arjun, Guru Hargobind, Guru Hari Rai.
Then I praise Hari Krishan, whose sight dispels all sorrows.
I remember Guru Tegh Bahadur, who brings the nine treasures into the home.
May they help us everywhere. (1)

The one who created the whole world first crafted the sword [*khaṇḍā*],
Made Brahma, Vishnu, Mahesa [Shiva], the whole play of nature,
Made oceans, mountains, the earth, and stabilized the sky without support,
Made the demons and the gods, and then caused conflict between them.
You created Durga and in so doing brought about the demons' destruction.
Ram obtained his strength from you and killed Ravan with his arrows.
Krishna obtained his strength from you and grabbed Kams by his hair and threw him to the ground.
All manner of sages and gods have performed austerities for ages,
But none could grasp you in your totality. (2)

The righteous *Satijuga* [*Satiyuga*] passed, then came the half-righteous *Treta* (*yuga*).
Discord danced over every head, and Nārad sounded the drum of conflict.
Mahikhasur and Sumbh were born to dispel the gods' pride.
They conquered the gods and ruled over the three worlds.
Mahikhasur proclaimed himself a great warrior, and donned a royal canopy over his head.
Indra, banished from his kingdom, looked towards Mt. Kailas.
Fearful of the demons, terror grew in his heart.
Indra approached Durga. (3)

One day Durga came to bathe, and Indra told her of his plight.
"The demons have stolen our power from us, and their proclamations resound through the three worlds.
"They sit in my house, Amarāvatī, and play their music. The demons have made all the gods flee.
"No one was able to conquer the demon Mahikh. Goddess Durga, I've come to you for shelter." (4)

Durga listened and roared with laughter. She sent for her demon-eating lion.
"Don't worry about anything," she said to the gods. The goddess was enraged, [ready] to kill the demons. (5)

Filled with rage, itching for a fight, the demons came to the battlefield.
Their swords and spears glared so brightly that no one could even see the sun. (6)

The drums and horns of battle resounded, and the weapons began to fly.

> The drums of war reverberated as the two sides faced one another. The goddess made her steel-lioness [sword] dance with her hand, and struck the demon Mahikh who was rubbing his belly, piercing his kidneys, innards, and ribs. I describe it as it feels in my heart; the blow she struck looked like a shooting star. (VDK 10)

As in CC 1, the poet here draws attention to the mental process of crafting the image of the goddess's actions in battle. The poet further sets the scene by describing how the demons' wives watched the battle from their balconies (VDK 11) as Durga sent more and more of their men to heaven and continued her fight with Mahish. In the battlefield, the towering warriors looked like the minarets of a mosque. Though the demon warriors would never allow the word "defeat" to pass their lips, Durga slew them all with her sword (VDK 15). Then, on the battlefield, Mahish thundered like a storm cloud, "Warriors like Indra ran away from me. Who is this pitiful Durga trying to fight me now?" (VDK 16).

Soon, though, the goddess's arrows made the towering-minaret warriors look as if they had been felled by lightning. In a compelling image, the poet describes the warriors lying on the battlefield with their hair flowing loose as looking like yogis with matted hair sleeping after taking marijuana (VDK 17). The poet continues this theme as he describes the blood flowing from wounded warriors' heads as being like the Ganges River flowing from Shiva's matted hair (VDK 18), recalling a similar comparison in CC 1.

Durga then pulled her sword from its sheath, lashing out at the demon Mahish. The blow she struck was so forceful it went through Mahish, breaking his skull, then his saddle and horse, piercing even further through to the horns of the bull who supports the earth, then even further to the tortoise that holds the bull. The battlefield flowed with blood and guts, and the poet proclaimed, "The tale of the sword [*teg*] will be told in all four ages" (VDK 19). As in the earlier goddess narratives, the poet has focused on the auspicious nature of the goddess's destruction of demons, here with special focus on the sword's central role in the story.

And so Durga slew the demon and made her lion dance in all the fourteen worlds. Yet even after describing the demon's demise, the poet continues to portray the battle scene: it was strewn with warriors who lay on the ground like Pathans who had reached a state of ecstasy listening to music, with other warriors wandering around dazed as if they were teetotalers who had mistakenly drunk strong liquor (VDK 20). Finally, the goddess Bhavani returned power to the gods and disappeared.

The gods' respite from demonic interference was brief, for soon, just as in the other goddess tales, the proud demons Shumbh and Nishumbh were born, and they set their sights on conquering Indra's capital city. Their army launched its assault, and the frightened gods again sought Durga's refuge. When the demons heard the news that Bhavani had reappeared, Shumbh sent for Dhumralochan, who proudly beat his drum and proclaimed that he would bring Durga to Shumbh (VDK 21–26). But his pride was no match for Chandi's double-edged sword, which sent him on his way to the city of Yam, god of death (VDK 27–28).

Shumbh, hearing that his warriors had fallen like stars from the sky, like mountains hit by lightning, next sent Chand and Mund to take on the goddess. But they were quickly dispatched by Durga's flying arrows (VDK 29–32). Angrily, Shumbh and Nishumbh convened a meeting. The demon warriors wrung their hands as they remembered their fallen comrades who had so easily run off Indra and his ilk only to be slain in an instant by the upstart goddess. Their next move was to enlist the demon Raktabij,[26] outfit him with armor, and send him into battle. Durga heard them coming, mounted her lion, and killed Raktabij's forces. They littered the battlefield like addicts on drugs, like people who had played Holi and then fallen asleep (VDK 33–34).

Raktabij managed to gather some more warriors, and they stood on the battlefield like minarets. Swords in hand, they rushed forward, shouting, "Kill! Kill!" Swords clanging on armor sounded as if a craftsman were shaping metal vessels with a hammer (VDK 35). Durga slashed at Raktabij's head. Still, more demons confronted her, and she killed each one as he approached. Blood gushed from their bodies like rainwater from a gutter, and new demon warriors arose howling from the blood. They too swarmed at Durga, their swords covering the battlefield like a dense winter fog, but she deflected their blows with her shield. Her unsheathed swords dripped with blood, and it looked as if all the goddesses had gathered together to bathe in the Saraswati River. But still, new demons arose from the blood (VDK 37–40).

The battle still raging, in her anger Chandi concentrated on Kalika, who then burst through her forehead and mopped up all the spilled blood before it could give rise to new Raktabijs. The moment of death passed over the warriors; so many lay dead it was as if their mothers had not even given birth to them (VDK 41–43). Hearing that yet another demon had lost the fight against Durga, Shumbh outfitted new forces.

The poet first used images from Islamic practice to capture this scene. The new warriors marched toward Durga like pilgrims [*hājīs*] going to the Ka'aba in Mecca. They issued arrows, swords, and daggers as invitation to the battle. One wounded warrior wandered around like a *qazi* [*qāzī*] teaching (Qur'anic recitation) in school, and another pierced by a spear bowed forward as if he were performing the Muslim prayer, or *namāz* (VDK 35). While it is worth noting that the poet has portrayed the demon forces with this Islamic imagery, they are depicted with Hindu imagery as well. In the next verse, the poet describes the warriors with their tangled hair marched in formation carrying tasseled spears as looking like a contingent of ascetics with matted hair going to bathe in the Ganges (VDK 46). Soon, the battlefield was strewn with heads, torsos, and arms like flowers in a garden, or like sandalwood trees sawn apart by a carpenter (VDK 48). As is so often the case in these goddess narratives, the scene of dead and dying enemy warriors is often compared to images of religious devotion, in this case both Islamic and Hindu.

Kalika became even more angry and slashed out at several thousand warriors with her sword; one goddess was able to defeat the entire demon force.[27] Hoping to turn the tide, Nishumbh donned his armor, made his horse prance in the battlefield, and took up the big bow that he had ordered specially from Multan. But Nishumbh and his Multani bow were no match for Durga's sword; it pierced through his body, his saddle, and his horse, and he fell to the ground. As Nishumbh fell, in one of the lighter moments of the composition, he offered praise to his brother Shumbh:

> Praise to the handsome Khān. May there forever be praise of your power.
> Cheers to the way you chew betel leaf. May there ever be mercy upon the Khān's consumption of intoxicants, and the way he makes his horse prance. (VDK 50)

As in earlier portions of VDK, the enemy demons here are portrayed with characteristics most typically associated with Islam (e.g., the title "Khān"). It should come as no surprise that there were still more demon warriors ready to take on the goddess.

The next wave of warriors brought arrows and muskets [*tuphangī*], and angels [*phareste*] came down from the sky to watch (VDK 51). Durga wielded her dagger and sword, felling demon after demon.

> The two sides came together to the pounding of war-drums.
> Durga took up her goddess-sword [*bhagautī*][28] and it blazed like fire.
> It pierced the demon-king Shumbh, the beloved [weapon] drank his blood.
> Shumbh fell from his saddle, and this simile came to mind.

That double-edged spear came out awash in blood,
Like a princess stepping out in a red sari. (VDK 53)

Durga, with weapons in all her arms, had killed Nishumbh and Shumbh. Their surviving warriors cried in frustration and fled without looking back, even as they were dying (VDK 54). The final verse invokes the benefits of reciting the story, although it is far less detailed than the closing verses of the first two goddess narratives:

Shumbh and Nishumbh were sent off to the abode of the god of death.
Indra was summoned to be recrowned as king, and a canopy was spread over King Indra's head.
The World-Mother's renown spread through the fourteen worlds.
This recitation of Durga's deeds [*Durgā-pāṭha*] has been composed entirely in stanza form [*pauṛī*].
Whoever sings it will not be reborn again. (VDK 55)

The Battles of the Goddess

All three goddess compositions in the Dasam Granth have the same basic narrative outline in which the goddess slays a series of demons whom the gods were unable to defeat. The goddess story thus depicts an ongoing struggle between the forces of good and bad in the cosmos, with no final resolution. Each version of the story suggests that the forces of good—in this case, the gods—must be ever vigilant and prepared to take on the demons. The demons, as representatives of that which is bad, against proper dharma, are constantly regrouping and developing new tactics to try to gain the upper hand against the gods and good people. The goddess plays a special role insofar as it is she alone who is able to solve demon problems that the gods cannot.

In each of the three goddess compositions in the Dasam Granth, the spotlight is on violent battles as the central theme and subject of poetic description. The battle imagery is unrelentingly gruesome, with the poet delighting in sketching images of shining swords and other weapons flashing as warriors wield them against their enemies, the sounds of swords and arrows whizzing through the air, the shrieks and cries of warriors, and gaping wounds, severed body parts, and flowing rivers of blood. The killing that occurs in these battles is auspicious, even to be celebrated, for it represents a triumph, however, temporary, of the forces of good, and allows good people to live well. Indeed, the poet frequently made explicit comparisons between these gruesome portrayals of demons' deaths with auspicious images such as Ram making offerings. As such, these goddess compositions reiterate a theme that was explicitly detailed in *Bachitra Natak*, namely, that in the cosmos there are gods and demons, and good people and bad people, and these relationships are parallel, and there is frequent battle on the part of the good to maintain the proper balance of dharma in the worlds of the gods and humans. Thus just as the gods must be ever vigilant against demons, so too must good people be ever willing to battle against the bad people in the world. In portraying these linkages between demons and enemies, the goddess compositions are illustrating a theme in Indian literature that goes back to Vedic times.[29] They also continually highlight the central role of leaders among both the gods and humans, and interestingly, the gods and demons hold court just as do human leaders. Rulers must be ever vigilant lest their enemies gain the upper hand.

In relation to other goddess narratives in Indian literature, each of these goddess compositions appears most directly related to the *Devi Mahatmya* portion of the *Markandeya Purana*, insofar as each relates the same sequence of battles against demons. Some Sikh authors have suggested other Puranic sources for these compositions, but without detailed arguments to illustrate the connections.[30] However, there are significant differences between *Devi Mahatmya* and the goddess compositions of the Dasam Granth.

One major difference between *Devi Mahatmya* and the goddess tales lies in the context. The Dasam Granth goddess tales have very little discussion of the frame story of the *Devi Mahatmya* and the larger context of the *Markandeya Purana*. For example, the *Devi Mahatmya* mentions the goddess and her future rebirth as Krishna, but this is not mentioned in the Dasam Granth goddess narratives. Nor do these narratives focus much on the characters of the king Surath (portrayed as a future Manu or progenitor and king of humans) and the Vaishya Samadhi as the audience for the story. Both Ashta (1959, 56) and Jaggi

(1966, 71) have noted that the Dasam Granth goddess compositions do not share the sectarian concerns of much of Puranic literature; that is, they do not appear to seek to promote goddess worship over worship of some other deity. Nor do these compositions have as many prayers and invocations to the goddess as do other forms of Puranic literature.

In addition to comparing the Dasam Granth goddess compositions to the *Devi Mahatmya*, it is also useful to consider the similarities and differences among the three. *Chandi Charitra* 1 and *Chandi Charitra* 2 are similar in both length and language, whereas *Var Durga Ki* is shorter and exhibits characteristics of Punjabi. There are significant stylistic differences among the three. *Chandi Charitra* 1 begins and ends with statements about poetic technique and is characterized by its extensive use of similes and the poet's frequent mention of how particular images arose in his mind and heart. *Chandi Charitra* 2 has less explicit mention of poetic technique, though its poet clearly sought to evoke as graphically as possible the sounds of battle and their effects, such as the demons' roars that were powerful enough to make pregnant women miscarry, and the poet chose words and rhythms that seem intended to capture the feeling of being on the battlefield itself. *Var Durga Ki* makes explicit the connection between the battles pitting gods versus demons and battles among humans in its depiction of demons who operate in a more human realm, for example, by describing demons with imagery associated with Islamic practice. Each of the three compositions employs images that compare the carnage of battle to everyday scenes, reflecting perhaps both the poet's vivid imagination and that the gory scenes of battle so frequently portrayed in the Dasam Granth were a common feature of the time, as is also suggested by the *Apni Katha* portion of *Bachitra Natak* in which battles are one of the central topics.

Why, one might ask, are there three separate versions of essentially the same story in the Dasam Granth? Unfortunately, there is no way to reach a definitive answer to this question; it is not entirely clear whether the three goddess compositions were meant to be grouped together, although *Chandi Charitra Ukti Bilas* and *Chandi Charitra* 2 are typically taken as part of the *Bachitra Natak Granth*. The possible answers to the question are also determined in part by whether one believes Guru Gobind Singh to have been the author of all three, or believes that one or more of them were the work of his court poets. The stylistic differences among the three compositions suggest that the three may in part have been exercises in varying types of poetic expression, likely meant not simply to be read but to be recited for an audience. An audience at the time would most likely already have been familiar with the basic outlines of the story of Durga, and part of the enjoyment of listening to different versions would be to savor the new images (especially from CC 1), to take in the evocative sonic qualities (CC 2) and enjoy the contemporary references (VDK). Poetic performance is well attested as a feature of courtly life; in courts with poets, there was likely to be an audience aware of the conventions of poetic theory, ready to savor the *rasa*, or flavor, of new compositions.

In the *Markandeya Purana*, Durga's battles with demons are presented in the form of a *mahatmya*, a type of text portraying the greatness of a deity or place that brings benefits to those who recite, read, or hear it. There is inherent value in the repetition of such texts, and this too may be a reason for telling the story more than once. Repetition and transmission of the *Devi Mahatmya* and associated texts have long been associated with devotion to the goddess. In Sikh exegesis, however, the issue of whether the Dasam Granth goddess compositions advocate devotion to the goddess or not has been extremely important.

The issue of whether the Dasam Granth's goddess compositions indicated devotion to the goddess on the part of Guru Gobind Singh and/or his followers is of course linked to the controversy within the biographical tradition surrounding Guru Gobind Singh about whether or not he worshiped the goddess before establishing the Khalsa. The majority viewpoint in recent years among Sikh commentators has been either to reject the statements in early biographies that Guru Gobind Singh worshiped the goddess or to argue that if he did so it was only to demonstrate the futility of such worship. Such readings of the Guru Gobind Singh biographical tradition in turn led to the argument that the Dasam Granth's goddess compositions were intended to inspire warriors in battle, not to inspire devotion to the goddess. Given the explicit emphasis on the poet's craft throughout these compositions, it seems plausible that another purpose of the composition was the art of composing poetry and the aesthetic experience of enjoying it, whether through reading or recitation.

A key component of the debate surrounding goddess worship and the Dasam Granth is the interpretation of the term *bhagauti*, which occurs in the first line of *Var Durga Ki*, "Prathami bhagautī simarkai Gurū Nānaka laī dhiāi," or "First I remember *bhagauti*, then I turn my attention to Guru Nanak." The word *bhagauti* also occurs in the invocatory phrase "srī bhagautī jī sahāi," or "with the assistance of revered *bhagauti*," found in some manuscripts at the beginning of various Dasam Granth compositions.

Bhagauti is a Brajbhasha form of the Sanskrit word *bhagavatī*, the feminine form of the word *bhagavat* (derived from the verbal root *bhaj*), which literally means "possessing *bhaga*," that is, possessing good fortune or prosperity and thus holy. In Sanskrit, *bhagavat* (masculine singular nominative *bhagavān*) is a term of address for the gods, and its feminine form *bhagavatī* is an epithet of the goddesses Durga and Lakshmi (see, e.g., Monier-Williams 1981, 743–744). Many Sikh commentators, however, have concluded that in the context of *Var Durga Ki* and elsewhere in the Dasam Granth, the word *bhagauti* should be understood primarily to mean "sword" and, by extension, the sword as manifestation or representation of divine power.

Jaswant Singh Neki and Giani Balwant Singh (1995, 319–322) have set forth what they term some of the "chequered semantic history" of this term in their entry on *Bhagautī* for *The Encyclopaedia of Sikhism*. They note that in the few instances in which *bhagautī* occurs in the Guru Granth Sahib, it means a devotee, and that it was in the *vars* of Bhai Gurdas [Bhāī Gurdās] that the term was first interpreted to mean "sword."[31] They go on to speculate that Guru Gobind Singh may have specifically chosen the feminine term *bhagauti* to complement the predominantly masculine terminology used for God in Sikh tradition. Other Sikh authors have also explored the complex symbolism that has developed around this term in Sikh thought. Nikky-Guninder Kaur Singh, in her feminist analyses of Sikh tradition, has particularly highlighted the complexity of the Durga/sword symbolism in the Dasam Granth (1993, 142–143), taking the image of the sword to be a "metaphor within a metaphor," arguing that for Guru Gobind Singh the sword was a metaphor for both the transcendent deity and for Durga and her female power. By making the wearing of a sword one of the obligations of those initiated into the Khalsa, the metaphor of the sword (with its attendant associations of female power) also became a concrete part of Sikh ritual and a sign of Sikh identity. Nikky Singh has further argued that the regular recitation of the line from *Var Durga Ki*, "I first recall *bhagauti*," in the Ardas prayer is another way of linking the sword, female power, and the transcendent God in everyday religious practice. This is part of her larger argument about the underemphasized feminine aspects of key Sikh symbols. Of the goddess sections of the Dasam Granth, Nikky Singh (2005, 119) wrote, "In his Durga compositions, the sword is personified as a female figure who appears in a variety of forms, combining princess, goddess, and lioness.... With the analogies to princesses and goddesses, the sword emerges as a fluid character, endowed with a status that is both secular and divine."

Pritpal Singh Bindra (2002, vol. 1, 13), in discussing the usage of the term in *Charitropakhian*, suggested that "generally Bhagauti is recognized and perceived in its material form. The 'sword' is construed as the embodiment of Bhagauti. But 'Bhagauti' has much deeper significance; it is Shakti, the Faculty and Integrity. It represents the celestial authority and eternal power. It is the latent prowess and capability." For Bindra, then, the goddess is more an abstract figure than she would be in Hindu myth. Both Nikky Singh's and Bindra's analyses stress that *bhagauti* in the Sikh context should be taken in a metaphoric rather than literal sense, drawing a contrast between Hindu and Sikh interpretations of the goddess.

Such interpretations of the term *bhagauti* thus focus on its symbolic significance rather than its identification with the goddess Durga of Hindu mythology, positing a specifically Sikh usage of the term. *Bhagauti* is understood not as a distinct deity but as a quality or characteristic of divinity that may be explored through the medium of goddess mythology. In such readings, the goddess Durga functions rather like an image that serves only to point the viewer or reader to something indescribable that lies beyond the realm of any distinct god or goddess who may be pictured in anthropomorphic or gynomorphic form. Thus in Dasam Granth discourse, Sikhs have developed a distinct interpretation of the term *bhagauti* and, by extension, the role of the goddess.

In addition to such symbolic readings of the term *bhagauti*, some Sikh authors (see, e.g., Neki and Singh 1995, 321) have also looked to the context in which the term is used to argue that Durga and *bhagauti* are not the same, pointing in particular to the first several lines of the second verse of *Var Durga Ki*:

> The one who created the whole world first crafted the sword [*khaṇḍā*],
> Made Brahma, Vishnu, Mahesa [Shiva], the whole play of nature,
> Made oceans, mountains, the earth, and stabilized the sky without support,
> Made the demons and the gods, and then caused conflict between them.
> You created Durga and in so doing brought about the demons' destruction. (VDK 2)

On this reading, the opening line of the composition, "prathami bhagautī simarkai," is linked to the creator, the one who created Durga, rather than seeing this creator, Durga, and *bhagauti* as identical.

The issue of the relationship between Durga and the sword remains central in debates about the Dasam Granth in part because various types of swords are such key symbols for Sikhs, particularly the curved sword [*kirpān*] that is one of the Five Ks to be worn by those initiated into the Khalsa, and the *khaṇḍā* symbol, which is formed by one straight and two curved swords and a discus or *chakkar* (Sanskrit *chakra*). It is worth noting that there are intriguing parallels between the mythology and symbology of Durga and Khalsa tradition. The goddess Durga's mount is a lion, or *singha*; "Singh" becomes the name for Khalsa-initiated men. The goddess wields a sword to defend the good; the Khalsa Sikh wears a sword as well.

Nonetheless, one key distinction Sikh commentators have made between Hindu goddess mythology and this same mythology in a Sikh context is that the Hindu mythology emphasizes devotion to the goddess, whereas the Sikh goddess narratives emphasize battle. While the goddess compositions of the Dasam Granth do contain verses praising the goddess, battle is clearly the primary concern. Most Sikh commentators have suggested that the goddess compositions must be taken primarily as inspiring tales for warriors heading into battle. Jaggi (1966) argued that the major focus of the Puranic compositions in the Dasam Granth such as the goddess tales was the promotion of heroism and the expression of heroic sentiment [*vīra-rasa*], along with sentiments of fear and terror [*raudra* and *bhayānak rasas*], rather than the concern with bhakti, or devotion, and the role of a devotee's chosen deity [*iṣṭha deva*] that is a central feature of Puranic literature. The emphasis on *rasa*, the sentiments evoked in the compositions, also suggests a more direct linkage with the aims of the types of poetry composed at royal courts throughout Indian history, meant for the aesthetic enjoyment of those at the court.

The centrality of battle is clear when the Dasam Granth goddess narratives are compared to the *Devi Mahatmya*. There is another theme at work, however, that has received less attention, and that is the parallel between the situation of the gods, with Indra as their king, threatened by demons, and the situation of Guru Gobind Singh and his followers, threatened by neighboring chieftains. In the world of Indra and the gods, there are shifting alliances and shifting balances of power. When Indra and the other gods lose control over their kingdoms, they must create new alliances and seek the assistance of the goddess. The demon-kings, too, hold court and receive and give gifts to pursue their own ends. Similarly, the *Bachitra Natak* narrative of Guru Gobind Singh's life illustrates the ever-shifting balances of power and allegiances in the Punjab hill region as different factions sought power and went to battle against one another. It is thus possible to read the goddess compositions in the context of the *Bachitra Natak* as having not simply a military but an equally significant political component. The political component places the battles of Guru Gobind Singh in the context of the battles of the gods, and most especially the goddess in her many forms, as necessary for the defense of the good. The goddess brings death to those who have improperly usurped power—indeed, in CC 1 she is explicitly compared to Yam, the god of death—and thus her role in battle is auspicious. *Bachitra Natak*'s explicit reference in its closing lines to the story of the goddess suggests that, taken together, the compositions explore the necessity for battle to defend proper order at all levels of the cosmos, from the heavens to earth. Worldly battles in a sense thus may have a spiritual component insofar as they are waged to create and sustain an environment in which the good may prosper.

One aspect of the Dasam Granth and its goddess compositions that has yet to be explored fully is the relationship between the goddess

Durga and the role of the king or ruler, a theme that has been highlighted in scholarship on Hindu goddess mythology. In the *Devi Mahatmya*, Indra's position as king of the gods was usurped by demons, and he sought assistance to regain his rule and preside over a kingdom in which he and the other gods could properly receive the sacrifices offered to them. Coburn (1984a, 159–160) has shown that in the *Devi Mahatmya* episode in which the gods create the goddess, she is depicted according to the classical Indian model of a king as described in texts such as the *Laws of Manu*. As such, she is a figure of both cosmic and worldly power.

Similarly, Gupta and Gombrich (1986) have shown that kings in India have often been associated with goddesses or the feminine principle, and argue that "for at least the last thousand years, perhaps longer, the concept of power in its political and social application has been intimately connected with tantric theology" (Gupta and Gombrich 1986, 123) insofar as power or shakti is central to kingship. Gupta and Gombrich are not arguing that kings necessarily engaged in esoteric tantric practice, but rather that the tantric conception of power as symbolized in goddesses "became almost universally current in the Hindu community" (Gupta and Gombrich 1986, 132). In turn, the goddess Durga in particular came to be depicted with royal insignia such as the discus or *chakra*, and trumpet of Vishnu. As the slayer of the buffalo demon Mahish, she was especially associated with victory in battle and depicted with the royal emblem of the lion. A king's throne is the *siṃhāsana*, or lion's throne (Gupta and Gombrich, 1986, 132).

Once again, if the Dasam Granth goddess compositions are read in the context of *Bachitra Natak*, we may posit a connection between the role of the goddess as protrectress of the cosmos and the Sikh Gurus as protectors as well, not only of their own followers but others, as in the case of Guru Tegh Bahadur, who gave his life to protect those who wear the sacred thread and forehead mark. As noted earlier, both the *chakkar* or *chakra* and the *singha*, or lion, remain important in Sikh symbolism.

In an analysis of the role of goddess worship in small kingdoms in southern Orissa, Burkhard Schnepel (1995) showed that royal patronage of goddesses was especially important during the founding period of local dynasties, and that as kingdoms grew in power, their focus shifted from local goddesses to Durga. There was an important connection between the religious realm of ritual worship of the goddess and political power.

How might this example of Orissan kingdoms apply to the Dasam Granth? The narrative of *Bachitra Natak* shows that Guru Gobind Singh, with his forts and army, his royal court, held a position that was similar to, or at least could be perceived as similar to, that of a local king. He entered into alliances with and in some cases fought against neighboring local kings, the Punjab hill chiefs, suggesting that they saw him in this role. The Punjab hills were and remain an area in which the Shakta traditions of worshiping the goddess remain very popular. In this context, the stories of Durga likely had special valence. Local rulers in Indian tradition have often been associated with the goddess Durga; Durga's insignia are much like royal insignia. Importantly, this link between royal insignia and Durga's insignia suggests that goddess mythology for both Sikhs and Hindus is not simply about religious belief and devotion but also about political power and legitimation.

To make such comparisons is to venture into somewhat treacherous territory in the context of Sikh historiography, in which the issue of "Hindu" connections or influences is highly vexed. Arguably, however, the similarities between the mythology and symbolism of the goddess Durga and the portrayal of Guru Gobind Singh in the Dasam Granth need not imply that Guru Gobind Singh was participating in or somehow advocating Hindu traditions. Such an argument is possible both for those who believe that Guru Gobind Singh composed the goddess narratives and for those who believe he did not.

First, it is important to keep in mind that the conceptions of religious boundaries that existed in Guru Gobind Singh's time are not the same as those that have developed in colonial and independent India. Someone living in Guru Gobind Singh's time would likely not have understood the terms "Hindu" and "Sikh" in the quite the same way that people would now (indeed, even now there is not complete consensus on how to understand such terms). Second, it is equally if not more important to remember that contemporary notions of religion are not necessarily the same as those that existed in Guru Gobind Singh's time. The concept of dharma, found in the Dasam Granth and throughout Indian tradition, is far broader than the current notion of "religion"; it may encompass dimensions of political and military power as well, or more broadly, general cultural conceptions about the proper social order. Dharma is not an exclusively Hindu term; it has been used by other religious traditions that arose in India (e.g., Buddhism), each tradition giving the term a new interpretation. Perhaps we may read the goddess narratives in the Dasam Granth not simply as inspiration for warriors in battle but also as a means of indicating both the religious and temporal power (*miri-piri*) that had first come to be vested in the Sikh with the sixth Guru, Guru Hargobind. That is, the "Hindu" mythology and the goddess's role in maintaining proper cosmic order or dharma was perhaps more politically than religiously relevant to Guru Gobind Singh and his followers. The *Bachitra Natak* narrative of the Sikh Gurus in the context of God's ongoing efforts to maintain dharma suggests a process within Sikh tradition of formulating a new conception of dharma that gives new shades of meaning to a long-standing cultural concept. Thus the goddess narratives focus primarily on battle, not on ritual worship of the goddess.

Reading the goddess narratives this way also sheds light on the poetic enterprise of the Dasam Granth. Each of the goddess compositions, CC 1 in particular, in part is focused on the art of poetic expression and draws upon classical Indian literary conventions such as the use of the *rasas* or sentiments to be evoked in artistic expression. This emphasis on skilled poetic composition is also indicative of one of the traditional responsibilities of Indian rulers—the sponsorship of the arts. One of the classical topics for Indian poetry, or *kāvya*, is the gods; to compose poetry about their deeds may be as much an exercise in poetic artistry as religious devotion, again suggesting that it may be more fruitful to read the Dasam Granth goddess and other "Hindu" mythological material as indicative of participation in the broad realm of Indian culture—dharma in its broadest sense—rather than looking for a solely religious reading of the text and its topics of concern. Such an approach is also useful for reading the "tricky tales" of *Charitropakhian*, the subject of the next chapter.

4

The Tricky Tales

CHARITROPAKHIAN ["STORIES ABOUT BEHAVIOR/CHARACTER"; also known as *Triā Charitra*, or "The Behavior of Women"] is the lengthiest, most controversial, and least studied portion of the Dasam Granth. Pritpal Singh Bindra, who has published an English translation of most of *Charitropakhian*, subtitled his work "tales of male-female tricky deceptions," and other Sikh commentators have similarly characterized these stories with names such as the "so-called sexy tales" (Grewal and Bal 1967, 93–94). For many Sikh commentators, the basic and most difficult question in Sikh interpretation of the Dasam Granth overall has been what to do with these stories, particularly since they occur in a text that some people term "the second scripture of the Sikhs." Given that they constitute roughly 40 percent of the entire Dasam Granth, it is difficult, though not impossible, to ignore them.

This chapter will examine the stories of *Charitropakhian* and consider how this composition may be understood in the context of the Dasam Granth as a whole. Many Sikh commentators have seen these stories as completely different in character from the rest of the text, lacking any apparent connection with the more theologically oriented themes of other compositions. In fact, many published versions of the Dasam Granth omit *Charitropakhian* along with the Persian *Hikaitan* on the grounds of their controversial, arguably obscene nature. Surindar Singh Kohli (2005, vii), for example, would not have his English translation of *Charitropakhian* and the *Hikaitan* published in his Dasam Granth translation without the permission of the Shiromani Gurdwara Parbandhak Committee.[1]

The graphic nature of some of the *charitras* has diverted attention from the ways in which *Charitropakhian* in fact does fit in thematically with the rest of the Dasam Granth. The autobiographical narrative of *Bachitra Natak* and the goddess compositions discussed in the preceding chapters are connected by the themes of a cosmic order in decline, and the need for constant vigilance and battle on the part of both the gods and humans to restore and maintain that order. A close analysis of the overall structure of *Charitropakhian* reveals that it too bears thematic connections to other compositions within the Dasam Granth, and the presence of these stories may in fact reveal something about the overall organizing themes of the Dasam Granth as an anthology. Like *Bachitra Natak* and the goddess tales, *Charitropakhian* too is concerned with the issue of dharma, in this instance primarily the personal dharma or duties and obligations of a ruler, and also makes connections between the maintenance of proper order in the world of the gods and the world of humans. Paying more attention to this composition can enrich our understanding of the text as a whole.

Just as with two of the goddess compositions within the Dasam Granth (CC 1 and CC 2), the title of *Charitropakhian* indicates a concern with the issue of *charitra* or behavior, deeds, and adventures (see, e.g., Monier-Williams 1981, 212). An *upākhiān* is a subordinate story or episode, and in this context refers to the fact that 402 of the 404 *charitras* are situated within a frame story. Some Sikh commentators have seen the first and last *charitras*, each of which addresses a lengthy series of battles between gods and demons, as separate from those that fit within the frame story. As with other portions of the Dasam Granth, there is speculation that *Charitropakhian* may not have been preserved in its final form, owing to the content of the first and last *charitras*, some inconsistencies in numbering within the text (see, e.g., Bindra 2002, vol. 1, 13; Jaggi 1966, 156), the inclusion of the *Benti Chaupai* (which many Sikhs recite as part of their daily prayers) within *charitra* 404, and the fact that there is no definitive conclusion to the events described in the frame story.

The opening *charitra*, which is referred to as *Chandi Charitra* at the end of its forty-eight verses, is a benediction to the goddess. As such it is clearly connected to the earlier goddess compositions in the Dasam Granth.

You are the sword-bearer, you are the cutting sword.
You are the arrow, the sword, the curved knife, the dagger.
You are to the east, south, west.
Wherever I look, there you stand. (1:1)

You are Yogamāyā, you are Saraswatī [Bākabānī].
You are the beautiful one, you are Srī Bhavānī.
You rule as Vishnu, Brahma, Rudra.
You are the mother of the universe, you always rule victoriously. (1:2)

You are born as the gods, the Daitya and Yakshas demons. You have created Turks and Hindus in this world.
You have taken form [*avatarī*] in this creation as the various paths.
You are the mouth from which debates about the Vedas are spoken.[2] (1:3)

You are the one with the frightful form, the one with four eyes.
You have a beautiful young form, you have a terrifying form.
You recite the four Vedas. You slew the demons Shumbh and Nishumbh. (1:4)

After these opening lines proclaiming the goddess as the supreme power in the cosmos, the lines that follow mention the goddess taking many other forms, including avatars of the god Vishnu such as Narasingha, Varāha, Ram, and Krishna (CP 1:5–6). She is described as the originator and destroyer of the universe (CP 1:7), and slayer of demons such as Chand, Mund, and Raktabij (CP 1:7–10). She recites the protective mantra *kaucha* [*kavacha*] (CP 1:10). As in the earlier goddess narratives, there are verses describing the goddess's prowess in battle. At one point, the poet proclaims, "There is no way to describe the splendor of Kali taking sword in hand" (CP 1:26). And, just as in other descriptions of the goddess's battles, the poet evokes the sights and sounds of battle, describing the beating of war drums, the weapons (including the *tupak* or matchlock rifle) (CP 1:33), the headless warriors who roam the battlefield, and the jackals, vultures, and ghosts who come to feast on the flesh of the wounded and dead (CP 1:18–40). Thus, however one interprets the theological implications of the demon-slaying goddess and her sword, there are clear thematic connections between this account of the goddess and the others in the Dasam Granth. Such connections, however, have been overshadowed by the concerns about the characterization of women and obscenity that have dominated the discourse concerning *Charitropakhian*. These concerns, in turn, have kept discourse on the composition enmeshed in the controversy over authorship, and whether Guru Gobind Singh indeed composed these stories.

In the closing lines of the first *charitra*, the poet invokes the familiar theme of an era of decline as he asks for the goddess's assistance as he turns to the topic of women.[3]

> How can someone who doesn't know how to swim cross the ocean
> Without taking your name as his boat? (1:42)
> If they seek your aid, the dumb will recite the six Shastras, the lame will climb mountains, the blind will see, and the deaf will hear. (1:43)
> The mysteries of pearls, wombs, kings, and women cannot be solved.
> Nonetheless, with your grace, I will hold forth just a bit. (1:44)
> First, propitiating you, I will speak with whatever power my intellect holds,
> Poets, if you perceive any flaws, please don't laugh at me. (1:45)
> Having first recalled *bhagautī*, I will now describe matters concerning women.
> May you flow through me like a river so that my words rise up as your waves. (1:46)
> You transformed me from a blade of grass into Mt. Meru, there is none kinder to the weak [*garība nivāja*] than you.
> O lord, forgive me my mistakes, for I have no other to forgive me than you.
> Those who serve you find their homes instantly filled with wealth.
> In this *kaliyuga*, all must rely only upon the swordbearing goddess Kali. (1:47)

After this benediction linking praise of the goddess to matters of women, the narrative shifts to the frame story for the stories that constitute the majority of *Charitropakhian*. The second *charitra* relates that there was a king named Chitra Singh who was so wealthy and handsome that an *apsara* [*apsarā*; a female celestial being capable of changing shape][4] on her way to visit Indra was completely captivated and told her messenger she would take a dagger to her heart or poison herself unless she could be with this man. The two married, had a handsome son named Hanwant Singh, and spent their time enjoying one another's company. But sadly one day the *apsara* returned to Indra's heaven, and Chitra Singh was devastated. He immediately set out to find a woman who looked just like his departed *apsara*, and after circulating sketches of her far and wide, located a candidate in a rival kingdom. To win her, he and his son had to fight a battle against her father, the king of Oḍacha. The rival king died in the battle, and Chitra Singh married his *apsara*-lookalike daughter named Chitramati [Chitramatī]. Chitramati, however, had designs on her stepson, Hanwant Singh. She conspired to bring her stepson to her own quarters and declared her desires, mentioning that her husband did not satisfy her. But her stepson rejected her advances. Chitramati, angered, scratched her own face, tore her clothes, and told her husband that his son had tried to have his way with her. Enraged, Chitra Singh vowed to kill his son. His ministers convinced him not to and explained that no one has as yet understood women's natures [*charitra*: as deed, character, nature, behavior] (CP 2:30). The king relented and put his son in prison instead. The next morning, the king brought his son out of the prison, and the ministers began relating stories, continuing for days thereafter. The structure of *Charitropakhian*, with a series of stories embedded within a frame story, bears striking connections with Sanskrit story literature, a topic explored later in this chapter. The frame story also shows intriguing parallels to the story of Puran Bhagat popular in the Punjab, in which a prince named Puran Bhagat is born and then kept in seclusion for twelve years. When he finally emerges from seclusion and meets his stepmother, Luna, she attempts to seduce him. When Puran Bhagat rebukes her advances, Luna tells her husband that his son had tried to have his way with her. Angered, the king orders that his son be executed. Puran's hands are severed, and he is thrown into a well to die. In the celebrated Qadir Yar version of this story, just as in *Charitropakhian*, there are periodic asides about women's treacherous natures.[5]

The tales in between the opening verses praising the goddess and the final battle scenes and prayers of the last *charitra* include retellings of popular Indian romance stories, accounts of seduction and amorous intrigue from Hindu mythology, some stories about clever thieves, and many, many stories about women who concoct elaborate schemes to pursue illicit and/or extramarital liaisons. There is no apparent organizational structure for these themes, other than occasional brief references to the minister continuing to tell the stories over many days.

While the stories sometimes defy strict classification, one breakdown (Loehlin 1971, 49) of their basic topics is that, leaving aside the opening and closing *charitras*, 269 of them address the deceitfulness of women; 78 portray the bravery, devotion, or intelligence of women (there are women, for example, who disguise themselves as men and fight valiantly in battle); 26 chronicle the deceitfulness of men; ten explore gambling, drinking, and opium usage (some coming out in favor of such activities, others against); and a remaining nineteen present versions of well-known folktales.

Many of the *charitras* concern women and men associated with royal households. They are full of stock images of beauty and power found in classical Indian poetry; a woman's beauty is so great that it rivals the moon or is the real cause of Brahma having four heads; men have teeth so glorious that they make elephants jealous; royal cities are so lush and luxurious that they rival the cities of the gods. Lust is a powerful force throughout the *charitras*; women cast their eyes upon handsome men, and all their sense and propriety falls away as they fall down, overcome by their insatiable passion. Previously honorable women conspire to arrange meetings with the objects of their desires, often by sending a maid to arrange the tryst.

Perhaps the most common theme in the *charitras* is the means by which women hide their illicit liaisons. Sometimes they get caught in the act of love and make up wild stories to hide what is happening or divert attention from their misdeeds (through blindfolding their husbands; rolling lovers into carpets; digging underground tunnels that allow lovers to sneak away; hiding lovers in drums, water pots; and so forth). Sometimes they ply family members with wine, cannabis, and opium[6] so that they may continue to meet their lovers in secret while their families are indisposed; sometimes they kill their husbands, parents, lovers to avoid being found out; sometimes they conspire to have their fathers or husbands give them away to their lovers by devising a curse or disguising their lovers as sadhus [*sādhus*]; sometimes they adopt disguises that allow them to sneak off to meet their lovers (particularly memorable is *charitra* 392, in which a young lady arranges to have herself shot out of a cannon directly to her lover's house, protected from injury by the power of a special mantra), or dress their lovers as women and keep them in their rooms; women with ugly husbands who announce that they have undertaken to perform prayers and pilgrimages to make their husbands better looking, in the meantime kill the ugly husband, and then install their handsome lovers as their miraculously "cured," new and improved husbands on the grounds that their prayers worked. A number of the *charitras* describe ardent, athletic lovemaking, often pursued according to the dictates of the *Kokashastra* [*Kokaśāstra*] (e.g., *charitras* 29, 247, 251, 252, 256).

The *charitras* are for the most part overwhelmingly cynical in their portrayal of religious activity, for so often it is a guise for some illicit activity, or religious leaders themselves (particularly Muslim judges, or *qāzīs*) are shown to be rather dimwitted. Indeed, skepticism about religious figures is such a recurring theme throughout the *charitras* that John Campbell Oman (1984, 83–91) included summaries of five *charitras* in his study *The Mystics, Ascetics, and Saints of India* to demonstrate that the tales show "that although the Indians feel that *sadhuism* is honorable and respectable, they are none the less quite alive to the great convenience of the *sadhu's* habit, as a disguise, for the successful conduct of amatory intrigues." The ascetic's garb as a useful disguise has a long and colorful history in Indian tradition; Kautilya's treatise on statecraft, the *Arthashastra* (Rangarajan 1992, 158), recommends that kings dress spies as ascetics in order to determine which subjects are happy and which are discontented.

The stories describe events mainly in India but also abroad (e.g., *charitra* 331, which mentions a king named Phirangi Rai who attacked the English [*angrejan*]). Some characters are identified by caste, most often Khatri, but also Jaṭ. Other characters are identified by ethnicity or religion (e.g., Pathans and Mughals). Some are versions of tales found in Sanskrit and vernacular literature from throughout India, such as the story of Nala and Damayantī (*charitra* 157), and Krishna's romancing of

Rukminī (*charitra* 320). Others are popular tales of romance such as Hīr and Rānjhā (*charitra* 98, which ends happily here, unlike Wāris Shāh's celebrated 1766 version), Sohinī and Mahīwāl (*charitra* 101), Sassī and Punnū (*charitra* 109), Mirzā and Sāhibān (*charitra* 129), and Yusuf and Zulaikha [Zulaikhā] (*charitra* 201).[7] By far, however, the majority of characters are kings, queens, princes, princesses, and their associates, and the frame story at least depicts the initial audience as a king and his son.

Charitra 3, the first that the minister tells the king and his son, gets right at the heart of many people's discomfort with these stories because it is likely to seem rather crude to many readers. There was a beautiful young village woman with an old, fat lover and a young, thin lover. As in many of the stories, there are observations about human character:

> A young woman falls under the spell of a young man, and an old man falls under the spell of a young woman.
> Everyone understands this is how things are in the world. (CP 3:6)

The young lady enjoyed lovemaking with the young man, but whenever she made love with the old man, she regretted it. Once, while she was enjoying herself with the young man, the old man came knocking at her door. She convinced her young lover to leave, telling him that someone had come to capture them, and that he should escape by jumping over a wall. Then she got up quickly as the old man came in. As she got up, the old man saw apparently unmistakable evidence of her recent sexual activity on her body. The old man asked her to explain, and she replied that she became uncontrollably aroused on seeing him. The poor old fool puffed up with pride, convinced of his attractiveness (CP 3:7–13).[8]

After hearing this first *charitra*, the king put his son back in jail, and the next morning, the storytelling resumed. Subsequent tales elaborate on the complex arts of deceit in portrayals of women who manage multiple lovers without them finding out about one another, women who scheme to seduce the men they desire, even women who kill members of their own families rather than be caught in their duplicity (see, e.g., *charitras* 9, 10, 11). Occasionally, in the midst of these rather grim portrayals of human nature, the storytelling minister throws in a few words of advice for the king on the futility of understanding women:

Steal a woman's heart, but don't let her steal yours.
Keep her captivated by giving her untold riches day after day.
Neither the Gandharvas, Yakshas, serpents, Shiva's attendants, gods, nor demons could fathom the mystery of women; what hope is there for men? (CP 10:12–13)

However wise and clever a man may be, none can fathom the clever characters of women.
A man who tells a woman what is in his heart will find that old age devours his youth, and that the god of death will steal his very life.
The *smritis*, Vedas, and *Kokashastra* all state that secrets should not be revealed to women, but that one should always try to discover theirs. (CP 13:8–10)

The general message seems to be that men must recognize that women are mysterious and clever, and that relationships with them require careful management. Subsequently, there are occasional references to Chitra Singh and the frame story; for example, at the beginning of *charitra* 30, Chitra Singh tells the minister that these stories are like nectar to his ears and asks for more.

The Anup Kaur and Anandpur *Charitras*

Charitras 21 through 23 are of particular interest because some people have argued that they depict an incident from Guru Gobind Singh's own life (see, e.g., Nara 1985, 44–48). These tales take place in the village of Anandpur on the banks of the Satadrava or Sutlej River, where Guru Gobind Singh did indeed live for some time. The main male character in these *charitras* is most frequently referred to as a *rāi*, or ruler, and once as a Guru. The *charitras* note that disciples [Sikhs][9] visited Anandpur regularly; once, a rich man's wife named Anup Kaur [*Nūpa Kuari*] came to visit. She was pierced by love's arrow and fell for the ruler [*rāi*] of the place. She sent for one of the ruler's servants, a man named Magan Das, and told him that if he arranged for her to meet the ruler, she would bestow great wealth upon him. Magan liked the idea of wealth, so he agreed to a ruse that would convince the ruler to visit

Anup Kaur. Magan fell at the ruler's feet and told him that he had obtained a special mantra that the ruler wanted to learn, and that he would share it only if the ruler did as he requested (CP 21:3–9).

And so the ruler donned the garb of an ascetic and set off for the woman's house, his mind focused on *bhagauti*. In the meantime, Anup Kaur got dressed and sent for flowers, betel leaf, and wine. When her guest arrived, she asked him to make love to her. The ruler was perturbed, realizing that while he had come for a mantra, he was being presented with something quite different. Casting his argument in terms of dharma, he told the woman that he would not honor her request for fear of bringing shame to his family, that he would not turn away from his wife, and that he could not hope to find a place among righteous kings [*dharamrāja*] if he were to acquiesce to the lady's demands (CP 21:16–17).

Anup Kaur countered with her own argument that a man who refuses a woman tormented by lust should be thrown in hell. The ruler replied that she should be ashamed of herself for trying to seduce a man at whose feet she worshiped, but she pointed out that women who worshiped Krishna also made love with him, and that Brahma had made humans out of the five elements and created desire between them. The lively exchange continued, but the ruler steadfastly refused the woman's advances, noting his fear of hell, his wish not to perform bad deeds, and his desire to maintain a good reputation. The lady, in turn, argued that even if people were to find out that he had engaged in relations with her, they would be afraid to say anything critical. But the ruler provided further objections; he was born as a Kshatriya in a respected clan, and if he were to be with this woman, he would be reborn into a family of low status (CP 21:18–32).

Then matters took an even more serious turn, for the lady threatened to poison herself, and the ruler worried that if the lady were to swear an oath on *Bhagauti* he would have to accede to her wishes and consequently be consigned to hell. In the midst of this heated discussion, the minister telling the story commented that women are undependable, forsaking one man for another, ever willing to expose themselves to a man they desire.[10] The ruler was in a difficult situation, for he realized that he had no disciples [*sikh*] with him, and that if he were to flee, the woman might catch him. He decided to offer her fulsome praise and try to make his getaway, wishing fervently that one of his disciples would rescue him. But it was to no avail; the lady renewed her demand for passion and once more threatened to poison herself. Still, he tried to explain that his Guru had taught him to be only with his wife, and not even to dream of visiting another woman's bed, citing examples of the consequences. When Indra did, he was punished with a thousand marks, when the moon did, he was blemished, when Ravan did, he lost all ten of his heads, and when the Kauravas did, they lost their entire army. He continued presenting his case, stating that loving someone else's woman is like a sharp dagger, and that the man who does so dies a dog's death (CP 21:44–53).

> Young lady! Women come to visit me from all over.
> Considering me as Guru, they bow their heads and request their hearts' desires.
> In my heart I consider my disciples [*sikhya*] to be my sons, their wives my daughters.
> Pretty lady, tell me, how could I possibly be involved with them [in the way you wish]? (CP 21:54)

At this point, frustrated and angry, the young lady shouted out, "Thief! Thief!" awakening her servants. Frightened, the ruler fled, leaving behind his shoes and cloak (CP 21:55–60).

The story continues in *charitra* 22. Everyone in the vicinity was awakened by the cry of "Thief!" and they quickly caught the fleeing man, brandishing swords and shrieking that he should be killed. They tugged at his beard, pulled his turban from his head, and thrashed him with sticks. He fell to the ground unconscious, and someone tied him up. Eventually, he was able to flee, the woman's brother taking his place in jail (CP 22:1–9).

The next morning, the ruler left his house and convened his court. That same morning, the lady's love had completely turned to anger, and she showed everyone the shoes and cloak the ruler had left behind. In his assembly or court [*sabhā*], the ruler proclaimed that his shoes and cloak had been stolen, and that any disciple who could tell him what had happened to them would be saved from death (CP 23:1–3).

> Hearing those words from the Guru's mouth, the disciples [*sikhya*] could not conceal what they knew, and told him about the woman with the shoes and the cloak. (CP 23:4)

Then the ruler asked that they bring the lady, the cloak, and the shoes to him. When she arrived, he asked her why she had stolen his things and then proclaimed that were she not a woman, he would have had her executed. The lady turned pale, her heart was pounding, and she could not speak. The ruler had her taken to his house, and then the next morning he met with her, noting that they had each put the other in a difficult situation. They agreed to exonerate one another, and the woman was given a stipend every six months (CP 23:5–12).[11]

These *charitras* are concerned with the need for a ruler to follow the dictates of dharma in his personal conduct; indeed, at one point the *rāi* noted that if he were to acquiesce to the lady's demands, he would be unable to take his place among righteous kings or "dharma rajas." Here, matters of dharma are explicated in the form of a story rather than a rule or prescription. The focus of Sikh exegesis has been to debate whether these stories are indeed about Guru Gobind Singh. Jaggi (1966, 158–161) discusses the Anup Kaur *charitras* at some length, arguing that they cannot be an authentic record of events in Guru Gobind Singh's life. His argument is based largely on the assertion that the events described are not in keeping with Guru Gobind Singh's character.[12] Others, however, have interpreted the Anup Kaur *charitras* as cautionary tales for men. Devotional singing, or *kīrtan*, may be performed with reference to this story using verses 51–54 from *charitra* 21, discussed earlier, in which the *rāi* explains that his Guru taught him never to be with anyone but his own wife.[13]

Charitra 49 also takes place in Anandpur. There was a barber's wife named Nand Matī whose husband was a fool and never admonished her though she had many men visiting their home for carnal pleasure while he was away. She always praised him as a good disciple of the Guru (in the poet's words, "that fool always spent his time with me/us"), and he became proud of his saintly ways, making no effort to change his wife's wayward behavior (CP 49:1). As in the earlier *charitras* that take place in Anandpur, there is mention of the "Guru," but he is not named.[14]

Charitras Concerning Historical Figures

There are several *charitras* concerning historical figures, including the Mughal emperors. *Charitra* 48 explores the relationship between the emperor Jahangir and his wife, Nur Jahan. Completely enamored of his wife, Jahangir always acceded to her wishes and one day took her and her friends hunting. The deer in the forest were so overcome by Nur Jahan's beauty that they fell to the ground without even being struck by arrows. But the outing turned treacherous when a tiger attacked. Jahangir was unable to shoot it, but one of the ladies in the hunting party killed the threatening tiger with a single bullet. He was grateful to have been saved but later heard the ladies at the court discussing how a woman who could shoot a tiger would fear no man. From then on, Jahangir was afraid of the woman who saved his life (CP 48). In this *charitra*, the storyteller has portrayed the main male character as being wary of women, even one whose skill and cunning saved his life.

Charitra 82 is another interesting example of a story concerning historical figures; in this instance, a woman uses her powers of deceit to aid her husband rather than cuckold him. After the Mughal emperor Jahangir died, his son Shah Jahan became ruler. Shah Jahan was angry with Dariya Khan and wanted to kill him but could not get his hands on him. He would mutter about it in his sleep, and when his wife heard him, she decided to take matters into her own hands. She sent for a clever friend whom she enlisted to bring Dariya Khan to the palace somehow. The young lady thereupon went to see Dariya Khan and told him that the queen was madly in love with him. Dariya Khan was thrilled at the prospect of meeting a woman who loved him and therefore agreed to the friend's plan that he should be snuck into the palace in a large cooking pot.

When the cooking pot arrived, the queen informed her husband, Shah Jahan, that the enemy who kept him awake at night now lay hidden in the palace in a pot, mistakenly thinking he was soon to romance the queen. The husband and wife decided they would have the friend take the pot to Chandni Chowk (in Delhi) and present it to a *qazi* (Muslim judge) and his staff, asserting that the pot contained a ghost [*bhūta*]. The friend did so, whereupon the *qazi* decreed that the ghost must be buried alive lest it torment another poor soul, and thus Shah Jahan and his wife were victorious over this enemy (CP 82). Here is an instance of a clever woman assisting her husband rather than deceiving him (though she does of course wield her powers of deception on another man), and both of them manipulating an unsuspecting religious figure to bring about their wish.

The Pros and Cons of Intoxicants

Charitra 266, one of the longer tales, presents a lengthy debate about image worship between a cannabis-quaffing princess and a Brahman priest. A just king named Sumati Sain engaged a Brahman priest to educate his four brave sons and beautiful daughter. One day, the feisty young princess arrived earlier than her brothers to meet with the Brahman and saw that he was performing worship of a *shalagram* [*śālagrāma*] stone that in this story is described as an image of the god Shiva.[15] The young princess laughed and asked the Brahman why he was worshiping a stone. A spirited debate ensued in which the young lady opined that anyone who considered God to be in a stone could never understand the true nature of God, and then went on to describe what she saw as the hypocrisy of the pious:

> Priest, you read a couple of Puranas and you're quite pleased with yourself.
> But you haven't read the Purana that eradicates all wrongdoing.
> You pretentiously perform austerities, but you're thinking about money day and night.
> Foolish people assent to your views, but I don't believe them. (CP 266:23)

She then told the priest she was not interested in learning any of the worthless mantras he sold to others. The priest, in turn, asserted that she could not understand what he was talking about because she had drunk *bhang* [*bhānga*; cannabis].

> Listen, Brahman, your words are full of ego and you don't understand what I'm saying.
> It's not as if drinking *bhāng* makes the intellect go away, and what intellect do you have even though you haven't drunk *bhāng*? (CP 266:37)

The princess continued berating the priest for his unceasing quest for money and denounced the whole class of priests who traveled far and wide reciting various sacred texts in exchange for money and gifts, who proudly studied in Kashi, who wore matted hair, or shaved their heads, or pierced their ears with heavy wooden earrings.

> They don't believe in the Mother or Mahakal,
> Those fools believe in earthen idols, and they die believing in them.
> (CP 266:53)

After a torrent of such criticisms, the Brahman replied that she was naive and did not realize that everyone bowed their heads before Brahmans, even kings (CP 266:71–72). The princess, however, remained unconvinced and returned to elucidating her views on the merits of cannabis for warriors whom it made strong in battle, able to tear a tusk from an elephant, and its dangers for those of weaker constitutions such as the Brahman, who, the young lady averred, would fall flat on his face like a corpse if he were to drink cannabis (CP 266:81). She asked the Brahman whether he would still be worshiping a Shiva *linga* when Death had ensnared him in his net and told him he should only worship Mahakal:

> I am his disciple, he is my spiritual guide [*pīr*]. I have made my very being his disciple.
> It is through him that I am called a young lady. He alone is my protector, and I worship him alone.
> Brahman, I believe in Mahakal, not stones.
> I believe a stone is a stone, and people think this is bad.
> (CP 266:80–81)

The princess reiterated the theme of the futility of the Brahman's acts in the face of death, asking what book he would have when he was dying—the *Bhagavat Purana* or the *Bhagavad Gita*—or whether he would seek Ram's or Krishna's assistance. She told him that all the gods—Shiva, Brahma, Vishnu, Indra—are under Kal's power, as are demons, Hindus, and Turks. Sometimes the demons defeat the gods, sometimes the gods defeat the demons, but the lord [*purakh*] who kills them all was her protector (CP 266:101–104).

To prove her point, she picked up the image and threw it at the Brahman, smashing his teeth. The Brahman angrily vowed to tell the king what his daughter had done, but she grabbed hold of him and dunked him in a river, proclaiming him purified. She told the Brahman that she would tell her father the Brahman tried to molest her and that he would have his hands chopped off. This prospect frightened the Brahman enough that he fell at her feet and agreed to do whatever she wished. She made him renounce his wealth and declare that he would never again worship stones, only Mahakal. He tossed his images in the river and became a disciple of Mahakal, the young lady having made him drink wine and *bhang* (CP 266:105–125).

This *charitra* is both theologically and sociologically intriguing. The young lady expresses her devotion to the Mother and Mahakal (a theological theme that will be revisited in the closing *charitra*) and challenges the image worship of the Brahman priest. The theme of rejecting image worship and ritualism, as well as the potentially exploitative power of priests, is found in other Sikh sources. The young lady, however, is not entirely a sympathetic character as she quaffs *bhang* and injures the priest with his own image. As with so many of the other *charitras*, this is an example of a clever woman who nonetheless does not appear to be a suitable moral exemplar.

Another *charitra* concerned with the use of intoxicants tells of a Pathan named Maigal Khan who lived in Batala and spent his days and nights senseless from drinking wine. One rainy season, as dark clouds and lightning filled the sky, young ladies played on swings and sang so sweetly that cuckoos felt ashamed to sing. Among them Maigal Khan caught sight of the beautiful Ritu Raj Prabha [Ritu Rāja Prabhā] and immediately fell madly in love; it was as if he had been struck by a dagger. He sent for an old woman to act as his go-between, promising her riches if she could arrange a meeting with the enchanting young woman whose beauty he extolled:

> Mangoes grow where the nectar of her tears has fallen, apricots have sprouted from the nectar that drips from her tongue.
> Just a taste of the honey from her sweet face could make a man live forever.

> The moon, whose light the whole world requires, takes its place in the skies only having glimpsed her nose.
> Grapes and pomegranates are modeled on her teeth, and sugarcane on her lips. (CP 183:10)

The old lady conspired to meet the beautiful young woman, Ritu Raj Prabha, by offering to push her swing, and then she brought her to see Maigal Khan. The clever young lady told him she had come for him, but that it was her time of the month and that she would have to wait a couple of days. Then, she instructed him, he should drink wine and pleasure her with his embrace; she would meet him in his daughter's bed at midnight.

A couple of days later, Ritu Raj Prabha slipped away from Maigal Khan's daughter's bed before he arrived, and he was in such a drunken state that he mistook his daughter for Ritu Raj Prabha, and had his way with her despite her despairing cries. Only when the effects of the wine wore off did he realize what he had done and let his daughter go. He conceded that Ritu Raj Prabha had saved her own virtue and ability to be ever faithful to a husband [*patibratā*], and sighed:

> How can a man be saved from committing sins; first there is wine,
> then there are young women, and then too much wealth in the home.
> Only Ram can save a man. (CP183:19)

Thus while the young princess in the previous *charitra* outwitted a Brahman priest while she was under the influence of cannabis, here another young woman used a Pathan's weakness for wine to outwit him. This *charitra* is also another example of the rather sexually explicit nature of these stories that has troubled many readers.

Fighting Women

There are quite a few *charitras* in which women demonstrate skill in fighting and disguise. In *charitra* 96, a Pathan woman disguised herself in her husband's clothes and turban after he announced he was too afraid to take on attacking forces. The woman locked her husband in a cellar and fought off the attackers herself. When she was hit by arrows, she tore them from her flesh and shot them back at the enemy. Victorious, she freed her husband from the cellar, gave him back his horse and turban, and bade him farewell. The woman was both stronger and braver than her husband, and she rejected him when she realized his weakness.

Charitra 126 describes a fort under siege by a man named Abdul Nabi. After several days of losses, a small force continued fighting, and women assisted. One of the women shot Abdul Nabi dead. But soon thereafter her own husband died in the battle, and the enemy fighters told her she would now become their woman. The woman agreed but said she first had to cremate her son and husband. As the cremation fire burned, she grabbed one of the men and pulled him into the fire, taking her own life as well. This, then, is a rather different sort of female character than in other *charitras*, one willing to sacrifice her own life rather than be subject to the men who killed her family.

Devotion and Disguises

In many *charitras*, religious devotion serves as the pretense for secret liaisons. *Charitra* 24 is the story of Sumer Kaur, a beautiful princess born to a king and queen in a northern kingdom. She was married to a king in the south, had two sons and a daughter, but then her husband died. Alone, she pined for love as the pangs of separation stabbed at her heart, and then she was pierced by Kāma's arrows of love. She called for a handsome man and made love with him. They continued their affair, but it became increasingly difficult to sneak the man in to see her without arousing suspicion. One night, he dressed as a woman so that he could visit her. Sumer Kaur then revealed her plan, instructing her lover to bathe in a spring, announce that he had had a vision of Krishna, and then fall silent.

The man did as he was told, and as soon as people heard that he had a vision of Krishna, they began bringing him offerings and calling him a Guru. Hearing of the new "Guru's" fame, Sumer Kaur took a group of her friends to visit him. She had him detail every aspect of Krishna's appearance and then pleaded with him to return to her home so that she might serve him. She thus managed to install her lover as her Guru, and no one was the wiser. The minister ended the tale with these words: "No one can understand the deeds of a fickle woman. Not even the moon, the sun, gods, demons, Brahma, Vishnu, or Indra" (CP 24:1–49).

In *charitra* 214, a princess named Guljar Mati took a handsome lover but feared what would happen if her virtuous parents were to find out. She told her young man to take her away; he agreed and asked her to take money for them from her father's treasury. She left home, leaving behind a letter announcing that she had gone to bathe at a sacred pilgrimage site, and that she would meet them again if she survived the journey. She spent many years enjoying her man, but when the money ran out, she abandoned him and went home. There, she fell at her parents' feet, bestowing upon them a portion of the benefits she had accrued from her many years of performing religious acts at pilgrimage sites. Her father was pleased, thinking that his daughter had erased the sins of his past lives through her pious acts (CP 214:1–14). The theme here is of women who use religious fervor as a cover for secret passions.

In a slightly different take on the ways people may be deceived by acts of devotion, *charitra* 328 tells of a king and queen, and a dog handsome as a lion. When the king threw a rock at the dog and killed it, the queen, who was quite fond of the dog, was upset. The king dismissed her grief, told her they had thousands of other fine dogs, and teased her that she treated this dog as if it were a Muslim holy man [*pīr*]. So the queen named the departed dog Kutub Shah and had a shrine constructed for him. She began making offerings at the grave and told people that Pir Kutub Shah had fulfilled her desires. Soon many others came to make offerings, including *qazis*, sheikhs, and Sayyads whose beards brushed the grave as they kissed it and made offerings; this *charitra* thus pokes fun at the unsuspecting ritualistic piety of religious authority figures (CP 328:1–9).

Aligunj Mati, a princess, is the main character of *charitra* 257. Out for a stroll with her friends, she caught sight of a handsome king named Tilak Mani and vowed to one of her friends that she would forsake all her jewelry and become a *yoginī* in saffron clothes unless she could meet this object of her desire. Her companion advised her to send a clever friend to entice the king. Aligunj Mati enlisted a young woman and sent her off adorned so beautifully that she looked like the moon among the stars. The young woman found Tilak Mani out hunting; when he saw her, he concluded her beauty was such that she had to be the daughter of some celestial being. The enticing young friend wore a necklace with a letter attached that promised Tilak Mani a woman even more beautiful than she. Intrigued by this prospect, Tilak Mani vowed to leave behind his kingdom and find this woman for himself. Taking Aligunj Mati's friend in his chariot, he went to find the woman of his dreams.

So that he might meet her, Tilak Mani adopted the guise of a yogi and set up camp beneath Aligunj Mati's window. By day, she came to give him offerings; by night, they met secretly and made love. No one realized the ascetic was really a king. When the situation became unbearable, Aligunj Mati went to her father the king and said something so cruel that he sentenced her to forest exile. She cried to show her grief but inwardly exulted. Her father's servants took her to the forest, where her lover soon joined her. First, they made love, then he put her on his horse and took her back to his city (CP 257:1–29).

Charitra 403, at eleven verses relatively short compared with other *charitras*, briefly reminds readers and listeners of the frame story as the narrator begins, "Listen, king, I'll tell you another *charitra*." It is the story of a king named Rai Singh who lived in the city of Andavati [Andāvatī], and himself wrote *charitras* and then read them to women. A beautiful woman named Shivamati heard of this and vowed that she would seduce him and then get him to write a *charitra* about her. She did spend time with the king, then returned home and told everyone about it. But they did not believe her story at first and were convinced she was not telling the truth about her tryst when she said that she had told the story just to see how they would react. She declared that of course no one would cavort with a man during the day and then tell everyone; she would keep it a secret. So no one believed she really had spent time with the king. Then, she wrote him a letter and asked that he put her *charitra* in his book [*grantha*] (CP 403:1–11). This *charitra* suggests not only that women are skilled at the various arts of deceit depicted in these stories but that they take some pride in those skills.

Charitra 404

After 402 such stories, the narrative shifts to the final and, at 405 verses, the longest *charitra*. There is no explicit transition between this last *charitra* and those that precede it, nor is there a reference to the frame story. Like the opening *charitra*, it is more focused on the world of the gods than that of humans, and it too bears comparison to similar such narratives in other portions of the Dasam Granth. While the opening *charitra* centered on the goddess, and its closing lines linked it to the stories about women that follow, this final *charitra* describes Mahakal's [in this *charitra* a.k.a. Kal, Kalā, Kalikā, Kalakā, Asidhuj] battles with demons and does not have any explicit references to the stories that have preceded it. Thematically it has much in common with the battle narratives of the goddess compositions that occur earlier in the Dasam Granth. Although it is but one of 404 *charitras*, it is in fact longer than either *Chandi Charitra* 1 or 2.

Charitra 404 opens with a description of King Sati Sandhi, who lived during the *satyayuga*, the first of the four eras. He was made king of all the gods, and Brahma himself anointed him with a *tilak* on his forehead. This king slew all the demons and allowed the gods to live without fear for many years. But then a demon named Dīragh Dāṛ was born who amassed a large army and went to battle against the gods.

The gods assembled an army to defend themselves, choosing Sūrya the sun as their general. The moon and Kartikeya led forces as well. What follows is a battle scene reminiscent of so many others others in the Dasam Granth, with details of the sights and sounds of war—streaming blood, severed limbs, the air thick with arrows and other weapons, vultures, ghosts, and vampires shrieking in delight at the feast of flesh and blood. Various words for anger and killing recur throughout this *charitra* (recalling the *rudramaī rasa* of CC 1), and as the poet continued to describe the protracted, gory battle, he noted more than once that he did not have the power in his tongue to tell it all, and that he feared that his book would become too long.

Indeed, just this opening battle raged on at some length until all the fighters on both sides were slain, and then the two opposing kings continued fighting for another twenty years until they killed one another (CP 404:1–27). Out of that terrible fighting arose a great conflagration, from which a young woman [*bālā*] emerged. Laughing, she took up arms. Her beauty was so great the sun and moon felt shy before her, and she soon realized there was no male suitable to be her lord [*nātha*]. Thus she vowed that she would wed only the lord of the world Kalikā Devā, and serve him at his pleasure. She began focusing on this goal and drew many *jantras* [Sanskrit *yantra*] or mystical diagrams. Then, the World-Mother Bhavani took mercy on her and promised that the Formless One [*nirankār*] would indeed become her husband. Bhavani instructed her to concentrate firmly on him that night and then do whatever he told her. At midnight, her lord issued his command, "When the demon Swās Bīraj has died, then you will be wed to me" (CP 404:28–35).

And so the young woman set off for battle, surrounding the demon's fort with her forces, sounding her battle drum. The demon, disturbed from his sleep, wondered what sort of upstart attacker was after a demon such as he, who had defeated the demon Raktabij in battle, not to mention Indra, the sun, the moon, Ravan, and even Shiva. The young woman, now referred to as Dulaha [Dūlaha Kumārī], paid her respects to her weapons and began shooting arrows. But this demon was a tough opponent; out of his breath, blood, and marrow countless new demons sprang to life. When demons filled the earth as far as the eye could see, Kal [here Kalakā] appeared before the young woman. She fell at his feet and pleaded for assistance. Kal laughed and took up his sword to protect the world. He too began slaying demons right and left (CP 404:36–56).

Subsequent verses detail yet another protracted battle. New demons arose from the marrow and breath of the old, and elephants and horses emerged from the blood that flowed from their wounds. In the midst of the demon forces, Kal stood firm like a minaret [*munāra*]. As the slaughtering continued, the gods grew fearful. Vishnu trembled and disguised himself in women's dress; Shiva fled into the jungle. Mahakal's blows against the demons served only to create more and more of them, so many that the poet could not describe them all as the fourteen worlds became filled with demons. As the battle wore on, Brahma, Vishnu, and all the other gods sought refuge with Mahakal, praising him as the ruler of all worlds, destroyer of pride, protector of the downtrodden, infinite, timeless, fearless, unborn, indestructible, without parents or relatives. Interestingly, they also praised him as the slayer of Chand and Mund, whom the goddess Chandi slew in the Dasam Granth's three goddess compositions (CP 404:57–83).

The fearful gods continued their lengthy praises of Mahakal, noting that he created Brahma, Vishnu, Shiva, and the sage Kashyap. With the gods pleading at his feet, Kal laughed, took mercy on them, and pledged his protection. He then resumed battling demons, saving the lives of good people. As the fighting raged on, Mahakal wiped the sweat from his body, and as it fell to the ground, from it arose two bards [Bhaṭācaraja and Ḍhāḍhi Sain], who began praising Mahakal and composing verses. From yet more of his sweat falling on the ground was created Bhūm Sain. (These three sweat-born individuals do not figure prominently in the remainder of the *charitra*.) The battle was so fierce that entire worlds were destroyed, leaving only the underworld (CP 404:84–112).

The depiction of the battle scene continues relentlessly as angry demons gave birth to ever more demons through their flowing blood and oozing marrow. Even when wounded, missing eyes and limbs, they still wandered the skies, some drinking liquor and eating human flesh. At times the battle is described as being between the demons and Kali, though commentators have taken "Kali" in this context to refer to Mahakal.[16] The descriptions of battle, nonetheless, are very much reminiscent of those in the goddess compositions. Rivers of blood flow, jackals and vultures feast on flesh, ghosts and other spirits cackle and dance, and the sounds are so horrific that it seems like the final day of cosmic destruction [*parlo*]. The poet here too occasionally made the kinds of comparisons so typical of *Chandi Charitra* 1; several times, for example, the bloodstained clothes of the demons are compared to those of people who have been throwing colored dye on one another during the festival of Holi (e.g., CP 404:133). The cosmic battle had everyone's attention; the wives of the gods and demons watched, and from time to time the *apsarases* would give weapons to the warriors. As in *Var Durga Ki*, there are occasional references to Islamic practice. Some of the fallen demons are described as martyrs or *sāhīds [shāhīd]* (CP 404:167). And, the battle scenes are compared to everyday scenes; dazed warriors fall to the ground like yogis deep in meditation, rutting elephants look like mountains, horses swimming in the rivers of blood look like swarming crocodiles, and swords glint and gleam like fish (CP 404:170–171).

Mahakal displayed his powers throughout the battle, including the ability to absorb weapons and enemies into his own body. But the demons too exhibited remarkable creative powers. Not only did they create new demons from their flesh and blood as they were wounded and slain in battle, but some of the demons angrily emitted fire from which Pathans bearing bows were created, and the newly created Pathans in turn blew fire from their mouths that created Mughals. The Mughals then breathed in anger, and from that breath were created Sayyads and Shekhs. All then mounted horses and joined the fray, striking out at Mahakal (CP 404:198–200). They were quite drunk on wine, and more and more of these barbarians [*malechas*] came into being; the poet even listed some of their names. None of them, however, could defeat Mahakal, who first slew the Pathans, cutting many of them into pieces, then the Mughals, then the Sayyads, who died like moths in a flame. The Shekhs saw their likely fate and fled in fear, but feeling ashamed returned to fight. They, however, were like deer being hunted by a tiger. Seeing the carnage, ghosts and vultures arrived to feast, as more and more warriors fell like trees uprooted by a storm (CP 404:201–227).

In *Bachitra Natak* and the goddess compositions, the battles of the gods versus the demons were compared to the battles that good people must wage against bad; in *Var Durga Ki*, there was even a hint that Pathans and Mughals were like demons. But here in *charitra* 404 the comparison between demons and Mughals and Pathans is more explicit, for it was the demons who gave birth to them out of their own bodies. The equation of demons and Mughal and Pathan forces is driven home by the listing of their names as well. The demons in *charitra* 404 are like Raktabij, the demon who figures prominently in the goddess mythology with his ability to create new versions of himself with every drop of his blood that is spilled. In the goddess stories, he can be defeated only when the bloodthirsty goddess Kali laps up each and every drop of his blood. The demons in *charitra* 404 multiply at an even more alarming rate, and they arise not only from blood but also from flesh, marrow, and fiery breaths. A reader or listener might deduce that the poet was comparing the cosmic struggle of the gods versus the demons to the more earthly struggle of those who battled the Mughals and Pathans, and perhaps also that the gruesome battle scenes were drawn from not merely imagination but personal experience.

At this point in this *charitra*, the goddess Kali does not appear to lap up all the demons as she does in versions of the *Devi Mahatmya* narrative in which the demon Raktabij keeps reproducing himself. Instead, Mahakal, in these scenes named Asidhuj or "Sword-Banner," utters the mantra *huam*, which creates diseases that afflict the demons. With a hint of humor, the poet promised to name the diseases for the pleasure of Ayurvedins. As readers and listeners learn of the leprous sores and other painful afflictions that began to torment the demons, once again the poet expressed his fear that his book would become too long. But this was not a signal that the battle would finally end, for Mahakal still wished to fight the demons. He thus created special herbs to heal the afflictions he had visited upon the demons, and the war heated up yet again as the demons regained their health. The demons attacked with a fire-weapon, and Kal countered with a water-weapon. The demons' breeze-weapon was matched by a mountain-weapon, their cloud-weapon by a wind-weapon, and so forth; Kal had a weapon to meet each of theirs. The result was once more a battlefield littered with fallen warriors in bloodstained clothing, looking like Muslim mendicants [*malang*] who had consumed *bhang*, their fallen horses reminding the poet of *qazis* leaning forward as they prayed (CP 404:248–268).

The same images recur again and again—new demons emerged from blood, flesh, marrow, even thought, and Mahakal kept slaying them with an impressive array of weapons that included rifles. Demons shouted out, "Kill! Kill!"; severed body parts were strewn across the battlefield, and torrents of blood flowed as ghosts, witches, jackals, vultures, crows, and other carrion eaters feasted and shrieked with joy. The battle seems never-ending. At one point, Dulaha appears again, riding on a lion, causing the demons to flee in fear as she chops them into tiny pieces, shredding their banners and severing their limbs, grabbing some by the hair and tossing them to the ground (CP 404:331–332). As Mahakal and Dulaha continued their fight, fallen demons lay on the ground like minarets toppled by an earthquake, and swords and spears glinted like fish caught in a net. The blood spurting from the warriors' wounds reminded the poet of a fountain in a garden; the blood pooled to form a second Lake Mansarovar (CP 404:342–359). As in the goddess compositions, the poet compares the carnage of a battle in which demons are killed to everyday scenes.

Dulaha and Mahakal continued to fight the demons, and then Mahakal thought of a mantra he could use to defeat them. He pulled all the demons in close so that no new ones could be born, and gave a command to Kali to eat them all (CP 404:363–364). There is some difference of opinion as to who exactly Kali is in this context, and whether this is the same as the character Dulaha.[17] If this story parallels others about demons who constantly reproduce themselves when wounded, then perhaps the figure is indeed Kali, who happily laps up blood; here, the figure whom Mahakal commands here must not only drink blood but eat the demons whole.

At last there was but one demon left alive, a frightened king. The poet noted that only those who seek Mahakal's refuge may be saved, but the proud demon instead decided to challenge Mahakal to a fight. He battled on, wounded, shooting arrows even as vultures snatched pieces of his oozing intestines and flew into the sky. Then Mahakal shot 20,000 arrows at him, and finally, flowers showered from the skies as the last demon fell to the ground, his head severed, his body riddled with arrows. Everyone praised Mahakal as the king of all worlds and the destroyer of enemies (CP 404:365–376). After the suggestion that the last demon standing might have saved himself by seeking Kal's refuge, but instead died fighting, the *charitra* shifts to verses of praise.

At the conclusion of Kal's battles against the demons, there is the phrase "kabyo bāca bentī chaupaī," or "the poet spoke verses of supplication." Verses 377–401 constitute the important Sikh prayer popularly known as *Benti Chaupai*, which may be recited daily (particularly during evening prayer), for protection, and as part of Khalsa initiation rites. As such it is typically separated from the context of the lengthy battle story that precedes it in *charitra* 404.

> Give us your hand in protection, that all our heart's desires may be fulfilled.
> May our hearts forever rest at your feet, may you forever protect my life. (377)

> May you destroy all my enemies. Give me your hand that I might be saved.

Creator, may my family, servants, and disciples [*sikhya*] be ever happy. (378)
May you give me your hand in protection. May you destroy all my enemies today.
May my hope be fulfilled that I always thirst to remain your devotee. (379)

May I rest in concentration on no one but you. If I have a wish, may you alone fulfill it.
May you carry my servants and disciples to the other shore. May you single out each and every one of my enemies and destroy them. (380)

May your hands save me. May you destroy my fear of death.
Forever remain on our side. Protect me, O Revered Sword-Banner Lord [*srī asidhuj jī*]. (381)

O Protector, protect me. You are the beloved Lord and aid to good people.
A friend to those in need, destroyer of the wicked. You are the Lord of all fourteen worlds. (382)

After additional verses in a similar vein, this final *charitra* concludes with lines in which the poet praised the lord who assisted him in completing this *granth*:

Lord Whose Sign is the Sword, I am under your protection. Give me your hand that I may be saved.
May you grant me your assistance everywhere. May you save me from enemies and error. (401)
The World-Mother [*jagamātā*][18] took mercy on me, and I completed this book one splendid evening.
The one who takes away all the body's misdeeds, the one who destroys enemies and error. (402)

When the Sword-Banner Lord was generous, only then did I complete this book.

May [those who read or recite it] attain their heart's desires, may no sorrows reach them. (403)

A mute person who hears this will find his tongue.
A fool who puts his mind to it will become clever.
The man who recites these verses but once will be free from sorrow, pain, and fear. (404)

First, say seventeen hundred *sambat*, then add half of one hundred, and then three [i.e., 1753 Samvat, i.e., roughly 1696 C.E.].
On Sunday, the eighth day of the light half of the month Bhādrav [August–September], this book was completed on the banks of the Satudrava [Sutlej] River.

With these lines *Charitropakhian* comes to a close. There is no conclusion to the story of Dulaha and her desire to marry Kal. Interestingly, the text also concludes without any explanation of how the king and his son responded to these stories. We do not learn whether or not the king went through with his plan to execute his son, or whether he somehow punished or rejected his scheming wife. As a result, some commentators have wondered whether the composition is incomplete or missing some parts, or perhaps is composed of sections that were not meant to go together. If the date is correct, *Charitropakhian* was composed several years before the establishment of the Khalsa in 1699.

In his discussion of the closing *charitra*, Jaggi (1965, 187–188; 1966, 183) noted that while the story seems Puranic in style and has some characters mentioned in other sources (e.g., Sati Sandhi or Satyasandha as Dhritarashtra's [Dhṛtarāṣṭra] son and Mahakal as one of Kartikeya's attendants in the *Mahabharata*, Mahakal as one of Shiva's avatars in the *Shiva Purana*), the story of the battle as described here is not found in Puranic sources. For Jaggi, this was further evidence that there were multiple poets involved in producing *Charitropakhian* haphazardly stitching together disparate stories. He also argued that the story of Mahakal and Kali suggested the theological perspective of Shakta Tantra, an issue to be explored in the following chapter. Commentators who conclude that Guru Gobind Singh could not have authored this composition have generally taken divergences from traditional stories such as those in *charitra* 404 as indicative of authorial shortcomings. It is worth considering, however, that some of the events in the closing *charitra*, especially the creation of Pathans, Mughals, and so forth in an otherwise "Puranic" context, may represent a creative effort on the poet's part to link the themes of divine and worldly battle, a linkage that is implicit in other portions of the Dasam Granth.

Understanding the *Charitras*

As noted earlier, the content of *Charitropakhian* has been seen as so problematic that many editions of the Dasam Granth omit it entirely (e.g., those published by the Publications Bureau of Punjabi University), and many Sikh authors have dismissed it as unworthy of sustained analysis. Khushwant Singh (1977, vol. 1, 316), for example, expressed the view that "it is most unlikely that the Guru as the spiritual leader of his people would have ever allowed his name to be associated with a composition of the type of *Pakhyāṇ Caritr*. His lofty character and the value he set on Spartan living do not go with the prurience of the kind found in some of the passages of the Dasam Granth." Pritpal Singh Bindra undertook English translation of *Charitropakhian* in part to demonstrate that its contents are so shockingly obscene that they could not possibly have been composed by Guru Gobind Singh. The content of these stories is thus a significant component of the evidence cited by those who believe Guru Gobind Singh did not compose the entire Dasam Granth.

Among those who believe that Guru Gobind Singh did compose these stories, however, the most frequent explanation for their content is that the stories were meant to serve as the basis for moral instruction for a restricted audience of male soldiers, far from home and in need of guidance. Virtually all Sikh commentators (themselves nearly all male) have argued that these stories could only have been intended for a strictly male audience; certainly the context of the stories being told by the king's ministers suggests a male audience. However, while many *charitras* end with some general statement about how no one can understand the character of women, and how it is dangerous for men to reveal their secrets to them, the moral implications of the stories are not drawn out in any greater detail than this within the composition itself.

In this regard the *charitras* are quite similar to the stories in collections such as the Sanskrit *Panchatantra*, which, as Edgerton (1965) argued, illustrate practical wisdom and shrewdness rather than advocating a particular moral code. The frame story of *Charitropakhian* shows that the *charitras* were presented orally, and perhaps the written text was also intended primarily for oral presentation, which could have included discussion of the moral import of particular *charitras*. Still, those who consider Guru Gobind Singh the author of these tales and who make the moral instruction argument typically do not explore what the specific morals of particular stories might be beyond a rather vague notion of "feminine wiles." Dharam Pal Ashta, for example, wrote:

> Such stories may not be a pleasant reading, but they do imply lessons of warning to the reader against feminine wiles. Most of them belong to the upper classes among whom the women lead, for the most part, an easy and idle life, and few being ill-matched or oversexed take to intrigues to break the monotony of their dull life. (Ashta 1959, 153)

In a similar vein, Giani Ishar Singh Nara (1985, 49–50) concluded that Guru Gobind Singh did author these stories because "sex appeal is a matter which, due to undisciplined mind, most people are likely to fall prey to. He wanted to put his Sikhs on the guard against vily [*sic*] conduct of women, so that, while living in society as householders, they might keep their conduct above board.... Unless varying life situations are presented in their contexts, it becomes difficult to understand the realities, good as well as bad." Tāran Singh (1967, 251–262) took a slightly different approach and argued that Guru Gobind Singh sought to portray every aspect of life and human behavior; he also suggested that one way of reading the *charitras* is through a more metaphoric interpretation of the female characters as the human body, and the male characters as the intellect.

Thus as with other compositions in the Dasam Granth, authorship has been the dominant issue shaping the interpretation and analysis of the stories of *Charitropakhian*. In the case of those who have argued that Guru Gobind Singh did not author the stories, the need for sustained analysis of them is diminished because the stories are not the work of the Guru. Such arguments are typically based on a specific understanding of the character of Guru Gobind Singh (e.g., Pritpal Singh Bindra's paper "Could Guru Gobind Singh Write Such Things?" [2000]) and/or a specific understanding of the spirit of the Sikh faith that becomes the criterion against which to judge various portions of the Dasam Granth. There are also text-critical arguments regarding authorship, such as analysis of the use of pen names within *Charitropakhian* (the names "Ram," "Siam," and "Kal" occur in a number of the *charitras*), part of the larger argument that some portion of the Dasam Granth was the work of court poets by these and other names, and not Guru Gobind Singh.

In the context of this ongoing authorship debate, the options for understanding *Charitropakhian* as a text in its own right, and as a part of the Dasam Granth as a whole, have become limited. If the stories are rejected as a part of Sikh scripture or literature on the basis of their obscenity, the discussion comes to a standstill. The argument that the stories were intended only for the moral instruction of Guru Gobind Singh's army also usually does not include any detailed analysis of what morals the stories teach, nor does it address the perplexing question of what exactly a diverse group of soldiers was supposed to learn from stories of conniving women who were mostly affiliated with royal households, given that these were not likely to be the kinds of women these soldiers would meet.

Due to its content, *Charitropakhian* has remained perhaps the most controversial composition within a text that is controversial to begin with. And because the controversy over the stories is almost always framed within the authorship debate, the discussion of the stories has not moved forward. One way to move beyond this seeming impasse is to frame the stories differently, within long-standing Indic traditions of storytelling and performance in general, and courtly literature in particular. From this perspective, the structure and contents of *Charitropakhian* may begin to make more sense, and also generate a new set of potentially fruitful questions about such literature and storytelling, as well as evolving conceptions of Guruship and kingship in the Punjab region.

Many, indeed most, interpreters of *Charitropakhian* have already employed the tactic of identifying the wide-ranging sources of the *charitras* with very broad strokes. There is not much controversy in noting that stories in *Charitropakhian* about Krishna and the *gopis*, Nala and Damayanti, and romances such as Hir/Ranjha, Sohni/Mahinwal, and Yusuf/Zulaikha are part of larger Indian, Middle Eastern, or in some cases more specifically north Indian and Punjabi traditions. For example, in the introduction to their 1999 English translation of portions of the Dasam Granth, Drs. Jodh Singh and Dharam Singh (1999, vol. 1, xi) note that *Charitropakhian* "is a collection of stories of Indian as well as foreign origin" and that "writing about women's wiles was the in thing in Hindi Literature of the Guru's days." Jaggi (1966, 164–165) argued that the roots of some of the stories lie in Puranic literature, and he further saw the influence of "left-handed Tantra" in *Charitropakhian*. Dharam Pal Ashta (1959, 151) charted eight main sources for the *charitras*,[19] including the epics, Puranas,[20] *Panchatantra*, *Hitopadesha*, Rajput stories, Persian texts, and events from immediate history under Pathan and Mughal rule. In his survey of Punjabi literature, Mohan Singh, attributing the stories largely to court poets, wrote:

> The *Tiria Charittar* of Ram and Shyam is, like the Italian *Cento Novelle Antiche*, an encyclopaedia of almost all Panjabi, non-Panjabi, Indian and non-Indian tales known to Mediaeval India, in mixed Panjabi and Braji.... It is a veritable mine of history, mythology, geography and legendary lore, of customs and prejudices, which ought to be utilized by all folk-lorists and mediaeval historians. The narration is brief and rapid; phraseology apt and pregnant; style, adequate generally and at required place impassionate, elaborate or sententious; psychology, extremely interesting so far as the woman huntress is concerned; and amassing of facts, most remarkable and inclusive. (Mohan Singh 1971, 69)

Thus scholars writing specifically about the Dasam Granth and more generally about Punjabi literature have noted the vast range of these stories. Yet while it has been widely acknowledged that the stories of *Charitropakhian* have their origins in Indian storytelling traditions, there has not been much attempt to push this analysis further.

There are clues within the stories themselves that suggest an affinity with the conventions of classical Indian story literature. The frame story itself involves a king, his ministers, and his son. The frame story also describes how Chitra Singh killed Chitravati's father but also indicates that he wed her "according to the *Shastras*." On a slightly different *shastric* note, the illicit lovers of these tales are frequently described as following the dictates of the *Kokashastra* in their amorous pursuits. The majority of the women (and men) behaving badly are queens and princesses. Thus these tales may be situated within the realm of long-standing Indic traditions of courtly literature for the moral instruction of kings and their associates, in which it is the king's ministers' responsibility to advise him and keep him from making poor decisions in both his political and personal life. The *Arthashastra* (Rangarajan 1992, 144), Kautilya's classic Sanskrit text on kingship and statecraft, notes that "a king who has no self-control and gives himself up to excessive indulgence in pleasures will soon perish, even if he is the ruler of all four corners of the earth [*Arthashastra* 1.6.4]." The king's personal conduct is thus a factor in his ability to fulfill his wider responsibility to ensure the propagation and protection of dharma within his realm. The Sodhak Committee Report (1897, chap. 1.11) briefly acknowledges this aspect of *Charitropakhian* in its characterization of the composition as a "treasury of *raj-niti* [*rāj nītī*; statecraft, politics] and practical knowledge." The need for kings to develop expertise in *nīti* is highlighted in the frame stories of two of India's most famous story collections, the *Panchatantra* and the *Hitopadesha*. Both begin with a frame story in which a king is in despair, fearing that his sons are not smart enough to complete a thorough study of statecraft. The king then enlists a wise scholar to educate his sons in six months using stories, rather than pursuing a lengthier, intensive instruction in classical texts.

Indian literature in both Sanskrit and various Prakrits from many parts of the subcontinent provides many examples of anthologies that contain sections similar to *Charitropakhian*. Produced at royal courts, such anthologies often seek to address the three human aims, or *purusharthas* [*puruṣārthas*], the *trivarga* of dharma, *artha*, and *kama* [*kāma*], a theme that is noted at the beginning of the *Panchatantra* as well. That is, they address matters of religious duty, the pursuit of material well-being, and love and desire. Dasgupta and De (1947, 367), in their study of the history of Sanskrit literature, noted that Sanskrit poetry very frequently addresses these matters of religious devotion, worldly wisdom, and love. The Dasam Granth in its entirety similarly incorporates all these themes.[21]

Historians of Sanskrit literature have also noted that in court anthologies, it is often *kama* that receives the most attention.[22] Similarly, *Charitropakhian*, which is clearly focused on *kama* and, to a somewhat lesser extent, *artha*, makes up a substantial portion of the Dasam Granth, with other compositions treating issues of dharma (which subsumes the other two *purusharthas* of *artha* and *kama*) in more detail.

In the world of kings and royal households in which many of the stories of *Charitropakhian* are set, women often lived as co-wives. In that environment, women were traditionally seen as particularly prone to deceit, for they had to conspire to gain and maintain the king's favor or look for diversion if they were not the king's favorite.[23] Thus the admonition to be wary of women was particularly relevant to kings; it is clearly reflected in the frame story in which Chitra Singh cannot believe that his new wife tried to seduce his son. The faithfulness of women was also of course important with respect to matters of succession.

Even beyond the particular environment of the royal court, the portrayal of women in India's story literature generally is very much akin to that in *Charitropakhian*. For example, J. A. B. van Buitenen's characterization of women as they are depicted in the stories that are part of the *Bṛhat Kathā* tradition preserved in texts such as the Sanskrit *Kathāsaritsāgara* ["Ocean of Story"][24] is equally applicable to *Charitropakhian*:

> While the more official literature likes to show the Indian woman in the light of dharma—the many saintly wives who retrieved their husbands from death, who followed them through the most outrageous perils—as striking examples of how a woman should behave, the story literature displays its women in the light of *artha*, of practical profit and wit. The result is a far more human picture. The woman of the story literature appears as a spirited, quick-witted, lusty creature who often can think rings around her men. The modesty so interminably enjoined upon her by the sacred writings is about as common as the frequency of the admonitions might lead us to suspect. If she is a wife, there is a constant suspicion that she might be unfaithful. (van Buitenen 1974, 210–211)

Just as the portrayal of women as quick-witted though potentially deceitful is common in Indian story literature, so too is the theme of a minister who uses stories to advise the king or princes, the *Panchatantra* and *Hitopadesha* being classic examples. The frame story of *Charitropakhian* is in some ways reminiscent of another example of Sanskrit story literature, the *Shukasaptati* [*Śukasaptati*], or "Seventy Tales of the Parrot," in which a parrot tells seventy stories on successive evenings to distract a young wife who is planning to go out to meet her lover while her husband is away on business.[25] In *Charitropakhian*, initially at least the stories are presented as being told on successive mornings when the king allows his son to be brought out of captivity for instruction. Pointing out such similarities of course does not prove a direct historical connection between *Charitropakhian* and such texts, but it does demonstrate that *Charitropakhian* is similar to a style of story collection with a long history in India, meant not necessarily for the moral instruction of armies but for the particular situation in which kings found themselves.

As such, the stories of *Charitropakhian* may be read as concerning the obligations of rulers, those to whom is entrusted the task of preserving the proper order of dharma. *Bachitra Natak* addressed the responsibilities of Guru Gobind Singh in the context of his dharma as a ruler who had to lead armies in battle in order to create a stable environment in which good people might flourish; the goddess compositions considered the maintenance of dharma through the lens of ongoing battles between gods and demons, and the rulers' battles and the gods' battles were explicitly equated with one another. In its opening and closing *charitras*, *Charitropakhian* addresses these exact same concerns and in the tales in between addresses the dharma of a ruler with respect to the issue of personal relationships, especially those between men and women. Further, this notion of the ruler's dharma is explicitly discussed in the Anup Kaur tales in which the ruler explains why he cannot pursue an extramarital liaison.

Viewed in this light of cosmic and personal dharma, there is indeed a thematic connection between the "tricky tales" of *Charitropakhian* and the rest of the Dasam Granth, and we may begin to see the text as a whole as an attempt at compiling as much knowledge about human endeavor and the cosmos as possible. As such, it is an important example of the continuation of such efforts in the vernacular languages of India, reflecting both the classical concerns of Sanskrit literature and the evolving conceptions of Brajbhasha literature. The stories of *Charitropakhian* frequently employ the conventions of Sanskrit poetry [*kāvya*] in their descriptions of characters (women's beauty in particular) and scenes as well as in use of metaphor and simile. But some of the conventions of what for lack of a better term we might call a "high" culture of Sanskrit learning are not in play. This seems particularly true for the many references to the *Kokashastra*, which on first reading might seem to refer to the twelfth-century Sanskrit text by Kokkoka more properly entitled *Ratirahasya*, but in fact seems more likely to be to a series of manuals containing artistic representations of sexual positions known as *Kokashastra*. Such manuals were commonly produced and circulated at royal courts in northern India. The references to *Kokashastra* in the *charitras* refer almost exclusively to sexual activity.[26] While the women of *Charitropakhian* are themselves almost always the seductresses, the Sanskrit *Kokashastra* is a more elaborate text that provides guidelines to men for wooing a woman who at first glance seems unattainable, part of which involves determining to which of four classes she belongs (*padminī*, *citrinī*, *śankhinī*, *hastinī*).[27] Neither the women nor the men in *Charitropakhian* seem the least bit concerned with such finer details of seduction and romance.

While the distillation of the finer points of *Kokashastra* into sexual positions alone may indicate a certain impoverishment with respect to classical Sanskrit tradition treating the issue of *kama*, the vast range of stories in *Charitropakhian* also demonstrates the enrichment of classical story literature by the specific cultural context of the Punjab and its folk traditions. Thus we find Nala and Damayanti, rendered many times in Indian literature, but also Hir and Ranjha, a classic Punjabi love story in which the main characters are Muslim. And in the stories related to royal courts, we meet not just Khatris but Pathans and Mughals as well. As such, *Charitropakhian* exemplifies a rich heritage of storytelling in the Punjab, a storytelling culture exploring practical wisdom and love, often bawdy, shared across traditional religious boundaries. Such boundary-crossing is evidenced not only in *Charitropakhian* but throughout the Punjab's vernacular storytelling tradition. In Waris Shah's 1766 version of the romance of Hir and Ranjha, for example,

Ranjha, a Jat Muslim, takes on the disguise of a Kanphat yogi so that he can secretly meet Hir. Interestingly, just as with *Charitropakhian*, some critics have chastised Waris Shah for pushing the boundaries of propriety in his vivid description of Ranjha and Hir's love.[28] In analyzing this storytelling tradition, it is necessary to acknowledge another set of sharp boundaries, namely, the line between propriety and obscenity, and the line between sincere religious behavior and blatant hypocrisy. Corrupt religious authorities of all stripes—Hindu, Sikh, Muslim—come in for sharp derision from all sides in this shared storytelling tradition. The *qazi* is easily duped, and the seemingly pious yogi may well be out to seduce young women.

In the context of studies of Sikhism in colonial and independent India, when the Dasam Granth was cast into a new category as a text with "scriptural" or "holy" status, the stories of *Charitropakhian* were an embarrassment to some Sikh reformers, leading to their frequent denunciation and even deletion in studies of the text as a whole. More recent conceptualizations of the nature of scripture seem to exclude the types of stories found in *Charitropakhian*. Yet an analysis of this composition in its entirety, in particular with close attention to the opening and closing *charitras*, reveals that the stories share many common themes with other compositions in the Dasam Granth, as well as with the broader Punjabi storytelling tradition. In fact, the nature of these stories suggests that a useful model for reading the Dasam Granth in its entirety is that of the courtly anthology that seeks to compile knowledge of the *purusharthas*, or human goals, an issue to which I turn in the concluding chapter.

Conclusion

Is the Dasam Granth a "holy book"?

It is worthwhile to return to a more pointed version of the question that opened this study of the Dasam Granth. It should be clear that there is no single conclusive answer for Sikhs as to whether or not the Dasam Granth is a "holy book," and that Sikhs and scholars have gone about answering the question of its "holiness" in a variety of ways. The genealogy and life story of a remarkable spiritual leader and the tales of avatars and goddesses who defeat demons can easily fit into many understandings of what a "holy book" might contain (though the avatar and goddess compositions are troubling to some). The "tricky tales," however, present more of a challenge as a component in a "holy book." *Charitropakhian* in particular appears to have inspired the popular distinction between portions of the Dasam Granth deemed "literature" and those deemed "scripture."

Many assessments of the text's holy status hinge upon an argument about authorship, which in turn has led to a variety of categorization schema for the Dasam Granth as a text in its entirety, none of which is particularly satisfying as a means of understanding the text as a whole. For those who believe that Guru Gobind Singh composed only some of the Dasam Granth, the primary categorization scheme includes some version of the following: compositions definitely composed by the Guru, compositions possibly composed by the Guru, and compositions produced by court poets. Such categorization schema thus are more focused on the issue of authorship rather than discovering any unifying principles or themes throughout the whole text. On the other hand, those who consider Guru Gobind Singh the author of the entire text often assert his authorship as the only necessary unifying principle. For example, in a brief statement at the beginning of Rattan Singh Jaggi and Gursharan Kaur Jaggi's 1999 edition of the Dasam Granth, Baba Virsa Singh (1999, vol. 1, i) suggests that accepting some parts of the Dasam Granth and not others is like telling someone you like their arms but not their head. He is thereby implying that the text is a unified whole to be taken as such because its author was Guru Gobind Singh.

The unrelenting focus on issues of authorship as the primary determinant of holy status has tended to overshadow consideration of key themes that run through the text as a whole, and therefore hindered understandings of why such a seemingly disparate set of compositions might have been compiled together. The paucity and disputed nature of the earliest evidence for the compilation of the text have meant that there is as yet no conclusive answer as to why these compositions were put together—it might have been because they were all considered to be the work of Guru Gobind Singh, or perhaps because they were works associated with his court. How or indeed even if the different parts of the Dasam Granth fit together has remained a challenging question.[1]

Absent definitive evidence about the original rationale for grouping these compositions together, both Sikh and Western historians have proposed a range of categories into which portions of the text may be placed. Rattan Singh Jaggi (1966) proposed four: compositions related to devotional or bhakti poetry, compositions praising weapons in Puranic style, Puranic compositions, and independent compositions. In his study of Sikh history, Khushwant Singh (1977, vol. 1, 313) also divided the Dasam Granth into four parts: mythological, philosophical, autobiographical, and erotic. W. H. McLeod (1976, 80) proposed four somewhat different categories: autobiographical works, works of militant piety, miscellaneous works, and works of legend and anecdote. Harjot Oberoi (1994, 95) used the categories of devotional poetry, biographical history, mythical narrative, and folktales and list of weapons. Jeevan Deol (2001a, 30) suggested that the Dasam Granth contains theological, mythological, and narrative works. As the rather general nature (e.g., "independent," "miscellaneous," "legend and anecdote," "folk tales," "narrative") and variation within the category schema suggest, there is as yet no scholarly consensus on how best to categorize the Dasam Granth in its entirety. Nor have scholars reached any agreement on how these categories may relate to one another or why such a diverse group of compositions came together in a single text. Nonetheless, there have been attempts to identify unifying themes in some portions of the Dasam Granth.

In his article "Eighteenth Century Khalsa Identity: Discourse, Praxis and Narrative," Deol (2001a, 31) noted that the warfare and conflict as well as the tendency to view the deity as weaponry are recurring motifs throughout the Dasam Granth. Deol (2001a, 32–33) focused particularly on the compositions within the Dasam Granth that are identifiable as part of the *Bachitra Natak Granth*, that is, *Bachitra Natak* itself and *Chandi Charitra* 2, *Chaubis Avatar*, *Brahma Avatar*, and *Rudra Avatar*, noting that if the intended unity of these compositions is taken into account, it "yields an organic whole which progresses from praises of Akal Purakh through an account of the life of Guru Gobind Singh to Chandi and the incarnations of Vishnu, Brahma and Rudra." Deol further suggested that reading the *Bachitra Natak Granth* as a whole shows that the avatar narratives are subordinate to the life story of Guru Gobind Singh and his mission to reestablish dharma. Deol (2001a, 39–40) went on to argue that the text became a Puranic metanarrative that was central to the development of Khalsa identity in the eighteenth century, situating the Panth "within a longer mythological time-cycle in which it is part of a larger design to fight the forces of evil" and creating a reinterpretation of dharma that included notions of rule and political sovereignty. Deol's analysis considers the Dasam Granth specifically in the context of eighteenth-century Khalsa identity formation and compares the developing concept of dharma relative to other north Indian religious movements of the time. He concluded (2001a, 40) that the Khalsa notion of dharma "valorizes ideas of rule and political sovereignty in a way that classical definitions and others contemporary to the Khalsa do not" because it embraces "wider political and cosmological claims," but he did not explore this intriguing claim in further detail.

If we broaden our consideration of dharma, however, it becomes clear that not only does the eighteenth-century Khalsa conception of dharma develop notions of rule and political sovereignty, but that the Dasam Granth itself may be read as a contribution to a long-standing discourse within Indian culture concerning the dharmic responsibilities of those who rule and/or have some type of spiritual authority. Examining notions of kingship along with other ideas about the roles of both spiritual and worldly leaders suggests that while the Dasam Granth does address the nature of rule and political sovereignty, particularly as it relates to spiritual leadership, it does so in a way that reveals both innovation and continuity with long-standing Indic traditions.

As Deol argued, the *Bachitra Natak* narrative of Guru Gobind Singh's ancestry and life is key to the broader themes that run through other portions of the text, particularly within the *Bachitra Natak Granth*. If we consider the narrative of Guru Gobind Singh's life in *Bachitra Natak* specifically in light of Indic discourse on the dharma of kingship and leadership in general, the presence of Dasam Granth compositions not part of *Bachitra Natak Granth* that have challenged interpreters, such as *Shastra-nam-mala* and particularly *Charitropakhian* and *Hikaitan*, begins to make more sense.

Bachitra Natak places Guru Gobind Singh in a lineage that includes kings, avatars, and gurus, situating the entire lineage in the cosmic framework of the *yugas*, or eras. In most such frameworks, the relative strength or weakness of dharma is a defining feature; indeed, in Puranic mythology the *yugas* are defined by the gradual weakening of dharma and the need for its periodic strengthening or restoration by avatars. As we saw in chapter 2, the theme of dharma is central to *Bachitra Natak* and its account of the Sikh Gurus in particular; Guru Nanak propagated dharma, Guru Tegh Bahadur sacrificed his life for it, and the Supreme Lord ordered Guru Gobind Singh himself to take birth and "set dharma in motion." The theme of dharma under threat runs through the goddess compositions as well. When the gods lose their power to demons, they cannot fulfill their responsibilities to oversee dharma, and "good people" cannot follow the proper path in their lives. In all these cases, battle must be undertaken in defense of dharma.

In much recent Sikh exegesis, the themes of dharma, particularly as they relate to the figure of the avatar, have raised the specter of excessive Hindu influence in much of the Dasam Granth. This is perhaps because commentators making such arguments are operating with an understanding of Hinduism that derives from colonial and postcolonial discourse about the nature of religious identity and Sikhism as distinct tradition as famously articulated in Bhai Kahn Singh Nabha's 1898 tract, *Ham Hindū Nahīn* (We Are Not Hindus). It is important to remember, however, that dharma is by no means strictly a "Hindu" concept, and that the Dasam Granth predates the colonial discourse on religious boundaries.

If we acknowledge that dharma is a broad, fluid concept adopted in a range of Indic religious traditions and not simply those associated with recent conceptualizations of Hinduism, we create more space to examine its articulation in Sikh tradition and can move beyond anachronistic notions of whether the Dasam Granth is in some way "Hindu" or not to a more nuanced analysis of the ways Sikhism has appropriated and modified Hindu ideas. As an example, many centuries before the beginnings of Sikhism, Buddhism developed its own understanding of dharma, which was distinct from then-current Hindu or Brahmanical notions of dharma. Even within sectarian Hinduism there are varying explanations of dharma and which deities are primarily responsible for its maintenance.

Central to most Indic dharmic discourse, however, is the importance of leadership figures who monitor dharma, be they kings, gurus, avatars, or deities. These leadership roles and the symbols that articulate their power often overlap. Avatars themselves in many theologies are in some way partially or entirely deities, and figures such as Ram are recognized both as kings and as avatars. Similarly, spiritual leaders such as the Buddha (like the Sikh Gurus, generally believed to have been born into the Kshatriya *varna*) have typically been represented with royal imagery, and rulers often assume the traits of spiritual leaders. The king is enjoined to rule with the wisdom of the sage in the ideal figure of the *rajarshi* [*rājarṣi*] described in Kautilya's *Arthashastra*. Among his many qualities, the *rajarshi* "is ever active in promoting the security and welfare of the people, [and] ensures the observance [by the people] of their dharma by authority and example" (Rangarajan 1992, 145). As discussed in chapter 3, studies of Indian kingship have noted the connection between Vishnu and kings, as well as the connection between the goddess and kings. The connection between the role of the goddess and the role of the ruler is clearly highlighted in several portions of the Dasam Granth.

Similarly, much of the epic literature that receives attention in the [Dasa]m Granth—in the form of stories from the Ramayana and

Mahabharata—is focused on questions regarding the dharmic responsibilities of those who would rule, and the battles that ensue when rule has been usurped. The Dasam Granth presents its own versions of some of those narratives of kingship, for example, in the *Gian Prabodh* accounts of Yudhishthira, Janmejaya, and other Mahabharata kings; in the *Chaubis Avatar* accounts of figures such as Manu, Ram, and Krishna; in portions of *Brahma Avatar*; and those discussed in more detail in previous chapters as well. *Zafarnama* too may be read in part as a condemnation of a ruler's failings and an analysis of the circumstances under which it is proper to wage battle against the reigning sovereign, in this case because of the Mughal emperor Aurangzeb's failure to keep his promises.

Battles are of course conducted with weapons, a key theme in many of the Dasam Granth's compositions. Weapons and their use are described throughout the text's many battle narratives and are the main topic of the lengthy *Shastra-nam-mala*. In this composition in particular, weapons provide a direct link between the world of the gods and the world of humans. The gods frequently bestow weapons with unique powers on humans, and *Shastra-nam-mala* also provides instructions on the mantras that a fighter may use to imbue his weapons with divine power. They are indispensable to the frequent struggles to maintain dharma that both the gods and humans pursue.

The fact that issues of kingship and rule recur throughout the Dasam Granth suggests that a central theme of the text is not simply weaponry, battle, and the inspiration of warriors but the role of the figure who leads battles for righteous causes. Just as the roles and symbols for spiritual and worldly leaders have intermingled throughout Indian history, so too was Sikhism evolving its own understanding of the Guru as a leader who wielded both temporal and spiritual authority. This intermingling of roles is typically traced to the sixth Guru, Guru Hargobind, who is credited with establishing the notion of the Sikh Gurus as the repository of both *miri* (temporal power) and *piri* (spiritual power), symbolized by two swords. Significantly, this idea is expressed in Perso-Arabic derived vocabulary, indicating that in the Punjab, which had been in direct and indirect contact with Islamic rule for many centuries, there was a range of ideas about leadership from which to draw.[2] As the narrative of *Bachitra Natak* and other sources concerning Guru

Gobind Singh's life make clear, the Guru lived his life in the context of the militarily oriented culture of the Punjab hill chiefs with their ever-shifting alliances and disputes among themselves and with the forces of the Mughal empire.

The office of Guru that Guru Gobind Singh assumed thus carried with it a complex set of interlocking associations—the traditional Indic idea of the guru as spiritual preceptor, the Sikh doctrine of the Guruship passing as light from one Guru to the next, the concept of Guru as expressed in the sacred words, or *bani*, of the Gurus, but also the Guru as a political leader, with training in weaponry and armed forces at his command. It is also clear that Guru Gobind Singh gave neighboring hill chiefs the impression that he was not just a spiritual leader but the leader of a military force with which to be reckoned. The dual nature of the Gurus' role is also captured in terms such as *sachchā pātishāh*, or "true king/emperor."[3] It therefore makes good sense that the compositions associated with Guru Gobind Singh should explore all these dimensions of Sikh Guruship as it had by then evolved.

The special mission of certain people to defend dharma—whether a king, an avatar, or even an avatar who rules as a king—is a theme that recurs throughout Indic explorations of leadership. Sikh conceptualizations of leadership were still evolving during Guru Gobind Singh's time, and they would shift substantially after his death brought an end to the line of human Gurus. The Dasam Granth articulates a new, distinctly Sikh role for the Guru and the concept of dharma, expressed in part through the need for Sikh leaders to protect Indian heritage as a whole. In *Bachitra Natak*, the Sikh Gurus are described in terms very much reminiscent of those used for the avatars of Hindu mythology. But it is crucial to note that later Gurus such as Guru Tegh Bahadur and Guru Gobind Singh also took on the role of a military and political leader. The Dasam Granth highlights the fact that their ancestors similarly fulfilled both roles, and this may be one reason the text focuses so much attention on avatars who ruled as kings. As such, the text illustrates both continuities with and innovations within traditional Indian conceptions of leadership and the role of the king. This is not to argue, however, that the Dasam Granth simply reflects a Sikh appropriation of classical Indic conception of kingship. Even in cases in which there is clear continuity with earlier ideas of kingship, there are also noteworthy differences.

The role of the king has long been associated with the Kshatriya *varna*, and in classical Indian texts concerning dharma one of the king's main obligations is to ensure that the members of each *varna* follow their proper responsibilities. There is some hint of this in *Bachitra Natak* insofar as the Sikh Gurus were all born into the Kshatriya *varna*, as well as in the text's discussion of the earlier time when the *varnas* had become mixed up, but there is no emphasis on Guru Gobind Singh taking the promotion of proper *varna* duties as part of his mission.

Significantly, the Dasam Granth also does not articulate any sense of divine kingship in the Gurus' role. In the *Bachitra Natak* account of Guru Gobind Singh's birth, for example, the Guru proclaims that those who consider him as lord [*paramesura*] will fall into the pits of hell (BN 32). Instead, there is the notion of the office of the Guru as carrying divinity, a divinity that in subsequent Sikh tradition would be vested in the *Adi Granth* and the Sikh *panth*, or community, itself. The Dasam Granth also places less emphasis on the traditional Indic notion that one of the king's key responsibilities is to protect Brahmans. This theme to be sure is reflected in the *Bachitra Natak* description of the reasons behind Guru Tegh Bahadur's martyrdom; perhaps we may read this as reflecting the ongoing trajectory of Sikhism's development into a community more clearly differentiated from various "Hindu" groups.

Another classic responsibility of the Indian king is the sponsorship of elaborate Vedic rituals. This theme is highlighted in several portions of the Dasam Granth, most notably in the *Gian Prabodh* descriptions of a series of kings and the sacrifices they sponsored. The sponsorship of rituals also involves the patronage of the male Brahman priests required to carry out the rituals. Such rituals serve as a means of demonstrating the king's power and authority both to his own subjects and to neighboring rulers, and also establish a connection between the king and the world of the gods to whom the sacrifices are offered. While the Dasam Granth certainly describes the Sikh Gurus' ancestors as having expertise in and sponsoring such rituals, it does not portray the Gurus themselves as sponsors of Vedic rituals. In the case of Guru Gobind Singh in particular, the Dasam Granth suggests a shift away from Vedic ritual to the ritual empowerment and use of weapons in battles waged for the protection of dharma. As *Shastra-nam-mala* demonstrates in particular, the ritual empowerment and use of various weapons is a key means of establishing a direct connection between divine and human worlds, and pursuing the protection of dharma at all levels. Indeed, there are several points at which the sight of enemies' wounds inflicted by weapons is compared to recitation of the names of God. It is also significant that a number of Dasam Granth compositions continue a theme expressed in many of the verses of the earlier Sikh Gurus, that of the wastefulness and ineffective nature of most religious ritualism be it Hindu or Muslim, as well as the inability of Hindu and Muslim texts, Puranas and Qur'ans, to capture fully the true nature of divinity.

There is no doubt that battle is a central theme throughout the Dasam Granth, for example, throughout the avatar narratives, the goddess compositions, *Gian Prabodh*, many of the *charitras* in *Charitropakhian*, and of course especially in *Bachitra Natak*. Indeed, the theme of battle in defense of the good particularly unites *Bachitra Natak*, the goddess compositions, and much of *Charitropakhian*. The violence of the battles between the goddess and demons and between the Guru and enemy forces is described in very similar terms.[4] Both are part of the ongoing struggle to maintain proper order in the cosmos. Sikh exegesis has tended to emphasize the notion that these battle stories were primarily meant to serve as inspiration for warriors. If we read them in the context of the types of literature traditionally produced in the courts of Indian kings, however, it becomes clear that they also continue a long-standing tradition of poetry in both Sanskrit and Indian vernacular languages extolling the battle exploits of rulers.

The literary anthologies extolling kings produced at royal courts often also included a wide range of other material that was quite often loosely organized along the lines of the *purusharthas*, or human aims, the classical *trivarga* of dharma, *artha*, and *kama*. As noted in chapter 4, this is also a potentially fruitful means of reading the Dasam Granth and is yet another instance of how the text reflects both continuity and innovation with respect to classical Indian literary tradition. For our purposes it is helpful once again to acknowledge but set aside the question of authorship and instead posit that the Dasam Granth represents an eighteenth-century example of an anthology composed of diverse materials. It is of course in some way associated with Guru Gobind Singh, who (like many Indian rulers), it is generally believed, both composed poetry himself and sponsored other poets in his court.

Indeed, there are several points within the Dasam Granth itself at which royal courts of both the gods and humans are described.

We may then ask a different series of questions about the Dasam Granth. How does this text relate to other anthology forms found in Indian literature, particularly those associated with royal courts? This is an area in which much research remains to be done both for Sanskrit and for the vernacular languages of the Indian subcontinent, but even a brief survey of what is known about royal anthologies suggests significant similarities with the Dasam Granth. For example, Winternitz's (1959, 67–68, 116–117, 156–184) study of Sanskrit *kavya*, or "ornate poetry," describes multiple anthologies containing compositions of a similar range to those found in the Dasam Granth, some of which are explicitly organized according to the *trivarga*. Many include historical poems honoring the royal patrons who sponsored poets, praising kings and detailing their victories in battle, as well as retellings of myth from the epics and Puranas, devotional poetry in praise of particular gods and goddesses, and lengthy sections containing erotic poetry. A number also include treatises on poetics. While there are no such treatises within the Dasam Granth, the frequent references to the nature of poetic expression, such as the use of metaphor and simile and mention of the *rasa* associated with a particular passage, indicate a relative degree of familiarity with *alaṃkāraśāstra* and traditional Indian theories of poetic composition and performance.

There are of course limitations to any argument regarding how and why the different compositions in the Dasam Granth may have been put together. For example, there were multiple versions of the text in circulation, with varying number and ordering of compositions, prior to the creation of the standardized print edition. We do not have fully conclusive evidence regarding the exact time, circumstances, or rationale for the compilation of the text that came to be known as the Dasam Granth. The evidence that the different compositions in the Dasam Granth may be organized according to the *trivarga* is of course circumstantial; the text itself does not explicitly indicate such a classificatory scheme. Depending on how one classifies particular compositions, the Dasam Granth does not necessarily perfectly fit the *trivarga* model (though arguably most forms of Indian literature, e.g., "Puranas," do not always perfectly fit the formal definition by which they are classified). Even individual compositions may address more than one of the *purusharthas* (e.g., the account of Krishna as avatar has both a dharmic and an erotic component). Nonetheless, reading the Dasam Granth as an example of the kinds of anthologies produced at royal courts does at least place the text in a more contextually and historically relevant framework than some of the other models that have been proposed. And, it shows that there was precedent for texts that contained a range of material from the devotional to the erotic, in part because these were the traditional topics on which both kings and court poets composed poetry. On such a reading, we may clearly classify some texts as fitting the category of dharma, such as *Jap*, *Akal Ustat*, *Gian Prabodh*, the avatar narratives and goddess compositions, *Savayye*, *Shabad Hazare*, and so on. Others incorporate both dharma and *artha*, most notably *Bachitra Natak* and *Zafarnama*. *Charitropakhian* and the Persian *Hikaitan* of course primarily represent the *kama* or erotic component and may be read in the context of a long-standing Indic tradition of warning kings of the danger of overindulgence in *kama*, as we saw in Kautilya's warning in the *Arthashastra* (1.6.4) that "a king who has no self-control and gives himself up to excessive indulgence in pleasures will soon perish, even if he is the ruler of all four corners of the earth" (Rangarajan 1992, 144).

The contents of the key compositions regarding Guru Gobind Singh's leadership role—*Bachitra Natak* and *Zafarnama*—are instances in which we may posit the evolution of a distinct Sikh articulation of the responsibilities of a ruler who has both a spiritual and a worldly component to his leadership. If we consider the *purusharthas* in a wider context, we may also note another area in which Sikhism developed its own articulation of human goals. The fourth *artha* of *moksha* [*mokṣa*], release from the realm of death and rebirth [*saṃsāra*], has most frequently been associated with renunciation [*sannyāsa*] in Indian religious traditions, an option in theory at least available only to males of the so-called twice-born *varnas*. Sikhism, however, though it had small renouncer groups in its early history, has explicitly rejected worldly renunciation in favor of the life of the householder as the best means of pursuing one's dharmic obligations. Similarly, Sikhism has largely rejected the classical Hindu model of *varnashrama* according to which one's obligations are determined largely by the *varna* into which one is born. At numerous points in *Charitropakhian* and elsewhere in the Dasam Granth, renouncers are the target of sharp ridicule. It is also possible to see a parallel between the goddess's relationship to the gods and the warriors' relationship to the greater society around him. The goddess is active, always ready to spring into battle, even when those battles disturb the gods' meditation. Similarly, the warrior battling on behalf of dharma is ever prepared to fight, active in the world rather than withdrawn from it like a renouncer.

Still, it is important to read the Dasam Granth not only in the context of Indian literature in general but also in the specific context of Sikh literature as it developed in the time of the Gurus. The first, Guru Nanak, established the tradition of composing devotional poetry set to music, and many of his successors continued this tradition, their compositions along with those of some other poets such as Kabir being compiled into the *Adi Granth*. Many Sikh commentators have wondered why Guru Gobind Singh did not add any of his own compositions to the *Adi Granth*. While Chhibbar's *Bansavalinama* reports that Guru Gobind Singh distinguished between the *Adi Granth* and the "play" of his own compositions, suggesting one possible reason, the existing evidence does not allow a conclusive answer to the question. But another possible answer lies in the relative predominance of compositions associated with leadership found in the Dasam Granth and its similarity to other anthologies produced at royal courts.

As discussed in chapter 1, that Guru Gobind Singh sponsored a number of poets at his court is widely attested in traditional accounts of his life.[5] Guru Gobind Singh's father, Guru Tegh Bahadur, had also sponsored court poets, some of whom likely continued as members of his son's court. Harmendra Singh Bedi (1993, 205) has charted the rise of sponsorship of poets in the Gurus' courts to the time of the fifth Guru, Guru Arjan, and described the four main categories of literature produced at the Gurus' courts as the compositions of the Bhatts (bards who praised the Gurus), poetic ballads or *var kavya*, Bhai Gurdas's compositions, and the works of the fifty-two poets in Guru Gobind Singh's court.[6] Sponsorship of poets at royal courts was a long-standing tradition among Indian rulers as well as Muslim rulers, including the Mughals. In many instances kings sponsored poets who were not adherents of the same religion as the ruler himself; thus a ruler might sponsor poetry on subjects addressing a different religion, and poets themselves have composed poetry addressing topics outside their own religious affiliation.

In the period of the Sikh Gurus, rulers at courts across north India sponsored and themselves composed poetry on topics similar to those found in the Dasam Granth, such as stories of the gods and goddesses and accounts of rulers' victories in battle (see, e.g., Keay 1933, 73–78). Louis E. Fenech's recent work *The Darbar of the Sikh Gurus: The Court of God in the World of Men* (2008) explores the nature of the Sikh Gurus' courts, and shows that there was an Islamicate component to the symbolism and organization of the courts. Fenech further argues that Guru Gobind Singh sought to replicate a kind of divine court on earth. This notion is certainly illustrated clearly in the Dasam Granth's frequent linking of the worlds of the gods and the world of humans, and the parallel responsibilities of the leaders of each, as well as the parallels between the battles each fights against enemies, be they demon or human. While the courts drew on both traditional Indic and Islamic symbols, the poetry composed in the courts was most frequently on topics traditional to Indian court poetry; indeed, the majority of the poets themselves seem to have been from Hindu or Sikh backgrounds.

As we have seen, the role of Guru Gobind Singh's court poets figures heavily in discussions of the authorship of the Dasam Granth, for the most common argument supporting the assertion that Guru Gobind Singh either wrote only some or none of the text is that some or all of it is the work of his court poets. In addition to the frequent occurrence of pen names such as Ram, Siam, and Kal, Jaggi (1966, 147) and other Sikh scholars have pointed to many verses in which the poet asks forgiveness for any mistakes in his work and asks that other poets correct them (see, e.g., KA 756, 834, 983–984), arguing that Guru Gobind Singh would not have composed poetry with errors. It is at such points that in-depth analysis of the text itself frequently comes to a halt, and for precisely this reason leaving aside the authorship debate can be tremendously useful for exploring the text in its entirety.

As discussed earlier in this chapter, the Dasam Granth shares much in common with Sanskrit and vernacular courtly anthologies produced over many centuries on the Indian subcontinent. Placing the Dasam Granth in the context of courtly literature also allows us to consider it in light of other Brajbhasha courtly compositions in the same period. Allison Busch's dissertation, "The Courtly Vernacular: The Transformation of Brajbhāṣā Literary Culture (1590–1690)" provides helpful information regarding this context. Busch (2003, 144–155) charts the rise of Brajbhasha as a "transregional language of courtly discourse" across much of north India beginning in the seventeenth century and argues (147–148) that social and cultural factors such as patronage from both Mughal and subimperial rulers created an environment in which Brajbhasha could travel. Brajbhasha was more accessible to Muslims than was Sanskrit. This shift to Brajbhasha in courtly contexts may be one reason that Sikh literature increasingly turned toward Braj rather than the early forms of Punjabi used by the first Sikh Gurus.

Busch (2003, 200–202) further describes how the shift to the vernacular Brajbhasha as a courtly language brought about the development of literature focusing on history in which political concerns were intermingled with aesthetic expression, often in the form of *mahakavya*, composed both by kings and by the poets whom they patronized in their courts.[7] While her work does not specifically address the Dasam Granth, it is clear that portions of the Dasam Granth, most notably *Bachitra Natak*, are examples of very much the same pattern. The Dasam Granth's retelling of classical mythology and the great epics such as the Ramayana and Mahabharata in an ornate poetical style continues a tradition that David Smith (1992, 35) noted in Sanskrit court literature in which *mahakavya* enjoyed great prestige as a means of updating "epic coverage of great kings, by attempting to raise contemporary monarchs and their dynasties to the epic plane" and providing "a framework for historical narrative." Busch, too, noted that the works of Braj historical *kavya* she studied were "perhaps most crucially about regional politics and the self-presentation of local kings" (2003, 252).

The focus on poetic ornamentation found throughout so many Dasam Granth compositions suggests its performative nature. Indian kings sponsored and composed poetry in part so that it could be enjoyed in performance, but the poetry also served as a means of performing, that is, legitimating, the office of king. This fact helps explain a key feature of the history of the Dasam Granth after its compilation, its prestige and popularity in the courts of the Sikh kings of eighteenth and early nineteenth centuries.

This also suggests that one potentially fruitful avenue for studying the Dasam Granth in subsequent Sikh history is its usage in the later Sikh kingdoms of the eighteenth and early nineteenth centuries, when the Dasam Granth was held in especially high regard.[8] Many of the Sikh rulers themselves sponsored the composition of poetry as well as translations of earlier texts, often on topics similar to those found within the Dasam Granth. Bedi (1993, 209) notes that the famous Sikh king Ranjit Singh was a great patron of poets, and that there were courts with poets at Patiala, Kapurthala, Nabha, Jind, and Sangrur. Like the Dasam Granth, this poetry was generally in some form of Brajbhasha and written in the Gurmukhi script.

Sikh history records that Guru Gobind Singh had proclaimed that after his death there would be no more human Gurus, that instead the *granth* (i.e., *Adi Granth*, subsequently known as *Guru Granth Sahib*) and the Sikh community, or *panth*, would hold that status. In the turbulent years that followed Guru Gobind Singh's death, Sikhs began to establish their own rule in the Punjab. It makes sense that the Dasam Granth would be especially popular during this era because it addresses concerns of worldly leadership throughout. Not only does it address such concerns, but it is also associated with a model leader, Guru Gobind Singh himself, suggesting that the text in and of itself could thus function as a potent symbol of Sikh political leadership. The ruler who honored the Dasam Granth would be symbolically associating himself with the authority that Guru Gobind Singh held as a leader.

The era of the Sikh kingdoms was one in which the boundaries between Hinduism and Sikhism were not always clear-cut. J. S. Grewal (1998, 104), for example, describes Ranjit Singh's Sikhism as having "something of a Hindu odour." One way to read the Dasam Granth and its popularity in the eighteenth and nineteenth centuries is to understand it as reflecting transitions—the transition from the period of the Sikh Gurus to the period in which *granth* and *panth* assume the status of Guru, and the transitional nature of the conception of Sikh kingship, which drew to varying degrees on both preexisting Indic and Islamicate notions of leadership, as well as taking on uniquely Sikh characteristics. Thus in the Dasam Granth we see some concern for the traditional responsibilities of the Kshatriya *varna* such as waging righteous battle, but limited concern for the protection of Brahmans, and an exploration of the traditional role of the avatar, along with Guru Gobind Singh's adoption of a new kind of role.

The immediate need for models of worldly leadership must have diminished as most of the Punjab came under either direct or indirect British rule in the middle and late nineteenth century. The colonial context raised a different set of concerns and brought new articulations of Sikh identity, as has been well documented in many studies of the Singh Sabha movement in colonial India. In this era, in which Sikh authors were addressing not only members of their own and other Indian religious communities but also the criticisms of British officials and Christian missionaries, new ways of defining Sikhism evolved. Often these new definitions incorporated Western conceptions of religious identity that involved very clear-cut boundaries between religions, and also appropriated models of religion based on a Protestant Christian understanding of what a religion entailed (most notably, some type of "scripture").

It is precisely during this colonial era that Sikh authors began to devote more attention to studying and analyzing the Dasam Granth, often implicitly evaluating it as an example of "scripture." It is at this time too that we begin to see increasing reliance on a Western post-Enlightenment conception of authorship in analyses of precolonial literature.[9] With this model of authorship, the author is presupposed to be a distinct, identifiable individual; significantly, this conception of authorship dovetails well with the compositions of the earlier Sikh Gurus, whose works are identifiable in the *Adi Granth*. It is less effective, however, for the Dasam Granth, in which authorship has yet to be definitively established. Such analysis, premised on a particular notion of authorship, is typical of Dasam Granth exegesis from the early twentieth century to the present. Similarly, it is during this period that there was increasing focus on conceptualizing the relationship between the Dasam Granth and "Hinduism."

In particular, analyses of the Dasam Granth often address the issue of Hindu influence, with an eye to either disproving the notion that such influence is present or suggesting that sections of the text with seeming influence cannot be the work of Guru Gobind Singh, and thus this question of influence is key to various authorship arguments.[10] However, these arguments typically oversimplify the Hindu concepts they seek to explore, often by taking very broad, fluid concepts and treating them as if they were both monolithic in nature and self-evident in definition. I have already argued that this is the case for discussions of dharma; it is also apparent in analyses of the so-called Puranic material in the Dasam Granth, as well as arguments regarding apparent Tantric influence. If, however, we acknowledge the fluid and variable nature of such broad categories, we once again leave room to consider whether the Dasam Granth may be interpreted as proposing new Sikh version of these concepts, and the discourse surrounding the text perhaps could move beyond the authorship impasse.

The scholar who has explored the Puranic components of the Dasam Granth in greatest detail is Rattan Singh Jaggi. In his book *Dasam-Granth Kī Paurāṇik Pṛṣṭhabhūmi*, Jaggi (1965, 116–124) analyzed classical definitions of Puranas such as the five *lakshans* [*lakṣaṇas*], or topics of creation: genealogies of gods, sages, and kings; cosmic cycles; and histories of royal dynasties. He also considered the issue of which texts make lists of the eighteen great or *Mahapuranas* and acknowledged the sectarian nature of Sanskrit Puranas and the fact that despite the classic definition, most Puranas are not actually focused on the five *lakshans*. Jaggi (1965, 198–207) argued that the Puranas were important throughout the whole period of the Sikh Gurus, not just during Guru Gobind Singh's time, and served as a way to communicate with Hindus.

A key question, however, is what exactly we learn from designating certain parts of the Dasam Granth as Puranic. While it does indicate a broad thematic similarity between portions of the Dasam Granth and the wider realm of Puranic literature, arguably, this designation has largely served more as a shorthand distancing strategy that implicitly links the so-called Puranic portions of the Dasam Granth with some notion of Hinduism and thereby calls their authenticity into question. One hint as to the limited utility of this usage of the term "Puranic" is that it is overwhelmingly broad. Jaggi (1965, 130), for example, argued that in order to understand the Puranic sources of the Dasam Granth it was necessary to look at the Ramayana and Mahabharata as well. He also suggested (207–212) that Puranic influence was responsible for the miracle stories found in the *janam-sākhī* literature describing the lives of the Gurus. It is clear that in this context "Puranic" has become so vast as to be relatively meaningless as a way to further our understanding of the Dasam Granth. The Puranas were composed over a period of centuries in different parts of India, promoting worship of different gods and goddesses, addressing differing social and sectarian concerns, and detailing varying accounts of dynastic and other forms of history.[11]

Jaggi (1965, 307–313) also noted significant differences between the Sanskrit Puranas and the so-called Puranic compostions of the Dasam Granth. These differences in fact bolster the argument that these compositions are more closely related to courtly literature because, as Jaggi explained, the Dasam Granth Puranic compositions are far more focused on use of *alaṃkāra*, or poetic ornamentation, exhibit more varied and complex use of meter, and on occasion introduce new stories within more familiar narratives. Like much other Brajbhasha literature of the time, they took well-known mythological themes, even specific texts (e.g., the explicit mention of the *Markandeya Purana* in *Chandi Charitra I*) and used these as the basis for a new literary creation.[12] Jaggi (1965, 262–263) also noted that the Dasam Granth compositions placed more emphasis on describing battles, which he attributed to the historical context in which Sikhs were fighting evil forces. While Guru Gobind Singh did indeed live in turbulent times of multiple conflicts, it is equally important to acknowledge that accounts of battles have long been a central topic for courtly literature.

It is by no means inaccurate to characterize portions of the Dasam Granth as "Puranic" insofar as they tell very similar stories. But to do so without taking into account the wide range of what "Puranic" may mean, and the varied contexts in which Puranas may function, has largely served as a means of characterizing some of the Dasam Granth as overly influenced by Hinduism. But if we note that the key concepts expressed in these Puranic narratives—kingship, leadership, avatars, deities, and the defense of dharma—and if we also recognize the wide range within which such concepts may be interpreted, it becomes possible to view the use of these concepts not so much as a function of Hindu influence but as an exploration of Sikh versions of them, not simply drawing upon a Puranic foundation but also expressing the typical concerns of courtly literature.[13]

Some Sikh interpreters have employed a similar distancing strategy by characterizing particular portions of the Dasam Granth, particularly the goddess compositions and *Charitropakhian*, as "Tantric." Jaggi (1965, 23, 86–87), following the work of Shamsher Singh Ashok and Giani Harnam Singh "Ballabh," made this argument in some detail. However, once again this argument is based on a fairly broad and vaguely defined notion of Tantra and does little to further our understanding of the text. The characterization of particular compositions as Tantric has instead served as a means of rejecting them as authentic compositions of Guru Gobind Singh. Essentially the argument is that "left-handed" [*Vāma-mārgī*] Tantra is characterized by a special regard for the goddess, the use of obscene vocabulary and discussion of sex, the worship of weapons, the use of liquor and other intoxicants, and eating meat, and that because these same features are found in certain portions of the Dasam Granth, it too bears Tantric influence. While regard for the goddess and the other features may indeed be characteristic of particular forms of Tantric practice, their presence in the Dasam Granth in and of itself does not conclusively indicate Tantra. Even if it does, the term is being used so broadly as to become virtually meaningless. It would be more productive to look much more closely at particular verses and specific descriptions and place them in the specific historical context of Tantric practice in the Punjab, particularly the Punjab hills. It is not enough to implicitly equate goddess worship or any mention of meat, sex, or foul language with Tantra; while such things may on occasion be indicative of Tantra, they also can be found in many other contexts.[14]

The use of "Puranic" and "Tantric" as analytic tools for the Dasam Granth has effectively functioned as a strategy to distance certain portions of the text from recent normative conceptualizations of Sikhism. Rather than exploring in detail how the Dasam Granth articulates themes found in Sanskrit and vernacular Puranic traditions, as well as in actual Tantric practice, many Sikh scholars have instead used the terms "Puranic" and "Tantric" as part of a larger argument regarding authorship of the text.

In his research, Jaggi frequently argued that the so-called Puranic and Tantric compositions in the Dasam Granth are full of mistakes—that is, they do not always relate the same characters and events in the same sequences as those found in earlier Sanskrit versions—and as a result cannot be Guru Gobind Singh's work. One premise at work here of course is that Guru Gobind Singh would not have made mistakes. But there are two other critical premises here. One is that there is some original form of Puranic and Tantric narratives against which later versions may be judged. Yet this is a difficult premise to defend, for while the different recensions of Puranic and Tantric texts may share the same overarching structure and characters, determining the "original" form is highly problematic. Not only is it difficult to determine precisely which written version of a Purana or a Tantra may be the earliest, but there is the further complicating factor of the interaction between oral and written versions of Puranic stories.

A second implicit premise is that an author of Guru Gobind Singh's caliber would not have taken Puranic and Tantric themes as his subject because they are not original. This is yet another example of applying a conception of authorship that has its roots in post-Enlightenment Western culture to a precolonial Indian text. Many studies of authorship in precolonial north Indian literature have noted that there is a very different conception of authorship at work that does not necessarily value originality and the individual identity of the author but rather values the representation of traditional themes in a new light.

Just as characterizations of certain portions of the Dasam Granth as "Puranic" or "Tantric" have reflected concern over possible Hindu influence, so too has the predominance of both avatar narratives and accounts of the goddess. If, however, we consider the avatar and goddess accounts as reflecting the Dasam Granth's overall interest in exploring the nature of leadership that combines a spiritual and a worldly component, we can see that this is another instance of the text exhibiting both continuity and innovation with earlier versions of the same accounts. As noted earlier, many of the stories of avatars presented in the Dasam Granth, notably Ram and Krishna, are about figures who ruled as kings.

Jaggi (1965, 223–225) argued that the Dasam Granth definitely accepts the notion of the avatar but with some unique characteristics, such as the unusual list of avatars of not only Vishnu, but also Brahma and Shiva. More challenging is the issue of whether *Bachitra Natak* presents Guru Gobind Singh as an avatar. In Sikh historiography, there has been a fair amount of discussion on this question. J. S. Grewal and S. S. Bal, for example, wrote:

> [Guru Gobind Singh] encouraged them [court poets] to translate the relevant portions of the *Ramayan* and the *Mahabbharat* to leave no room for any ambiguity and doubt in comprehending the avatars not only in all their glory but also their weakness. It is significant that his examinations of the avatars synchronised with the writing of the *Bachittar Natak*, his autobiography. It is evident that he had begun seeing himself in the image of an *avatar*. To him the *natak* and *leela* of his own life bore a close resemblance to the activities of saviours of earlier times. Gobind must have felt inspired on discovering himself in that light. But to be doubly sure on the point, he planned the *Bachittar Natak Granth* to underline the common factor of all the saviours, including himself. He composed verses on the lives of avatars and once more turned to Durga, 'an incarnation of Bhagauti (Sword) who is herself a symbol of power'. (Grewal and Bal 1967, 100–101)

It is possible to expand such analyses by acknowledging that the term "avatar" can have different shades of meaning; it is not a self-evident designation. As noted in chapter 2, even if one does read *Bachitra Natak* as presenting Guru Gobind Singh as an avatar, the text itself seems to assert that he is an avatar of a new stripe and that all previous such figures have failed in their missions.

The concept of the avatar is fluid and has had different valences in the history of Indian religions. Much like dharma, its usage is not exclusive to Hinduism; there are, for example, Jain avatars. In Hindu mythology, the lists of the avatars of even a single deity such as Vishnu vary in name and number. Some noted avatars such as Ram took on avatar status over time; others are not always presented as avatars in quite the same way (e.g., Krishna in the *Bhagavad Gita* as compared with the Puranas). There are complex theological distinctions among different types of avatars in Vaishnava sects. Defining a particular figure as an avatar has also been a way to appropriate the power associated with a rival tradition, exemplified in the inclusion of the Buddha and even Muhammad in many lists of the avatars of Vishnu. In more recent times, there has been an even further shift to a somewhat generic conceptualization of the avatar as a kind of "saint"; it is quite common for gurus and other spiritual leaders from the nineteenth century to the present to be deemed avatars by their followers.[15] Thus the Dasam Granth avatar narratives appear to reflect a stage in the ongoing transformation of the concept of avatar in Indian culture. Defining someone as an avatar, or at least in terms evocative of the avatar (which is clearly the case in many portrayals of the Sikh Gurus) also likely served as an effective rhetorical means of conveying the power and status of the Gurus to audiences beyond their immediate followers.

An additional key point of the concept of the avatar in the Dasam Granth, especially the portrayal of Guru Gobind Singh as a new kind of avatar in *Bachitra Natak*, is its linkage to the stories of the goddess. Guru Gobind Singh's battles as detailed in *Bachitra Natak* are explicitly linked to the goddess's battles with demons. As discussed in chapter 3, the *Devi Mahatmya* links the goddess and the king. In the Dasam Granth, there are linkages between the goddess and the avatar-like figure of the Guru, the goddess and the king, as well as an overlap between the role of the avatar and the king in the figure of the Guru. The goddess and the avatar both fight forces that challenge proper dharma.

It is perhaps not surprising that the goddess narratives retain significant rhetorical power in Sikh tradition even when people do not espouse belief in her. The goddess is something of an outsider to the Hindu pantheon; when the gods are in trouble, she is the option of last resort, a fierce fighter, a protector. She stands somewhat apart from the usual social order of the gods but is ready to step in when needed, even if the din of her battle disturbs the gods in their meditative endeavors. This is not unlike the way some Sikhs came to see themselves—fighters and defenders of Indian culture, but not exactly within the Hindu fold. The goddess's role as a protector against invading demon forces clearly must also have had special valence in the Punjab region, which was subject to numerous invasions by outsiders and as a result long periods of political instability and conflict. Thus the tales of the goddess can be meaningful even for those who profess no belief in the goddess whatsoever, for the goddess is the only one who can save the gods when they are too weak to defeat their enemies. Her position and story are thus analogous to some later understandings of Sikh identity and the place of the Sikh *panth* relative to Indic culture.

The analogy between the role of the goddess and some subsequent Sikh self-understandings is also illustrated in the move toward interpreting the term *bhagauti* as "sword" rather than "goddess." This interpretation highlights the fact that for many Sikhs what is most relevant about the goddess is her role as a defender, here abstracted to that of a weapon. This is yet another example of how Sikh tradition has taken a Hindu idea—here, the goddess—and given it a distinctively Sikh interpretation. As the Dasam Granth goddess compositions themselves demonstrate, the goddess is taken not so much as a divine being to be worshiped but as a powerful, multivalent symbol of Sikh power. And, as we saw in chapter 3, the linkage with the goddess subsequently persists indirectly in the symbols of Khalsa Sikh identity such as the lion and sword.

Once again, we may ask, is the Dasam Granth is a holy book? The answer to this question of course lies in part in how one defines what a "holy book" is. Often Sikhs have sought to determine the status of the Dasam Granth on the basis of authorship (a book authored by one of the Sikh Gurus is a "holy book"), or through comparison with the Guru Granth Sahib (a book similar in content to the Guru Granth Sahib is a "holy book"). But the authorship of the Dasam Granth has not been determined conclusively, and the Dasam Granth is not entirely like the Guru Granth Sahib in its content. Thus the question of its status as a "holy book" has remained challenging to the Sikh community, so much so that Sikh leaders at times have sought to silence any discussion of the status of the text.

We have seen that most of the discussion about the Dasam Granth has been framed in terms of issues of authorship; as such, it has focused on a limited set of questions that almost invariably leads to some sort of debate among those who have different answers to the authorship question. Much of the actual content of the text has been pushed aside in this ongoing dispute. Even when Sikh scholars have sought to address the content of the Dasam Granth, the most frequent analytical model used is one that seeks to determine whether the Dasam Granth shows too many signs of "Hindu" influence. This, too, is a question that tends to lead us back to an impasse concerning the relationship between Hinduism and Sikhism, cast in a model that often relies on vague characterizations of terms such as "Puranic" and "Tantric."

Another way some Sikhs have sought to answer the "holy book" question is by proposing that the Dasam Granth be divided into sections of scripture and sections of literature (or treating the Guru Granth

Sahib as scripture, and the Dasam Granth as literature), or characterizing the Guru Granth Sahib as the "New Testament" of Sikhism, the Dasam Granth the "Old Testament."[16] But when people try to interpret the Dasam Granth by dividing its compositions into different categories such as these, we are left with a series of disparate organizational models that were not relevant to the time period in which the Dasam Granth was composed, and which cannot account for why such a range of compositions would be compiled into a single text. It is no small irony that despite the many vehement criticisms some Sikhs have levied against Western scholarship on Sikhism, part of what has fueled the continuing controversy regarding the Dasam Granth among Sikhs themselves is the tendency to interpret the text using concepts of authorship and literature whose origins lie mainly in Western literary criticism, not to mention the strategy of using the model of the Christian Bible as scripture as a means of understanding the Dasam Granth.

As I have tried to show in this study of the Dasam Granth, both individual compositions with the text and the text as a whole make more sense when they are placed in the context of long-standing Indian conceptions of leadership and the literature that has been produced at royal courts. Indian literary tradition provides a better means of categorizing the different parts of the text, and Sikh tradition has its own model for further refining the categories. Perhaps "scripture" might better be understood as illustrative of Sikh dharma, even "in the spirit of *bani*," and "literature" might be better understood as illustrative of Sikh explorations of *artha* and *kama*.[17] Or we might think of the Dasam Granth as exploring both Sikh theology and Sikh statecraft, or *raj-niti*, what Sikhs have termed *miri-piri*, the twin concerns of spiritual and temporal leadership. With such a model, it is at least possible to imagine why the different parts of the Dasam Granth could be compiled together, irrespective of who actually composed them.

What can the Dasam Granth teach us about vernacular anthologies that address diverse themes? In this regard, the Dasam Granth is a specifically Sikh example of a widespread type of Indian literature. It is of interest in the broader study of Indian literature because it illustrates new conceptualizations of dharma, the role of avatars, and even new interpretations of the nature of Hindu deities. An especially intriguing question to pursue is what meaning the myths about different gods and goddesses have in the context of a religious tradition that acknowledges their existence to some extent but does not worship them. If one Indian religious community could use the tales of the goddess, for example, but not necessarily advocate her worship, might there have been similar examples in other times and places in India? Are stories about gods and goddesses always about belief and devotion?

The Dasam Granth, problematized as being of uncertain authorship and subject to undue Hindu influence, has not found a comfortable place in many of the dominant colonial and postcolonial conceptions of Sikhism. In part that is because the questions people have asked of it invariably lead to unending debates or unsatisfying answers. When we ask a different set of questions about the contents of the Dasam Granth, however, it becomes possible to see the text as reflective of a series of transitions—from poetry solely focused on spiritual concerns to poetry addressing both spiritual and worldly concerns as the Sikh Gurus took on spiritual and worldly leadership—and a transition from the era of the Sikh Gurus to an era in which *granth* and *panth* assumed that status, and Sikhs became rulers of their own kingdoms. The Dasam Granth, as an exploration of the responsibilities of rulers, was well suited to the Sikh kingdoms. The transition from the period of the Sikh kingdoms to British colonial rule, and then India's independence, however, was one in which the Dasam Granth lost some of its relevance, becoming a source of debate, a debate that has had the unfortunate consequence of obscuring what this text may teach us about the development of Sikhism and the wider realm of Indian conceptualizations of leadership.

NOTES

Chapter 1

1. Grewal's edited volume *The Khalsa: Sikh and Non-Sikh Perspectives* (2004) is a useful introduction, with articles examining accounts of the establishment of the Khalsa by Sainapat, Koer Singh, Chhibbar, Santokh Singh, Cunningham, Latif, Khazan Singh, Archer, Banerjee, and Teja Singh and Ganda Singh. See also part 2 of Grewal 1996, 39–72; Deol 2001a; Kaur 2000.
2. Many accounts of Guru Gobind Singh's life, for example, rely on Macauliffe's *Sikh Religion* (1909) and its account of the Guru. Macauliffe, however, did not provide complete citation of all his sources. For a discussion of Macauliffe's work and the sources upon which he relied, see Grewal 1998, 43–53.
3. For a brief treatment of this Shakta tradition, see Goswamy 1997.
4. For a more detailed discussion of the political climate in the Punjab region at the time of Guru Gobind Singh's birth, see Grewal and Bal (1967, 1–18) and appendix A, "Contemporary Hill Chiefs" (174–176) for a listing of the rulers in the region during Guru Gobind Singh's life.
5. Kesar Singh Chhibbar's *Bansavalinama* (10:1) places the Guru's birth earlier (Sammat 1718, i.e., 1661), as do many early Western accounts. E.g., Malcolm (1981, 34) wrote, "Guru Govind is stated, by a Sikh author of respectability, Bhai Guru Das Bhale, to have been fourteen years of age when his father was put to death." Thus with Guru Tegh Bahadur's death in 1675, the birth date becomes 1661 or 1662. Other early Western accounts such as Joseph Cunningham's 1849 *History of the Sikhs* (1990, 63) similarly place Guru Gobind Singh's birth earlier; Cunningham wrote that Guru Gobind Singh "was in his fifteenth year" at the time of his father's death. See also Gordon 2000, 35; Grewal and Bal 1967, 192 n. 1.

6. See, e.g., *Bansavalinama* 10:6–11 (125). According to Malcolm (1981, 144–145), Guru Gobind Singh was "brought up in the religion of Nanac," but "he appears from having been educated among the Hindu priests of Mathura, to have been deeply tainted with their superstitious belief." Some relatively late sources report that Guru Gobind Singh sent five Sikhs to Benares to collect all the traditional learning available and bring it back to the Guru's court.
7. Cunningham (1990, 74) wrote that Guru Gobind Singh gradually established a "virtual principality amid mountain fastnesses."
8. Many traditional sources record that Guru Gobind Singh had a third wife, Mata Sahib Kaur. However, some Sikhs have argued that in fact Jito and Sundari were the same person, and that the Guru was not married to Mata Sahib Kaur. See, e.g., http://www.sikhpoint.com/community/articles/GuruGobindAnd3Wives.php.
9. Traditional Sikh accounts of the establishment of the Khalsa report that Guru Gobind Singh called his followers to Anandpur for Baisakhi. He had placed five goats in a tent, and when his followers had assembled, he asked for volunteers who were willing to give their lives. He then took each of the five volunteers who came forward inside the tent, where he would behead one of the goats, and then return before the crowd of followers, who assumed that he was beheading the volunteers. Those five volunteers became known as the *panj piāre*, or five beloved, the first members of the Khalsa. Guru Gobind Singh then established a new rite of initiation into the Khalsa, in which he himself also took part. While the traditional understanding of the foundation of the Khalsa is that it was at this time that the Five Ks (uncut hair, comb, undergarment, steel bangle, and the sword, or *kirpān*) were instituted, earlier accounts such as Sainapati's *Gursobhā* (Grewal 2004, 38) instead mention five weapons: matchlock, bow and arrow, spear, sword, and dagger. Malcolm (1981, 38) wrote that Guru Gobind Singh's disciples were required to be devoted to arms, to wear steel, to wear blue clothing, to let their hair grow, and greet one another with "Wa! Guruji Ka Khalsah! Wa! Guruji ki futteh!" Malcolm (1981, 146–147) also listed the five weapons as "a sword, a firelock, a bow and arrow, and a pike."
10. See, e.g., Cunningham 1990, 67–68. Malcolm (1981, 39), on the authority of "one of the most respectable and best informed authors of that sect," wrote that Guru Gobind Singh spent time in devotion to a temple to Durga Bhavani in Anandpur, and that the goddess instructed him to "unloose his hair and draw his sword." According to Loehlin (1971, 4, following Macauliffe), the propitiation of the goddess took place at Naina Devi near Anandpur. A pandit from Benares attempted to manifest the goddess but failed. Guru Gobind Singh threw a huge amount of ghee into the fire, brandished his sword, and announced that the sword was the true goddess of power.

11. Disturbances in the Punjab have also adversely affected ongoing research into the text; Jaggi (1966, 24) noted that he was unable to locate certain journal articles regarding the *Dasam Granth* because the journal files were lost at the time of partition.
12. Malcolm (1981, 50–52) cites an account of the aftermath of these events according to which Guru Gobind Singh, "in despair, clasping his hands, called upon the goddess of the sword," in a footnote Malcolm referred to the goddess as "Bhavani Gurga" (presumably a misprint for "Bhavani Durga.")
13. See Malcolm 1981, 54–57, for one perspective on this phase in Guru Gobind Singh's life.
14. For a brief account of Bhai Mani Singh's life, see Gurmukh Singh 1997a.
15. The exact nature of Guru Gobind Singh's relationship with Bahadur Shah has been a source of debate in Sikh history, but the details of this debate are beyond the scope of this project.
16. For further discussion of the doctrine of *panth* and *granth*, see Grewal 1998, 186–193; Deol 2001a, 27–28.
17. For more detailed summaries of these compositions, see Ashta 1959, 35–168, "Brief Critical Study of the Works in the Dasam Granth."
18. See Jaggi 1965, 345–346, for a chart showing the ordering of compositions in four early manuscripts.
19. For a detailed discussion of the meters used in the Dasam Granth, see Loehlin and Jaggi 1995, 517–531.
20. The name "Brajbhasha" does not designate a single language with a standardized grammar; there is variation in the grammatical forms and vocabulary used throughout the Dasam Granth. Ashta (1959, 281) described the Braj of the devotional works of the Dasam Granth as incorporating "elements of Avadhi, Panjabi, Persian, Arabic and Dingal" but concluded that the "secular works" "are comparatively free from such admixture." See also Jaggi 1965, 318–327, for an analysis of the types of vocabulary used in the Dasam Granth.
21. Personal interview, Bhai Kirpal Singh, Gobind Sadan, New Delhi, December 2007.
22. See, e.g., Mohan Singh 1971, 66.
23. Ashta (1959, 38) reported that verses 211–230 in *Akal Ustat* are "an exact translation in twenty *Tribhangis* of the 30 *Tribhangis* in *Bhagwati Padya Pushpanjali Stotra* by Pt. Ram Krishen." See also Jaggi 1966, 82–83, 166–167.
24. For further discussion of the contents and ordering of the *Bachitra Natak Granth*, see Jaggi 1965, 272–273. Jaggi (1965, 1966) includes CC 1 as part of the *Bachitra Natak Granth*. In Jaggi and Jaggi's five-volume edition of the Dasam Granth from 1999, however, the designation does not occur at the close of the composition.
25. For an early English translation of portions of *Apni Katha*, see Malcolm 1981, 140–144. Ashta (1959, 41–42) argued that in content and form *Bachitra Natak* is similar to miracle narratives in Brajbhāṣā detailing the

live of gods, goddesses, and humans. Jaggi (1966, 142–143) notes that Giani Harnam Singh Ballabh compared the descriptions of battles in *Apni Katha* to those found in *Prithvī Rāj Rāso* and found significant similarities in style, language, number of verses, and number of dead in the battle.

26. Cunningham (1990, 76–77) concluded that Guru Gobind Singh had completed the *Apni Katha* portion of the Dasam Granth at Damdama in around 1705.
27. Cunningham (1990, 66), for example, described it as "an extant and authentic composition" of the Guru.
28. Some authors have identified additional Puranic sources for this composition such as the *Padma Purāṇa* and the *Devī-Gītā*, but without providing substantive evidence to bolster this argument. See, e.g., Trilochan Singh 1955, pt. 2, 36.
29. Nikky Singh (2005, 32) refers to *Var Durga Ki* as Guru Gobind Singh's first composition, completed in 1684. Other Sikh historians have considered *Jap* to be the Guru's first composition. For an introduction to the *var* in Punjabi literature, see Dharam Singh 1998b.
30. The story of Mahidī or Mīr Mahidī has connections to Shi'a tradition. For a brief discussion, see Harmendra Singh Bedi 1993, 234.
31. For a brief comparison of this list to the list found in the *Bhagavat Purana*, see Jaggi 1965, 220.
32. For a discussion of *Rudra Avatar* in comparison to Sanskrit Puranas that treat the avatars of Shiva, see Jaggi 1965, 221.
33. For a general discussion of how these accounts of avatars compare to the Sanskrit Puranas, see Jaggi 1965, 173–180.
34. As with many other Dasam Granth compositions, English translations of this *shabad* vary; here are four different translations for comparison:
    From http://www.sikhiwiki.org/index.php/Shabad_Hazare (translator not named):

    O my Love, listen to the plight of Your devotees.
    Separation from You Lord is—Just like covering of a diseased quilt in cold weather to feel warmth;
    It is just like living in high mansions, but invested with cobra snakes;
    Drinking water from a pot, pierces like a lance;
    And the cup strikes like a dagger;
    Eating meat is like being hit by butcher's knife.
    O Love, to be with You, I would prefer to sleep on the bare hard ground; while cursed is the living with others in Your forgetfulness.

From Duggal 1999, 116:

    Go and tell the plight of his devotees to my Beloved Lord,
    The luxury beds are an agony without Him,
    It's like living in a snake-pit yard.

The goblet is spike and the cup a dagger,
One receives the punches of the butcher hard.
I would rather live in disguise with my lover;
It's hell living in the strangers' ward.

From Shackle and Mandair 2005, 116:

Tell the Friend whom we all love
The state of His disciples:
Sickened by these quilts without You,
Our mansions are like snakes' nests.
Flasks are torture, cups are knives,
We're cut by butchers' choppers.
Longing for his simple bed,
We curse this rich existence.

From Mansukhani 1997, 149:

Please tell the dear friend—the Lord—the plight of his disciples.
Without you, the use of rich blankets is like a disease for us and the comfort of the house is like living with snakes.
Our water-pitchers are like stakes of torture and our cups have edges like daggers. Your neglect is like what animals suffer when they face butchers.
Our Beloved Lord's straw-bed is more pleasing to us than living in costly furnace-like urban houses.

35. For photographs of the *tupak* and other weapons of Guru Gobind Singh's era, see Madra and Singh 1999, 9–19.
36. Ashta (1959, 149 n. 1) is following the interpretation of Giani Harnam Singh Ballabh in his analysis of this verse.
37. Some printed editions use a variant style of numbering and end up with 405 *charitras*.
38. Deol (2001a, 31; 43 n. 15) describes a *Charitropakhian* manuscript that was apparently intended to be kept in a quiver. See also Jaggi 1966, 133, for a description of a *Charitropakhian* manuscript.
39. According to Loehlin and Jaggi (1995, 517), *hikait* 4 is the same story as *charitra* 52; *hikait* 5 is *charitra* 267; and *hikait* 9 is *charitra* 290. See also Loehlin 1971, 52–53.
40. For the chapter addressing those who consider Guru Gobind Singh the author of the entire text, see Jaggi 1966, 27–81, "Pūrab Pakkh"; for the chapter on those who consider him the author of only selected sections, see Jaggi 1988, 82–90, "Uttar Pakkh."
41. For a brief introduction to Sainapati and *Srī Gur Sobhā*, see Gurmukh Singh 1998b. For the full text with introductory remarks, see Ganda Singh, 1967. See also Deol 2001a; Grewal 2004, 35–45; Murphy 2007.

42. References here are to the version edited by Rattan Singh Jaggi (1995). Guru Gobind Singh is the subject of the tenth chapter of *Bansavalinama*, with occasional mention of him in later chapters as well.
43. For an example of such criticisms, see Daljeet Singh 1997.
44. Jaggi (1966, 29–30) believes that this may have been the date of the completion of the avatar portions of the text, but that it cannot refer to the entire Dasam Granth because the date of Guru Gobind Singh's letter to the Mughal emperor Aurangzeb, the *Zafarnāmā*, is 1763 V., or approximately 1706 C.E.
45. I am here using Jaggi's (1966, 169–171) extended quotation from *Mahima Prakash*.
46. For example, while the words in this letter are printed separately, they would have been run together in Bhai Mani Singh's time. The letter uses separate consonants in words in which they would have been conjoined in older Punjabi (e.g., the letter includes the words *karisan* and *charitar*, which in older texts are typically spelled *krisan* and *charitra*). There are 404, not 303, *charitras* as stated in the letter. Nor, according to Jaggi, is the quality of the handwriting consistent with what one would expect from an experienced scribe such as Bhai Mani Singh. In addition, Jaggi (1966, 39–45) notes that the letter's use of punctuation and marks indicating nasalization is characteristic of a later period. The letter also refers to sections of the *Krishna Avatara*, but not the same sections that are found in the manuscript attributed to Bhai Mani Singh.
47. For additional comments on Dasam Granth manuscripts, see Deol 2001a, 32–33; 43 n. 14; Kumar 2000, 137 n. 5.
48. In his early work, most notably his *Dasam Granth dā Kartritav* (1966), Jaggi argued that Guru Gobind Singh did not author the entire text. In 1999, Drs. Rattan Singh Jaggi and Gursharan Kaur Jaggi published an edition of the complete *Dasam Granth* with Gobind Sadan, an organization led by the late Baba Virsa Singh. Baba Virsa Singh considered the entire Dasam Granth to be Guru Gobind Singh's composition, and in the gurdwara at Gobind Sadan in New Delhi one finds both the Guru Granth Sahib and the Dasam Granth.
49. For Jaggi's full discussion of the manuscripts, see Jaggi 1966, 91–112. Jaggi argued that the Sangrūr Vālī Bīr differs substantially from the Bhāī Manī Singh Vālī Bīṛ, and that it appeared to be only about 180 years old. Jaggi also argued that the Paṭna V ālī Bīṛ is not as old as claimed.
50. The Motī Bāg V ālī Bīṛ and the Bhāī Manī Singh Vālī Bīṛ have pages said to be in Guru Gobind Singh's handwriting. Jaggi argued that the paper and style of letters used lead to the conclusion that they do not date to the Guru's lifetime (Jaggi 1966, 63–64, 95). Jaggi (1966, 113–139) also examined various other letters and manuscripts said to be in Guru Gobind Singh's handwriting and concluded that some of them were forgeries made to inflate the prices of the manuscripts.

51. Jaggi cited the following reasons for doubting the authenticity of the manuscript as Bhai Mani Singh's work: the manuscript is not all in the same handwriting; there are errors in the composition *Var Durga Ki* (Jaggi 1966, 93) which suggest that the copyist was not a Punjabi speaker, which seems highly unlikely for Bhai Mani Singh; Giani Gian Singh's 1880 *Panth Prakash* (Jaggi 1966, 305–306) states that the version of the Dasam Granth compiled by Bhai Mani Singh had only the Dasam Granth, but the Bhai Mani Singh Vālī Bīṛ begins with the Adi Granth (while Bhai Kānh Singh Nābhā's 1930 *Mahan Kosh* states that this manuscript included both the Adi Granth and the Dasam Granth, this does not necessarily prove that the manuscript is actually the work of Bhai Mani Singh).
52. For a listing of the occurrences of the phrase *srī mukhvāk pātshāhī das* and other similar phrases in the Dasam Granth, see Jaggi 1965, 347–352.
53. See, e.g., Loehlin and Jaggi 1995, 514–515; Grewal, 1998, 265.
54. The Sodhak Committee Report report is widely available online, e.g., at http://www.dasamgranth.org/dasamgranth/library/1897_report/1897report.pdf and http://www.sikh-heritage.co.uk/Scriptures/DasamGranth/1897report1of4.pdf.
55. Jaggi (1966, 15; 35–37) was critical of the Sodhak Committee's method. He argued that this report was not scientific in its approach, that it did not consult the oldest available manuscripts, and that its main goal was to ensure consistency in recitation of the text.
56. Grewal (1998, 262–265) summarizes one version of this argument as made by Daljeet Singh.
57. Ashta (1959, 12–16) makes this argument. According to Jaggi (1966, 16), the first Sikh author to make this claim was Bhāī Bishan Singh in 1902. For a detailed discussion and critique of this argument, see Jaggi 1966, 48–59. For a listing of the poets' pen names used in the Dasam Granth, see Jaggi 1965, 341–342. See also Jaggi 1966, fig. 3, 204–205; Jaggi 1965, 343–344.
58. For a 2003 article detailing disputes about such recitations, see http://www.tribuneindia.com/2003/20030523/main6.htm.
59. See, e.g., the 2006 Council of Khalistan press release entitled "Professor Gurtej Singh Exposes Dasam Granth Fraud," http://www.khalistan.com/PressReleases/PR120706_ProfessorExposesDasamGranthFraud.htm; and the December 12, 2007, article, "Exposé: Hindu Infiltration of Sikh Institutions at the Highest Levels," http://www.panthic.org/news/126/ARTICLE/3768/2007-12-26.html.
60. "News and Views: Resolution No. 3," *Sikh Studies Quarterly* 2 (3): 117.
61. This is not the first time that the Akal Takhat has weighed in on such matters; an earlier work by Giani Bagh Singh Ambalvi, *Dasam Granth Nirṇay*, published in 1977, led to his being excommunicated for questioning the authorship of the Dasam Granth, though he was later reinstated.

62. Satinder Bains, "Sikh High Priest Warns Writer of Controversial Book on Dasam Granth." Punjab Newsline, June 27, 2006, http://www.punjabnewsline.com/content/view/750/38/.
63. According to one online source, "Makkar announced that a committee of Sikh scholars has been established which will further work to raise awareness of Guru Gobind Singh Ji's Granth within Sikh circles—especially amongst those that deny it's [*sic*] authenticity." http://forums.waheguroo.com/current-affairs-news-announcements-f38-sri-akal-takht-sahib-resolution-on-current-dasam-granth-debate-etc-t24553.html#entry174137
64. For the full text of this statement, see http://www.sridasamgranth.com/#/internationaldgseminar/4527533394. I am grateful to Gurinder Singh Mann for providing me with information about the conference as well as the 2006 statement.
65. Varinder Walia, "Writer of Controversial Book Fails to Appear at Takht," http://www.tribuneindia.com/2006/20060821/punjab1.htm#5 (accessed April 9, 2008).
66. See, e.g., "Jathedar Iqbal Singh Roughed Up," http://www.tribuneindia.com/2008/20080607/punjab1.htm. The 2008 Gurmatta regarding the Dasam Granth was issued in response in part as a result of a larger controversy involving leaders of the regional *takhts* and their relative authority.

Chapter 2

1. The genealogical account of the Gurus is further elaborated in Kesar Singh Chhibbar's *Bansavalinama* (1769). It is briefly described in J. S. Grewal's 2004 article (in Grewal 2004), "Brahmanizing the Tradition: Chibber's *Bansāvalināmā*," 62.
2. Kohli (2005, 125) translates "Mahākāl Kālakā" as "the primal power, the supreme Kal." In contrast, Jaggi (1966, 141) stated that Mahākāl and Kālakā are the names of Shakta deities. In Sanskrit, the name Mahākāla generally refers to Shiva in his destructive form.
3. The battle of Bhangani is also described in a poem entitled "Pauṛīān Gurū Gobind Singh Kīān," in which the guru is described as an incarnation of God. For further description of this poem, see Ashok 1997.
4. *Malecha* [Sanskrit *mlechha*] comes from a verbal root meaning to speak indistinctly, i.e., a foreigner. The term, which may also be used to refer to people outside the varna system, generally has a negative connotation.
5. There are differing views as to how to translate the phrase "je je carita purātana lahe." Kohli (2005, 139) translates it as "all the wonderful things that were comprehended by the ancient sages," taking the word *purātan* as "ancient sages." Jodh Singh and Dharam Singh (1999, 203) render the line as "as much as performances as (of the so-called incarnations of God) I have seen," taking *purātan* as "incarnations of God." In their modern

Punjabi gloss, Jaggi and Jaggi (1999, vol. 1, 191) translate the line as "Whatever former births [*purātan janam*] I have seen." Bhai Randhir Singh (1995, vol. 1, 91) glosses the phrase "carit purātan" as "purāṇe hālat, kautak," i.e., olden times, wonders. In Sanskrit, the word *purātana* means "belonging to the past, former, old, ancient" (Monier-Williams 1981, 635).

6. The claim for *Bachitra Natak* as the first non-Muslim autobiographical memoir in India is challenged by the existence of a 1641 Hindi autobiographical work by Banarsi Das mentioned in Srivastava's (1979, 129) contribution to the volume *Historical Biography in Indian Literature* (in which Ganda Singh's article was reprinted). Some historians have described the edicts of King Ashoka as one of the earliest examples of autobiography in India; see, e.g., Kalyan Kumar Dasgupta 1979, 15.
7. For further discussion of various types of *praśasti* literature, see Dasgupta and De 1947, lxxx-lxxxvii; Ali 2004, 82–85.
8. Later eighteenth-century Sikh authors (e.g., Chhibbar) described the Gurus as avatars, suggesting that they read *Bachitra Natak* and other sources about the Gurus in this way.

Chapter 3

1. The identification of the languages of compositions within the Dasam Granth is, as with most compositions from the period, somewhat tentative. There is a range of verbal and nominal forms within the two *Chandi Charitras*, and *Var Durga Ki*, while exhibiting characteristics of Punjabi, is not modern Punjabi by any means.
2. For an introduction to the names and characteristics of the goddess in Puranic literature, see Kinsley 1978, 440–447.
3. The *Devi Mahatmya* is usually dated to approximately the sixth century C.E. See, e.g., Coburn 1991; Kinsley 1978, 490.
4. Ashta (1959, 235), e.g., describes CC 1 as a "free translation" of the *Durgā saptaśati* portion of the *Markandeya Purana*. Jaggi (1965, 331–332) argues that these compositions should not be taken as "translations" strictly speaking. Although Loehlin (1971) and others have linked one or more of the goddess compositions in the Dasam Granth to the *Devī-Bhāgavat-purāṇa*, or, more specifically, the *Devī-Gītā* portion of this text, there is little correspondence between the two. While the *Devī-Gītā* does use some epithets of the goddess that are found in, e.g., CC 2 [World-Mother], its outline and focus are significantly different from the Dasam Granth stories of the goddess slaying demons. The *Devī-Gītā* is a conversation between Himālaya and the goddess concerning the threat of the demon Tāraka to the gods, and includes chapters on the goddess and her role in creation, instruction in various forms of yoga, and Vedic and Tantric worship of the goddess. The Tantric worship illustrated in the *Devī-Gītā* includes use of special mantras, visualization practice, and making offerings. For a translation of the *Devī-Gītā* and commentary, see Brown 1998.

5. For a comparison of CC 1 and CC 2 in the Dasam Granth to their Puranic antecedents, see Jaggi 1965, 163–168.
6. Most translators have followed Bhai Randhir Singh's (1995, vol. 1, 92) translation of *kalā* as *shakti*.
7. Translators have interpreted the first part of this line, "tāmasatā mamatā namatā," in different ways. Jaggi and Jaggi (1999, vol. 1, 193) follow Bhai Randhir Singh (1995, vol. 1, 92), who took *mamatā namatā* to refer to the qualities of *rajas* and *sattva* because they follow mention of the *guṇa* of *tamas*. Singh and Singh (1999, vol. 1, 207), however, take *mamatā* in its more modern Punjabi sense of "maternal affection" and *namatā* to be a variant of *namrata*, or "humility." Kohli (2005, 64) takes *mamatā* to be "mineness" [i.e., Sanskrit *mama—tā*] and *namatā* as modesty.
8. Kohli (2005, 64) did not include the name of the king's companion, Samadhi, in his translation, although it does appear in the original text.
9. In *Devi Mahatmya* 1:64–69 (Coburn 1991, 37–38), Vishnu's sleep [*nidrā*] is personified as a form of the goddess who leaves Vishnu, allowing him to awaken and fight the demons. In CC 1:10, it is Chandi who leaves Vishnu so that he may awaken.
10. The story of Madhu and Kaitabh is also told in the fourteenth chapter of the *Chaubis Avatar* section of the Dasam Granth.
11. Although *Chandi Charitra Ukti Bilas* is divided into eight chapters, the verses are numbered continuously in most printed editions, and I have followed that convention here.
12. Both Singh and Singh (1999, vol. 1, 219) and Kohli (2005, 67) have translated the image as the moon surrounded by clouds, but it is more complex, a reference to a solar eclipse in which the moon appears as a black disk surrounded by the corona of the obscured sun.
13. A similar image occurs in *Devi Mahatmya* 2:51 (Coburn 1991, 53), which describes the lion roaming through the demon army like a forest fire.
14. For further discussion of the seven mothers or *mātṛkās*, see Kinsley 1978, 494–496. The mothers are also mentioned in the *Mahabharata*. The names and numbers of mothers may vary in different sources, but typically the list includes Brahmāṇī, Māheśvarī, Kaumārī, Vaiṣṇavī, Vārāhī, Nārasiṃhī, and Aindrī.
15. The exact nature of these gifts is unclear. The phrase is *megha aḍambara*. *Megha* means "sky," and *āḍambara* is a war-drum or may refer to the trumpeting of elephants. Singh and Singh (1999, vol. 1, 243) translate this as "a canopy and a war-drum"; Kohli (2005, 74) translates it as "a dreadful thundering trumpet and a canopy"; Jaggi and Jaggi (1999, vol. 1, 225) gloss it as a "canopied *ambārī*." In any event, it appears to have been a gift symbolic of royalty and battle.
16. *Brahma-kavacha* is presumably a reference to one of the *angas* or subsidiary texts appended to the *Devi Mahatmya* known as the *Kavacha-anga*, in which Brahma tells Markandeya about the armor of the goddess and how

recitation of its features bestows protective benefits to different parts of the reciter's body. See Coburn 1991, 99–117, for a discussion of the *angas*, and Coburn 1991, 175–179, for a translation of the *kavacha-anga*.

17. The phrase is *Sati Saiā*, 700 [*saptaśati*], i.e., a reference to the *Durgā Saptaśati*.
18. Bhai Randhir Singh (1995, vol. 1, 132) interprets this as the nectar that arose when the gods churned the milk-ocean.
19. Both Singh and Singh (1999, vol. 1, 319) and Kohli (2005, 98) translate *sivadūtī* as "Shiva's messenger," but it was Durga who enlisted Shiva as her messenger.
20. Interestingly, a number of the names and phrases that occur in this section have specific reference to the mythology of Durga, but translators and commentators have tended to take them in a more general sense.
21. There is some difference of opinion as to the meaning of the term *karoṭī* in this line. Jaggi and Jaggi (1999, vol. 1, 309) take it as "Kālī Devī"; Singh and Singh (1999, vol. 1, 329) translate it as "the protector like shield"; and Bhai Randhir Singh (1995, vol. 1, 151) glosses it as "hattha dī oṭa-ḍhāla sarūpā" or "she whose form is shield in hand." Monier-Williams (1981, 255) defines the Sanskrit word *karoṭi* as "basin" or "cup" and therefore "skull."
22. *Purāṇī*. Bhai Randhir Singh (1995, vol. 1, 152) takes this as "knowledge of the Puranas."
23. Singh and Singh (1999, vol. 1, 333) and Jaggi and Jaggi (1999, vol. 1, 313) take this to mean someone who abstains from war or who is not a soldier.
24. See Neki 1995 for an introduction to the development of the Ardas prayer.
25. Most commentators (e.g., Ashta 1959, 137) identify *Var Durga Ki* as exhibiting characteristics of western Punjabi or the Lahndi dialect.
26. Raktabij is here called *Sraṇvat Bīja*, presumably derived from the verbal root *sru* meaning to flow, gush, etc., as in blood.
27. The last phrase of this verse illustrates the challenges of translating this text, and the ways translators and commentators sometimes add new shades of meaning. The phrase is "sada rahimati tere vāra kau." With no embellishment, the words are "always-mercy [*sada rahimati*] -to-your-blow [*tere vāra kau*]." Singh and Singh's (1999, vol. 1, 359) rendering of the line is "May Akalpurakh ever bless her blows." Kohli's (2005, 109) translation is "O goddess; hail, hail to Thy blow." And in their modern Punjabi gloss, Jaggi and Jaggi (1999, vol. 1, 333) offer two possible readings: "Always commend [the goddess's] blow" or "the poet is a martyr [*kurbān hai*] to the goddess's blow." How might the line best be rendered in English? There is no specific reference to Akal Purakh, so Singh and Singh's translation seems to be adding something not in the line itself.
28. Bhai Randhir Singh (1995, vol. 1, 168) here glosses *bhagautī* as "goddess; sword"; Jaggi and Jaggi (1999, vol. 1, 335) translate it into modern Punjabi as *barchī* or spear, presumably because this is the term used for the

goddess's weapon later in the verse; Kohli (2005, 110) and Singh and Singh (1999, vol. 1, 61) both translate it as "sword."

29. See Krishna 2007 for an introduction to the role of demons in Sanskrit literature.
30. Jaggi (1965) argued convincingly that both CC 1 and CC 2 were based on the *Devi Mahatmya* or *Durgā-Saptaśati* portion of the *Markandeya Purana*; Ashta (1959, 130) made a similar argument. Other authors such as Trilochan Singh (1955, pt. 2, 36–37) have mentioned other Puranas such as the *Padma Purāṇa* and *Devī Bhāgavat Purāṇa* as possible sources.
31. See also the entry *Bhagautī* in Nabha 1990, 901.

Chapter 4

1. Similarly, when the Publications Bureau of Punjabi University published Bhai Randhir Singh's *Shabdārath Dasam Granth Sāhib* in 1995, it chose to omit *Charitropakhian* and *Hikāitān*. See Bhai Randhir Singh 1995, Taran Singh's "Introduction [*Bhūmikā*]," v. For English translations of selected *charitras*, see Loehlin 1971, 48–51, 86–87, 93–94.
2. My translation of the last line of this verse is tentative. Bindra translates this line, *tuhī bakrata te brahama bādo bakāhī* as "you have produced the altercating folks." In their Punjabi gloss, Jaggi and Jaggi translate the line as "from your mouth, you have created those who debate matters concerned with Brahma."
3. Macauliffe translated some of these lines (1990, vol. 5, 287, 289) but rendered the "God" of the verses as male, and *bhagautī* only as "sword."
4. The *apasarās* are the wives of the Gandharvas who live in the sky but often visit earth and have the ability to change shape at will. See, e.g., Monier-Williams 1981, 59. The modern Punjabi word is *apachcharā*.
5. Puran Bhagat survives in the well for twelve years and is then rescued by Gorakhnath. For further details and analysis of the story, see Qadir Yar 1983; Tahir 1988.
6. According to Malcolm (1981, 112), "The use of opium to intoxicate, is very common with the Sikhs, as with most of the military tribes of India. They also take Bhang [*Cannibis sativa*] another inebriating drug."
7. For a comparison of the *Charitropakhian* version of Yusuf and Zulaikha to the biblical and Qur'anic versions, see Loehlin 1971, 91–94.
8. For a similarly graphic story, see *charitra* 402.
9. Some commentators take the word *sikha* as used in this *charitra* to refer specifically to members of a Sikh community; others take it in its more general sense as "disciple."
10. The line is quite explicit; the woman reveals her *mūtra dhāma*, literally, "place of urine."
11. Oman (1984, 196–198) relates a slightly different version of this story according to which Anup Kaur disguised herself as a *sadhu* who had special knowledge regarding the goddess. This *sadhu* agreed to meet Guru

Gobind Singh on the condition that he arrive alone at midnight in ascetic garb. Guru Gobind Singh did as instructed but received no special knowledge from the *sadhu*, who soon left his company. Then the young Anup Kaur (having shed her disguise) appeared and made her proposition to Guru Gobind Singh, which he refused. As he was leaving, she cried out, "Thief!" and the Guru joined in her cry and managed to slip away. He later gave the ascetic garb he had worn to Bir Singh with the instruction that he establish a new sect of *sadhus* to be known as the Nirmalis. The Guru's experience with Anup Kaur in turn inspired him to compose the *charitras* concerning women as a caution to his followers.

12. Jaggi (1966, 158–161) further argues that it is unlikely a wealthy woman would have visited Anandpur and suggests that the stories may bear some relation to the Rajasthani *premākhiān* "*Ḍhola māru*."
13. See *Amṛt Kīrtan* 2006, 852. I am grateful to Pashaura Singh for providing me with this reference. For further discussion of the Anandpur *charitras*, see Taran Singh 1987, 254–256.
14. As part of his argument that Guru Gobind Singh did not compose these *charitras*, Jaggi (1966, 162) suggests that it is highly unlikely a woman such as Nand Mati would be living in Anandpur so soon after the town was established.
15. The *shalagram* stone is usually associated with the god Vishnu, but in this story it refers to an image of the god Shiva.
16. See, e.g., Jaggi and Jaggi 1999, vol. 5, 628–629; Jaggi 1966, 182; Paṇḍit Narain Singh Jī Giānī, 1998, vol. 8, 522.
17. In their modern Punjabi translation of the verse, Jaggi and Jaggi (1999, vol. 5, 669) simply repeat the word "Kali" in quotation marks; when this name appears in the goddess compositions, they take it as "Kali." In his modern Punjabi translation, Pandit Narain Singh Ji Giani (1998, vol. 8, 572) glosses "Kali" as "Kal," who is receiving a command from Mahakal. Bindra did not translate this verse.
18. I have given a literal translation of the term *jagamātā* here. Bindra (2002, vol. 2, 767) translated it as "Creator"; Pandit Narain Singh Ji Giani (1994, vol. 8, 580) translated it as "the Protector Lord Who Is Like the World's Mother" [*jagat dī mā vāng pālaṇ hāre prabhu*], presumably reading the epithet in a context in which the notion of the World-Mother, elsewhere a name for the goddess, is theologically untenable.
19. Ashta detailed the sources of particular *charitras* as follows:

    (1) Mahabharata (12, 320)
    (2) Ramayana (102, 152)
    (3) Puranas (108, 114, 115, 120, 123, 141, etc.)
    (4) Historical tales of Rajput women (89, 95, 99)
    (5) Panchatantra (128, 144, 161), Hitopadesh (78, 286, 313, 368)
    (6) Persian texts such as Bagho Bahar and Caahar Darvesh (66, 201, 353)

(7) Popular tales (32, 40, 68, 70, 72, 86, 93, 96–99, 101, 103, 106, 108, 109, 129–136, 151, 171, 176, 183, 186–201, 219, 346) and immortal romances (101, 109, 129)
(8) Pathan and Mughal times when crime and murder were common (19, 46, 82, 105, 185, 189, 195, 196, 207, 22, 246, 278, 297, 297, 332, etc.)

20. For a discussion of how the Purana-related stories in *Charitropakhian* relate to the Sanskrit Puranas, see Jaggi 1965, 183–186.
21. In his study of the Dasam Granth, Taran Singh (1987, 254) briefly alluded to the role of the *purusharthas*.
22. On such anthologies, see, e.g., Winternitz 1959, 172–184.
23. On courtly life, see Ali 2004.
24. See Jaggi 1965, 278, for his discussion of the connection between *Charitropakhian* and the Sanskrit *Bṛhat Kathā* tradition.
25. For an English translation of *Shukasaptati*, see Haksar 2000.
26. A similar reference to lovemaking according to the *Kokashastra* is found in verse 2205 of *KA*.
27. See Comfort 1964, 37, 55. Comfort noted that *Kokashastra* was used to refer to the Sanskrit text of that name, as a generic term for erotic literature, and for illustrated manuals depicting sexual positions. It seems likely that the many *charitras* which refer to lovemaking "according to the *Kokashastra*" are referring to the illustrated manuals rather than the Sanskrit text.
28. See Deol 2002 for further discussion of the notion of obscenity in Waris Shah's work.

Conclusion

1. The issue of the Dasam Granth as a whole is further complicated by the variation in total number and ordering of compositions within the earliest manuscripts, and the fact that some compositions found in some manuscripts are not included in typical printed editions. My argument here is focused on the Dasam Granth in its standard printed form.
2. For a more detailed analysis of the role of Islamicate imagery in the courts of the Sikh Gurus, see Fenech 2008.
3. For further discussion of Sikh usage of the term pātishāh, see Fenech 2008, 54–55.
4. The issue of violence in the name of what is good is a theme deserving further exploration in both Hindu and Sikh tradition. Weaponry and battle are central to Hindu mythology and iconography, though this dimension of the tradition has perhaps been overshadowed by more recent articulations of Hinduism that focus on Gandhian notions of ahiṃsa, or nonviolence.
5. For further discussion of the sources describing and in some cases listing the court poets, see Harmendra Singh Bedi 1993, 208, 245, 248.

6. For a more detailed discussion of the first three categories of court poetry named here, see Harmendra Singh Bedi 1993, 205–207.
7. For a broader discussion of these issues in Indian vernacular literature, see Pollock 1998.
8. Jaggi (1966, 10) noted that the Dasam Granth received the greatest honor in the PEPSU region, that is, the Patiala and East Punjab States Union area that was created after Indian independence, uniting several former princely states led by Sikh rulers.
9. For a range of analyses of Indian conceptions of authorship, see Ebbesen 1995; Novetzke 2003; Hawley 1988; and Rinehart 1999b. A classic study of Western conceptions of authorship is Foucault 1986.
10. For a more detailed discussion of the nature of "influence" and its applicability to Punjabi literature, see Rinehart 1999b.
11. In his insightful article "Purana as Brahminic Ideology," Velcheru Narayana Rao (1993, 99) notes that the emphasis in Puranas shifted over time to a more devotional focus in which narrators tell stories their audiences already know: "The emphasis is not on information but rather on a renewed opportunity to experience the divine. It is not communication but communion."
12. See, e.g., Busch 2003, 173–174.
13. "Purana," like "dharma," is a term that has been used in different Indian religions. There are, for example, Jain as well as Hindu Puranas. See, e.g., Jaini 1993.
14. One component of Jaggi's analysis (1966, 188–189), however, seems more substantive and worthy of further research, and that is the role of weapon worship in Tantric practice and in Dasam Granth compositions such as the *Shastra-nam-mala*.
15. For more on recent uses of the term "avatar," see Rinehart 1999a.
16. Along similar lines, a 2004 article about Gurbaksh Singh Kala Afghana compared his efforts to reform Sikhism to those of the Protestant Reformation led by Martin Luther. See Puneet Singh Lamba, "Gurbaksh Singh Kala Afghana: An Adi Granth Purist" http://www.sikhtimes.com/bios_071004a.html (accessed July 24, 2007).
17. In a June 6, 2008, resolution, Joginder Singh Vedanti, Jathedar of the Akal Takht, suggested a strategy of this sort with respect to specific passages in the Dasam Granth used in prayer and other rituals, characterizing the Dasam Granth as an essential part of the literature and history of the Sikh panth but not on a par with the Guru Granth Sahib.

REFERENCES

Ahluwalia, M. S. 1997. *Mahimā Prakāsh*. In Harbans Singh, ed., *The Encylopaedia of Sikhism*. Vol. 3. Patiala: Punjabi University, 16–17.

Ali, Daud. 2004. *Courtly Culture and Political Life in Early Medieval India*. Cambridge: Cambridge University Press.

Amṛt Kīrtan. 2006. 2nd ed. Amritsar: Khalsa Brothers.

Ashok, Shamsher Singh. 1997. *Pauṛīān Gurū Gobind Singh Kīān*. In Harbans Singh, ed., *The Encylopaedia of Sikhism*. Vol. 3. Patiala: Punjabi University Press, 330.

Ashta, Dharam Pal. 1959. *The Poetry of the Dasam Granth*. New Delhi: Arun Prakashan.

Ballantyne, Tony, ed. 2007. *Textures of the Sikh Past: New Historical Perspectives*. Oxford: Oxford University Press.

Banerjee, Anil Chandra. 1976. Guru Gobind Singh and the Shakti Cult. *Sikh Review* 24 (268): 21–29.

———. 1983. *The Sikh Gurus and the Sikh Religion*. New Delhi: Munshiram Manoharlal.

Banerjee, Indubhusan. 1963. *Evolution of the Khalsa*. Vol. 1, *The Foundation of the Sikh Panth*. Calcutta: A. Mukherjee.

Banga, Indu, ed. 1997. *Five Punjabi Centuries: Polity, Economy, Society and Culture, c. 1500–1990*. New Delhi: Manohar.

Barnett, L. D. 1957. Some Notes on Hindi Poetry in the Panjab. *Bulletin of the School of Oriental and African Studies, University of London* 20 (1): 73–75.

Barrier, N. G. 1970. *The Sikhs and Their Literature: A Guide to Books, Tracts and Periodicals 1849–1919*. Columbia, MO: South Asia Books.

Barrier, N. G., and Nazer Singh. 1998. Singh Sabha Movement. In Harbans Singh, ed., *The Encylopaedia of Sikhism*. Vol. 4. Patiala: Punjabi University Press, 205–212.

Bawa, Ujagar Singh. 1991. *Bichitra Naatik (A Part of Sikh Scriptures)*. Gaithersburg, Md.: Washington Sikh Center.

Bedī, Harmendra Singh. 1993. *Gurumukhī Lipi Men Upalabdh Hindī Bhaktisāhitya kā Ālochnātmak Adhyayan*. Amritsar: Guru Nanak Dev University.

Bedī, Kālā Singh, ed. 1965. *Vār Srī Bhagoti Jī Kī (Chaṇḍī dī Vār)*. New Delhi: Punjabi Book Store.

Bhasin, Rajinder Singh. 1999. *Guru Gobind Singh: The Prophet, Poet and Philosopher (A Biography)*. Delhi: Shilalekh.

Bhatia, Sardar Singh. 1998. Sukkhā Singh. In Harbans Singh, ed., *The Encylopaedia of Sikhism*. Vol. 4. Patiala: Punjabi University Press, 266–267.

Bhattacharyya, N. N. 1979. Historical Biographies in Early Indian Literature: A Brief Survey. In S. P. Sen, ed., *Historical Biography in Indian Literature*. Calcutta: Institute of Historical Studies, 29–32.

Bindra, Pritpal Singh. 2000. Could Guru Gobind Singh Write Such Things? Paper presented at Sikh Educational Conference, Toronto, California, September.

———. 2002. *Chritro Pakhyaan: Tales of Male-Female Tricky Deceptions from Sri Dasam Granth*. 2 vols. Amritsar: B. Chattar Singh Jiwan Singh.

Brown, C. Mackenzie. 1990. *The Triumph of the Goddess: The Canonical Models and Theological Visions of the* Devī-Bhāgavata-Purāṇa. Delhi: Sri Satguru Publications.

———. 1998. *The Devī Gītā, The Song of the Goddess: A Translation, Annotation, and Commentary*. Albany: State University of New York Press.

Busch, Allison. 2003. The Courtly Vernacular: The Transformation of Brajbhāṣā Literary Culture (1590–1690). Ph.D. diss., University of Chicago.

Coburn, Thomas B. 1984a. Consort of None, *Śakti* of All: The Vision of the *Devī Māhātmya*. In John Stratton Hawley and Donna Marie Wulff, eds., *The Divine Consort: Rādhā and the Goddesses of India*. Delhi: Motilal Banarsidass, 153–165.

———. 1984b. *Devī Māhātmya: The Crystallization of the Goddess Tradition*. Delhi: Motilal Banarsidass.

———. 1991. *Encountering the Goddess: A Translation of the Devī Māhātmya and a Study of Its Interpretation*. Delhi: Sri Satguru Publications.

Comfort, Alex. 1964. *The Koka Shastra: Being the Ratirahasya of Kokkoka and Other Medieval Indian Writings on Love*. New York: Stein and Day.

Cunningham, Joseph D. 1990. *A History of the Sikhs: From the Origin of the Nation to the Battles of the Sutlej*. Delhi: Low Price Publications. First edition 1849; revised 1915.

Dasgupta, Kalyan Kumar. 1979. Historical Biography in Sanskrit Literature. In S. P. Sen, ed., *Historical Biography in Indian Literature*. Calcutta: Institute of Historical Studies, 3–34.

Dasgupta, S. N., and S. K. De. 1947. *A History of Sanskrit Literature: Classical Period*. Vol. 1. Calcutta: University of Calcutta.

Dehejia, Vidya, ed. 1999. *Devi: The Great Goddess—Female Divinity in South Asian Art*. Washington, D.C.: Arthur M. Sackler Gallery.

Dehejia, Vidya, and Sagaree Sengupta. Poetic Visions of the Great Goddess: Tamil Nadu and Bengal. In Vidya Dehejia, ed., *Devi: The Great Goddess—Female Divinity in South Asian Art*. Washington, D.C.: Arthur M. Sackler Gallery, 99–117.

Deol, Jeevan. 2001a. Eighteenth Century Khalsa Identity: Discourse, Praxis, and Narrative. In Christopher Shackle, Gurharpal Singh, and Arvind-pal Singh Mandair, eds., *Sikh Religion, Culture and Ethnicity*. Richmond, Surrey: Curzon Press, 25–46.

———. 2001b. Text and Lineage in Early Sikh History: Issues in the Study of the Adi Granth. *Bulletin of the School of Oriental and African Studies* 64 (1): 34–58.

———. 2002. Sex, Social Critique and the Female Figure in Premodern Punjabi Poetry: Vāris Shāh's "Hīr." *Modern Asian Studies* 36 (1): 141–171.

Deora, Man Singh. 1989. *Guru Gobind Singh: A Literary Survey*. New Delhi: Anmol Publications.

Dimock, Edward C., Edwin Gerow, C. M. Naim, A. K. Ramanujan, Gordon Roadarmel, and J. A. B. van Buitenen. 1974. *The Literatures of India: An Introduction*. Chicago: University of Chicago Press.

Dīp, Dalīp Singh. 1988. *Guru Gobind Singh: Jīvan ate Chintan*. Chandigarh: Guru Gobind Singh Foundation.

Duggal, Kartar Singh. 1999. *Select Sikh Scriptures IV: Guru Gobind Singh*. New Delhi: UBS Publishers.

Dusenbery, Verne A. 1992. The Word as Guru: Sikh Scripture and the Translation Controversy. *History of Religions* 31 (4): 385–402.

Ebbesen, Jeffrey. 1995. The Question of Authorship in Indian Literature. In Patrick Colm Hogan and Lalita Pandit, eds., *Literary India: Comparative Studies in Aesthetics, Colonialism, and Culture*. Albany: State University of New York Press, 47–62.

Edgerton, Franklin. 1912. A Hindu Book of Tales: The Vikramacarita. *American Journal of Philology* 33 (3): 249–284.

———. 1942. Dominant Ideas in the Formation of Indian Culture. *Journal of the American Oriental Society* 62 (3): 151–156.

———. 1965. *The Panchatrantra, Translated from the Sanskrit by Franklin Edgerton*. London: Allen and Unwin.

Erndl, Kathleen M. 1993. *Victory to the Mother: The Hindu Goddess of Northwest India in Myth, Ritual, and Symbol*. New York: Oxford University Press.

Farquhar, J. N. 1920. *An Outline of the Religious Literature of India*. London: Oxford University Press.

Fenech, Louis E. 2000. *Martyrdom in the Sikh Tradition: Playing the "Game of Love."* New Delhi: Oxford University Press.

———. 2008. *The Darbar of the Sikh Gurus: The Court of God in the World of Men*. New Delhi: Oxford University Press.

Foucault, Michel. 1986. What Is an Author? In Hazard Adams and Leroy Searle, eds., *Critical Theory since 1965*. Tallahassee: Florida State University Press, 137–148.

Giānī Kartā Singh Jī Hitkārī. N.d. *Srī Dasam Granth Jī Dā Pāṭhāntar Darpaṇ, Hissā Do*. Lahore: Gurmat Tract Society.

Gordon, Sir John J. H. 2000. *The Sikhs*. Patiala: Language Department, Punjab. Rreprint of 1883 edition. Goswamy, Karuna. 1997. Religion and Art in the

Punjab Hills: A Study in Relationship, *c.* 1600–1850. In Indu Banga, ed., *Five Punjabi Centuries: Polity, Economy, Society and Culture, c. 1500–1990*. New Delhi: Manohar, 548–563.

Grewal, J. S. 1981. The Sikh Panth: 1500–1850. In David N. Lorenzen, ed., *Religious Change and Cultural Domination*. Mexico City: El Colegio de México, 193–198.

———. 1990. *The Sikhs of the Punjab*. Rev. ed. Cambridge: Cambridge University Press.

———. 1992. *Guru Nanak in Western Scholarship*. Shimla: Indian Institute of Advanced Study; Delhi: Manohar Publications.

———. 1993. *Guru Nanak and Patriarchy*. Shimla: Indian Institute of Advanced Study.

———. 1996. *Sikh Ideology Polity and Social Order*. Delhi: Manohar.

———. 1997. *Historical Perspectives on Sikh Identity*. Patiala: Publication Bureau, Punjabi University.

———. 1998. *Contesting Interpretations of the Sikh Tradition*. Delhi: Manohar.

———, ed. 2004. *The Khalsa: Sikh and Non-Sikh Perspectives*. New Delhi: Manohar.

Grewal, J. S., and S. S. Bal. 1967. *Guru Gobind Singh (A Biographical Study)*. Chandigarh: Department of History, Panjab University.

Grewal, J. S., and Irfan Habib, eds. 2001. *Sikh History from Persian Sources: Translations of Major Texts*. New Delhi: Tulika.

Gupta, Hari Ram. 1984. *History of the Sikhs*. Vol. 1, *(The Sikh Gurus, 1469–1708)*. New Delhi: Munshiram Manoharlal.

Gupta, Sanjukta, and Richard Gombrich. 1986. Kings, Power and the Goddess. *South Asia Research* 6 (2): 123–138.

Haksar, A. N. D. 2000. *Shuka Saptati: Seventy Tales of the Parrot*. New Delhi: HarperCollins.

———. 2007. *Subhāshitāvali: An Anthology of Comic, Erotic and Other Verse*. New Delhi: Penguin Books.

Hawley, John Stratton. 1998. Author and Authority in the *Bhakti* Poetry of North India. *Journal of Asian Studies* 47 (2): 269–290.

Ingalls, Daniel H. H., trans. 1965. *An Anthology of Sanskrit Court Poetry: Vidyākara's* "Subhāṣitaratnakoṣa." Cambridge, Mass.: Harvard University Press.

Institute of Sikh Studies, Chandigarh. 1990. *Some Recent Publications on Sikhism: An Evaluation*. Chandigarh: Institute of Sikh Studies.

Jaggī, Rattan Singh. 1965. *Dasam-Granth kī Paurāṇik Pṛṣṭhabhūmi*. Delhi: Bharati Sahitya Mandir.

———. 1966. *Dasam Granth dā Kartritav*. New Delhi: Panjabi Sahit Sabha.

———. 1967. *Guru Gobind Singh Jī dī Bānī vich Sutantratā dī Bhāvnā*. Chandigarh: Guru Gobind Singh Foundation.

———, ed. 1972. *Kesar Singh Chhibbar dā Bansāvalīnāmā Dasān Pātshāhiān Kā*. *Parkh: Research Bulletin of Panjabi Language and Culture*, 2. Chandigarh: Panjab University.

———. 1990. *Dasam Granth Parichay*. New Delhi: Gobind Sadan Institute for Advanced Studies in Comparative Religion.

———. 1991. *Dasam Granth Bāṇī Biurā*. Patiala: Publication Bureau, Punjabi University.

———. 1995. *Bansāvalīnāmā Dasān Pātshāhīān Kā*. In Harbans Singh, ed., *The Encyclopaedia of Sikhism*. Vol. 1. Patiala: Punjabi University, 279–280.

Jaggī, Rattan Singh, and Gursharan Kaur Jaggī, eds. 1999. *Srī Dasam Granth Sāhib: Pāṭh Sampādan ate Viākhā*. 5 vols. New Delhi: Gobind Sadan Institute for the Advanced Study of Comparative Religion.

Jaini, Padmanabh S. 1993. Jaina Purāṇas: A Purāṇic Counter. In Wendy Doniger, ed., *Purāṇa Perennis: Reciprocity and Transformation in Hindu and Jaina Texts*. Delhi: Sri Satguru Publications, 207–249.

Jhā, Śailendra Mohan. 1974. *Brajbolī Sāhitya*. Patna: Bihar Hindi Granth Academy.

Jolly, Surjit Kaur. 1988. *Sikh Revivalist Movements: The Nirankari and Namdhari Movements in the Punjab in the Nineteenth Century (A Socio-Religious Study)*. New Delhi: Gitanjali Publishing House.

Joshi, S. S., and Mukhtiar Singh Gill, eds. 1994. *Punjabi-English Dictionary*. Patiala: Publication Bureau, Punjabi University.

Karan, Pradyumna P. 1994. Patterns of Pilgrimage to the Sikh Shrine of Guru Gobind Singh at Patna. *Journal of Asian and African Studies* 46–47:275–284.

Kaur, Kuldip. N.d. *Chaṇḍī dī Vār: Kī is vār vich Durgā Upāsnā dī Prerna Mildī Hai?* New Delhi: Sundar Printing Press.

Kaur, Madanjit, ed. 2000. *Guru Gobind Singh and Creation of Khalsa*. Amritsar: Guru Nanak Dev University.

Keay, F. E. 1933. *A History of Hindī Literature* 2nd ed. Calcutta: YMCA Publishing House; London: Oxford University Press.

Kinsley, David. 1978. The Portrait of the Goddess in the Devī-māhātmya. *Journal of the American Academy of Religion* 46 (4): 489–506.

———. 1987. *Hindu Goddesses: Visions of the Divine Feminine in the Hindu Religious Tradition*. Delhi: Motilal Banarsidass.

Kohli, Surindar Singh. 1987a. Adi Granth. In Mircea Eliade, ed., *The Encyclopedia of Religion* Vol. 1. New York: Macmillan, 28–29.

———. 1987b. Dasam Granth. In Mircea Eliade, ed., *The Encyclopedia of Religion*. Vol. 4. New York: Macmillan, 241–242.

———. 1997. *Prāchīn Panth Prakāsh*. In Harbans Singh, ed., *The Encyclopaedia of Sikhism*. Vol. 3. Patiala: Punjabi University, 353–354.

———. 1998. *Srī Gurū Panth Prakāsh*. In Harbans Singh, ed., *The Encyclopaedia of Sikhism*. Vol. 4. Patiala: Punjabi University, 254.

———. 2005. *The Dasam Granth: The Second Scripture of the Sikhs Written by Sri Guru Gobind Singh*. Delhi: Munshiram Manoharlal.

Krishna, Nanditha. 2007. *The Book of Demons, Including a Dictionary of Demons in Sanskrit Literature*. New Delhi: Penguin Books.

Kumar, Davindra. 2000. Guru Gobind Singh's Contribution to the Indian Literature. In Madanjit Kaur, ed., *Guru Gobind Singh and Creation of Khalsa*. Amritsar: Guru Nanak Dev University, 127–139.

Loehlin, C. H. 1971. *The Granth of Guru Gobind Singh and the Khalsa Brotherhood*. Lucknow: Lucknow Publishing House.

Loehlin, C. H., and Rattan Singh Jaggi. 1995. Dasam Granth. In Harbans Singh, ed., *The Encyclopedia of Sikhism*. Vol. 1. Patiala: Punjabi University, 514–532.

Macauliffe, Max Arthur. 1990. *The Sikh Religion: Its Gurus, Sacred Writings and Authors*. 6 vols. Delhi: Low Price Publications. Reprint of 1909 edition.

Macdonell, Arthur A. 1971. *A History of Sanskrit Literature*. Delhi: Motilal Banarsidass.

Madra, Amandeep Singh, and Parmjit Singh. 1999. *Warrior Saints: Three Centuries of the Sikh Military Tradition*. London: I. B. Tauris Publishers in association with the Sikh Foundation.

———, eds. 2004. *"Siques, Tigers, or Thieves": Eyewitness Accounts of the Sikhs (1609–1809)*. New York: Palgrave Macmillan.

Malcolm, John. 1981. *Sketch of the Sikhs: Their Origins, Customs and Manners*. Chandigarh: Vinay Publications. Reprint of 1812 edition.

Mann, Gurinder Singh. 2008. Sources for the Study of Guru Gobind Singh's Life and Times: Facsimiles of Core Compositions in the Earliest Manuscripts of the *Dasam Granth*. *Journal of Punjab Studies* 15 (1–2): 229–311.

Mansukhani, Gobind Singh. 1997. *Hymns from the Dasam Granth*. 6th rev. ed. New Delhi: Hemkunt Press.

McInerney, Terence. 1999. Mysterious Origins: The *Tantric Devi* Series from Basohli. In Vidya Dehejia, ed., *Devi: The Great Goddess—Female Divinity in South Asian Art*. Washington, D.C.: Arthur M. Sackler Gallery, 119–135.

McLeod, W. H. 1976. *The Evolution of the Sikh Community: Five Essays*. Oxford: Clarendon Press.

———. 1984. *Textual Sources for the Study of Sikhism*. Manchester: Manchester University Press.

———. 1992. The Sikh Struggle in the Eighteenth Century and Its Relevance for Today. *History of Religions* 31 (4): 344–362.

———. 2000. *Exploring Sikhism: Aspects of Sikh Identity, Culture, and Thought*. New Delhi: Oxford University Press.

———. 2003. *Sikhs of the Khalsa: A History of the Khalsa Rahit*. New Delhi: Oxford University Press.

———. 2006. *Prem Sumārag: The Testimony of a Sanatan Sikh*. New Delhi: Oxford University Press.

M'Gregor, W. L. 1970a. *The History of the Sikhs: Containing the Lives of the Gooroos; The History of the Independent Sirdars, or Missuls, and the Life of the Great Founder of the Sikh Monarchy, Maharajah Runjeet Singh*. Vol. 1. Patiala: Languages Department, Punjab. Reprint of 1846 edition.

———. 1970b. *The History of the Sikhs: Containing an Account of the War bewteen the Sikhs and the British in 1845–46*. Vol. 2. Patiala: Languages Department, Punjab. Reprint of 1846 edition.

Miller, Barbara Stoler, trans. 1967. *Bhartrihari: Poems, with the Transliterated Sanskrit Text of the Śatakatrayam*. New York: Columbia University Press.
Monier-Williams, Sir Monier. 1981. *A Sanskrit-English Dictionary Etymologically and Philologically Arranged with Special Reference to Cognate Indo-European Languages*. Delhi: Motilal Banarsidass. Reprint of 1899 edition.
Murphy, Anne. 2007. History in the Sikh Past. *History and Theory* 46:345–365.
Nābhā, Bhāī Kāhn Singh. 1990. *Gurshabad Ratnākar Mahān Kosh*. Delhi: National Bookshop, 1990.
———. 1999. *Chaṇḍī dī Vār Saṭīk*. Amritsar: Dharam Prachar Committee.
Nara, Giani Ishar Singh. 1985. *Safarnama and Zafarnama: Being an Account of the Travels of Guru Gobind Singh and the Epistle of Moral Victory Written by Him to Emperor Aurangzeb*. Abridged and translated into English by Joginder Singh. New Delhi: Nara Publications.
Narang, Gokul Chand. 1946. *Transformation of Sikhism*. 3rd ed. Lahore: New Book Society.
Neki, Jaswant Singh. 1995. Ardās. In Harbans Singh, ed., *The Encyclopaedia of Sikhism*. Vol. 1. Patiala: Punjabi University, 184–188.
Neki, Jaswant Singh, and Giani Balwant Singh. 1995. Bhagautī. In Harbans Singh, ed., *The Encyclopaedia of Sikhism*. Vol. 1. Patiala: Punjabi University, 319–322.
Nesbitt, Eleanor. 1997. The Body in Sikh Tradition. In Sarah Coakley, ed., *Religion and the Body*. Cambridge: Cambridge University Press, 289–305.
———. 2005. *Sikhism: A Very Short Introduction*. Oxford: Oxford University Press.
News and Views: Resolution No. 3. *Sikh Studies Quarterly* 2 (3): 117.
Nijjar, Bakhshish Singh. 1972. *Punjab under the Later Mughals (1707–1959)*. Jullundur: New Academic Publishing.
Novetzke, Christian. 2003. Divining an Author: The Idea of Authorship in an Indian Religious Tradition. *History of Religions* 42 (3): 213–242.
Oberoi, Harjot. 1992. Popular Saints, Goddessees, and Village Sacred Sites: Rereading Sikh Experience in the Nineteenth Century. *History of Religions* 31 (4): 363–384.
———. 1994. *The Construction of Religious Boundaries: Culture, Identity and Diversity in the Sikh Tradition*. New Delhi: Oxford University Press.
———. 1995. The Making of a Religious Paradox: Sikh, Khalsa, Sahajdhari as Modes of Early Sikh Identity. In David N. Lorenzen, ed., *Bhakti Religion in North India: Community Identity and Political Action*. Albany: State University of New York Press, 35–66.
Olivelle, Patrick. 1997. *The Pañcatantra: The Book of India's Folk Wisdom*. Oxford: Oxford University Press.
———, trans. 2006. *The Five Discourses on Worldly Wisdom by Viṣṇuśarman*. New York: New York University Press and the JJC Foundation.
Oman, J. C. 1984. *The Mystics, Ascetics and Saints of India: A Study of Sadhuism, with an Account of the Yogis, Sanyasis, Bairagis and Other Strange Hindu Sectarians*. New Delhi: Cosmo Publications. Reprint of 1903 edition.

Padam, Piārā Singh. 1968. *Dasam Granth Darsan*. Patiala: Sardar Sahit Bhavan.

Pandit Nārāin Singh Jī Giānī. 1994–19987. *Sri Dasam Granth Sāhib Jī Saṭik*. 8 vols. Amritsar: Chattar Singh Jīvan Singh.

Pintchman, Tracy. 1994. *The Rise of the Goddess in the Hindu Tradition*. Albany: State University of New York Press.

———, ed. 2001. *Seeking Mahadevi: Constructing the Identities of the Hindu Great Goddess*. Albany: State University of New York Press.

Pollock, Sheldon. 1998. The Cosmopolitan Vernacular. *Journal of Asian Studies* 57 (1): 6–37.

———. 2001. New Intellectuals in Seventeenth-Century India. *Indian Economic and Social History Review* 38 (1): 3–31.

———, ed. 2003. *Literary Cultures in History: Reconstructions from South Asia*. Berkeley: University of California Press.

Prasād, Kālikā, Rājvallabh Sahāy, and Mukundīlāl Śrīvāstava, eds. 1984. *Bṛhat Hindī Koś*. Varanasi: Jñānamaṇḍal Limited.

Qadir Yar. 1983. *Puran Bhagat: Rendered into English Verse by Taufiq Rafat*. Lahore: Vanguard Books.

Qureshi, Waheed. 1980. A Survey of Panjabi Language and Literature. *Panjab Past and Present* 14–15: 98–120.

Ramdev, J. S. 1967. *Guru Gobind Singh: A Descriptive Bibliography*. Chandigarh: Punjab University.

Rangarajan, L. N. 1992. *Kautilya: The Arthashastra*. Edited, rearranged, translated, and introduced by L. N. Rangarajan. New Delhi: Penguin India.

Rao, Velcheru Narayana. 1993. Purāṇa as Brahminic Ideology. In Wendy Doniger, ed., *Purāṇa Perennis: Reciprocity and Transformation in Hindu and Jaina Texts*. Delhi: Sri Satguru Publications, 85–100.

Renou, Louis. 1964. *Indian Literature*. Translated from the French by Patrick Evans. New York: Walker.

Rinehart, Robin. 1999a. *One Lifetime, Many Lives: The Experience of Modern Hindu Hagiography*. Atlanta, Ga.: Scholars Press.

———. 1999b. The Portable Bullhe Shah: Biography, Categorization, and Authorship in the Study of Punjabi Sufi Poetry. *Numen* 46 (1): 53–87.

———. 2004. Strategies for Interpreting the *Dasam Granth*. In Pashaura Singh and N. Gerald Barrier, eds., *Sikhism and History*. Delhi: Oxford University Press, 135–150.

Rocher, Ludo. 1985. The Kāmasūtra: Vātsyāyana's Attitude toward Dharma and Dharmaśāstra. *Journal of the American Oriental Society* 105 (3): 521–529.

Saināpati. 1967. *Sri Gur Sobhā*. Edited by Ganda Singh. Patiala: Punjabi University.

Sattar, Arshia. 1994. *Somadeva: Tales from the Kathāsaritsāgara*. Translated from the Sanskrit. New Delhi: Penguin Books.

Satyendra, G. S. 1967. *Braj Sāhitya kā Itihās*. Allahabad: Bharati Bhandar.

Schnepel, Burkhard. 1995. Durga and the King: Ethnohistorical Aspects of Politico-Ritual Life in a South Orissan Jungle Kingdom. *Journal of the Royal Anthropological Institute* 1 (1): 145–166.

Sekhon, Sant Singh. 1993. *A History of Panjabi Literature*. Vol. 1. Patiala: Publication Bureau, Punjabi University.

———. 1996. *A History of Panjabi Literature*. Vol. 2. Patiala: Publication Bureau, Punjabi University.

Sen, S. P. 1979. *Historical Biography in Indian Literature*. Calcutta: Institute of Historical Studies.

Shackle, Christopher, and Arvind-pal Singh Mandair, eds. and trans. 2005. *Teachings of the Sikh Gurus: Selections from the Sikh Scriptures*. London: Routledge.

Shackle, Christopher, Gurharpal Singh, and Arvind-pal Singh Mandair, eds. 2001. *Sikh Religion, Culture, and Ethnicity*. Richmond: Curzon Press.

Shackle, Christopher, and Rupert Snell, eds., 1992. *The Indian Narrative: Perspectives and Patterns*. Wiesbaden: Otto Harrassowitz.

Shamsher Singh Ashok. 1966. *Dasam Granth Bāre: Sri Dasam Granth Te Hor Rachnāvān: Ik Adhiaian*. Amritsar: Bhai Fakir Singh and Sons.

———, ed. 1999. *Gurbilās Pātshāhī Das Krit Kuir Singh*. Patiala: Publication Bureau, Punjabi University.

Shiromani Gurdwara Prabandhak Committee. 1998. *Das Granthī*. Amritsar: Shiromani Gurdwara Prabandhak Committee.

Siddhu, Seva Singh, and Amrit Pal Kaur, eds. 1998. *Guru Gobind Singh Vishesh Aṅk. Khoj Patrika* 47.

SikhiWiki. N.d. Shabad Hazarey. http://www.sikhiwiki.org/index.php/Shabad_Hazare. Accessed January 3, 2010.

Singh, Bhāī Randhīr. 1995. *Sabdārath Dasam Granth Sāhib*. 3 vols. Patiala: Publication Bureau, Punjabi University.

Singh, Bhāī Santokh. 1989–1992. *Srī Gur Pratāp Suraj Granth (Kavi Cūḍāmaṇī Bhāī Santokh Singh)*. 14 vols. Edited by Dr. Vīr Singh. Patiala: Bhāshā Vibhāg.

———. 1999. *Jīvan Birtānt Das Pātshāhiān Arthāt Sūraj Prakāsh*. 14th. ed. Amritsar: Dr. Chattar Singh Jivan Singh, 1999.

Singh, Daljeet. 1997. Dasam Granth: Its History. In Daljeet Singh and Kharak Singh. *Sikhism: Its Philosophy and History*. Chandigarh: Institute of Sikh Studies, 710–722.

Singh, Darshan. 1996. *Sikhism: Issues and Institutions (In the context of Dr. W. H. McLeod, Dr. Pashaura Singh, Dr. H. S. Oberoi and the Likes …*). New Delhi: Sehgal Book Distributors.

Singh, Dharam. 1998a. *Dynamics of the Social Thought of Guru Gobind Singh*. Patiala: Publication Bureau, Punjabi University.

———. 1998b. Vār. In Harbans Singh, ed., *The Encyclopaedia of Sikhism* Vol. 4. Patiala: Punjabi University, 406–407.

Singh, Fauja. 1996. *Gurbilās Pātshāhī 10*. In Harbans Singh, ed., *The Encyclopaedia of Sikhism*. Vol. 2. Patiala: Punjabi University, 135–136.

Singh, Ganda, ed. 1967. *Kavi Saināpati Rachit Srī Gur Sobhā*. Patiala: Punjabi University.

———. 1979. Biography in Panjabi Literature. *Panjab Past and Present* 8–9:115–126. Reprinted with a new concluding paragraph in S. P. Sen, ed. 1979. *Historical Biography in Indian Literature*. Calcutta: Institute of Historical Studies, 157–171.

———. 1996. Hukamnāmā. In Harbans Singh, ed., *The Encyclopaedia of Sikhism*. Vol. 2. Patiala: Punjabi University Press, 289–291.

Singh, Giānī Giān. 1987. *Panth Prakāsh*. Patiala: Bhāshā Vibhāg Panjāb.

Singh, Dr. Gopal. 1988. *A History of the Sikh People (1469–1988)*. 2nd rev. ed. New Delhi: Allied Publishers.

Singh, Gurbaksh "Kālā Afghānā." 1995. *Bippran kī Rīt ton Sachch dā Mārag*. 6 vols. Amritsar: Sri Akal Sahay Society.

Singh, Gurcharan. 1990. *Studies in Punjab History and Culture*. New Delhi: Enkay Publishers.

Singh, Gurmukh. 1997a. Bhāī Manī Singh. In Harbans Singh, ed., *The Encyclopaedia of Sikhism*. Vol. 3. Patiala: Punjabi University, 39–41.

———. 1997b. *Gurbilas Patshahi-Chhevin Krit Bhagat Singh*. Patiala: Publication Bureau, Punjabi University.

———. 1998a. *Sarabloh Granth*. In Harbans Singh, ed., *The Encyclopaedia of Sikhism*. Vol. 4. Patiala: Punjabi University, 57–58.

———. 1998b. *Srī Gur Sobhā*. In Harbans Singh, ed., *The Encyclopaedia of Sikhism*. Vol. 4. Patiala: Punjabi University, 236–238.

Singh, Gursharan. 1997. *Guru Gobind Singh: God's Warrior Saint*. Amritsar: Shri Darbar Sahib, 1997.

Singh, Gurtej. 1997. Two Views on Dasam Granth. In Daljeet Singh and Kharak Singh, eds., *Sikhism: Its Philosophy and History*. Chandigarh: Institute of Sikh Studies, 704–709.

Singh, Harbans. 1961. *Aspects of Punjabi Literature*. Ferozepore Cantonment: Bawa Publishing House.

Singh, Jagjit. 1996. Gurmat Granth Prachārak Sabhā. In Harbans Singh, ed., *The Encyclopaedia of Sikhism*. Vol. 2. Patiala: Punjabi University, 155–156.

Singh, Jodh. 1970. *Srī Dasam Granth Sāhib Hindī Anuvād Sahit Nāgarī Lipyantaraṇ*. 4 vols. Lucknow: Bhuvan Vāṇī Ṭrast.

Singh, Jodh, and Singh, Dharam, trans. 1999. *Sri Dasam Granth Sahib: Text and Translation*. 2 vols. Patiala: Heritage Publications.

Singh, Kartar. 1990. Chandi di Var: A Composition of Guru Gobind Singh Ji. *Sikh Review* 38 (9): 10–15.

Singh, Khushwant. 1977. *A History of the Sikhs*. Vol. 1, *1469–1839*. Delhi: Oxford University Press.

———. 1987. Gobind Singh. In Mircea Eliade, ed., *The Encylopedia of Religion*. Vol. 13. New York: Macmillan, 331–333.

Singh, Kuldip. N.d. Compilation of "*Dasam Granth*": A Scientific Analysis. http://www.sikhreview.org/august2003/moral3.htm. Accessed January 24, 2008.

Singh, Lāl, ed. 1999. *Choṇvīn Bāṇī Dasam-Granth*. Patiala: Publications Bureau, Punjabi University.

Singh, Mahīp. 1969. *Guru Gobind Singh aur Unkī Hindī Kavitā*. Delhi: National Publishing House.

Singh, Manmohan. 1997. *Dasam Granth Vich Mith [Myth] Rūpāntaran*. Amritsar: Lok Sahit Prakashan.

Singh, Mohan. 1971. *A History of Panjabi Literature (1100–1932)*. 3rd ed. Jullundur: Bharat Prakashan.

Singh, Nikky-Guninder Kaur. 1990. Guru Gobind Singh's Idea of Durga in His Poetry: The Unfathomable Woman as the Image of the Unfathomable Transcendent One. *Ultimate Reality and Meaning* 13:243–267.

———. 1992. The Myth of the Founder: The Janamsakhis and Sikh Tradition. *History of Religions* 31 (4): 329–343.

———. 1993. *The Feminine Principle in the Sikh Vision of the Transcendent*. Cambridge: Cambridge University Press.

———. 1995. *The Name of My Beloved: Devotional Poetry from the Guru Granth and the Dasam Granth*. San Francisco: HarperCollins.

———. 2005. *The Birth of the Khalsa: A Feminist Re-memory of Sikh Identity*. Albany: State University of New York Press.

Singh, Pashaura. 1996. Scriptural Adaptation in the Adi Granth. *Journal of the American Academy of Religion* 64:337–357.

———. 1998. Recent Trends and Prospects in Sikh Studies. *Studies in Religion/ Sciences Religieuses* 27 (4): 407–425.

———. 2000. *The Guru Granth Sahib: Canon, Meaning and Authority*. New Delhi: Oxford University Press.

Singh, Puran. 1966. *Guru Gobind Singh: Reflections and Offerings*. Chandigarh: Guru Gobind Singh Foundation.

Singh, Raījasbīr. 1999. *Khālsā Sirjnā te Dasam Granth*. Amritsar: Vigiān Bhāratī.

Singh, Sher. 1967. *Social and Political Thought of Guru Gobind Singh*. Delhi: Sterling.

Singh, Sukkhā. 1989. *Gurbilās Pātshāhī Dasvīn*. Edited by Gursharan Kaur Jaggi. Patiala: Bhāshā Vibhāg.

Singh, Tāran. 1967. *Dasam Granth: Rūp te Ras*. Chandigarh: Guru Gobind Singh Foundation.

Singh, Trilochan. 1955. The History and Compilation of the Dasm Granth, Parts 1–4. *Sikh Review* 3 (4): 51–60, 3 (5): 33–41, 3 (6): 44–52, 3 (7): 23–29.

Smith, David. 1992. Construction and Deconstruction, Narrative and Anti-Narrative: The Representation of Reality in the Hindu Court Epic. In Christopher Shackle and Rupert Snell, eds., *The Indian Narrative: Perspectives and Patterns*. Wiesbaden: Otto Harrassowitz, 33–59.

Soḍhak Committee. 1897. *Report Soḍhak Committee*. Amritsar: Gurmat Granth Prachārak Sabhā.

Srivastava, Hari Shanker. 1979. Historical Biographies in Hindi Literature. In S. P. Sen, ed., *Historical Biography in Indian Literature*. Calcutta: Institute of Historical Studies, 127–139.

Swynnerton, Charles. 1892. *Folk Tales from the Upper Indus*. Islamabad: National Institute of Folk Heritage.

———. 1908. *Romantic Tales from the Panjab with Indian Nights' Entertainment.* London: Archibald Constable.

Syed, Najm Hosain. 1986. *Recurrent Patterns in Punjabi Poetry*. Lahore: Punjabi Adbi Markaz.

Tahir, M. Athar. 1988. *Qadir Yar: A Critical Introduction*. Lahore: Pakistan Punjabi Adabi Board.

Thapar, K. S. 1996. *Gurbilās Pātshāhī Dasvīn*. In Harbans Singh, ed., *The Encyclopaedia of Sikhism*. Vol. 2. Patiala: Punjabi University, 136–137.

Trumpp, Ernest. 1989. *The Ādi Granth: Or The Holy Scriptures of the Sikhs*. Delhi: Munshiram Manoharlal. Reprint of 1877 edition.

van Buitenen, J. A. B. 1957. Dharma and Moksha. *Philosophy East and West* 7 (1–2): 33–40.

———. 1959. *Tales of Ancient India*. Chicago: University of Chicago Press.

———. 1974. The Story Literature. In Edward C. Dimock, Edwin Gerow, C. M. Naim, A. K. Ramanujan, Gordon Roadarmel, and J. A. B. van Buitenen, eds., *The Literatures of India: An Introduction*. Chicago: University of Chicago Press, 210–211.

Vidiārthī, Devinder Singh, ed. 1983. *Sri Guru Gobind Singh Abhinandan*. Amritsar: Guru Nanak Dev University.

Vidyāratan, Dr. Ran Singh. 1928. *Dasam Granth Nirṇay, Arthāt Dasam Pātshāhi de Lok Prasiddh Dasam Granth dī Bāni da Kram anusār Nirṇay te Vichār*. Patiala: Manager Pustak Bhandar.

Whitney, William Dwight. 1885. *The Roots, Verb-Forms, and Primary Derivatives of the Sanskrit Language*. Leipzig: Breitkopf and Härtel.

Winternitz, M. 1959. *A History of Indian Literature*. Vol. 3, *Fasciculus 1: Ornate Poetry*. Translated from the German by Miss H. Kohn. Calcutta: University of Calcutta.

Index